CHAPTER I
THE COUNTRY

With the single exception of Brazil, Argentina is the largest country in South America. It is about one-third the size of the United States. It is as large as the United States east of the Mississippi River, with a state the size of Texas added. The area is one million one hundred and thirty-eight thousand square miles. It is twelve times as extensive as the British Isles and five times the size of France. Argentina extends over thirty-three degrees of latitude, its northern limit being one degree within the Tropic of Capricorn. Buenos Aires, the capital, is about as far south of the equator as Atlanta is north, and is as far east of Washington as Newfoundland. It has a frontage on the Atlantic of sixteen hundred miles, almost as long as our own Atlantic shore. Its width varies greatly. The widest place is about nine hundred miles, and then it decreases again to the south until the mainland at its southernmost point is only one hundred and fifty miles across. The Argentine portion of Tierra del Fuego is a triangle about fifty-five miles on each side. The most of its limitations are natural boundaries, either of rivers or mountains. The national boundary between Chile and Argentina, which has been the cause of so much contention, is the backbone of the continent, and its longitude is still east of New York.

The topography of Argentina is very varied. Some, perhaps, think of it only as a flat and level country. This is true of the pampas, where for hundreds of miles there is scarcely a rise as high as a barn. Argentina probably contains the greatest stretch of level and fertile plains in the world, whose possibilities have hardly been touched upon. But Argentina is not all level. It contains within its borders the very highest mountain peak in the world outside of the Himalayas, mighty Aconcagua, which pierces the ether up to a height of twenty-four thousand feet. It also possesses Tupungato, another lofty peak of the Andean range. The pampas are entirely treeless except for groves which have been planted by man. But Argentina does not lack timber, for there are tracts larger than many European kingdoms which are covered with fine forests. The climate is equally diversified. One may broil in the wilderness of the Chaco, and shiver with the cold in Southern

Patagonia. In fact there is almost as much difference in the climate as you would find between Sicily and Iceland. On the Andes slopes there is very little rain, but up in the territory of Misiones you reach the region of tropical downpours. Thus it is that you can find a representative type of almost any kind of climate and almost every variety of soil.

The Rio de la Plata is the second largest river system in the world. It is one of the three main outlets from the interior of South America to the sea, and carries almost twice as much water as the Mississippi. At its mouth the river is one hundred and eighty miles across from Cape San Antonio, Uruguay, to Cape Santa Maria, in Argentina. A little further inland, which some consider as the real mouth, the distance is one hundred and forty miles. Opposite Montevideo the width has narrowed down to sixty-five miles, and at Buenos Aires it is about twenty-eight miles from shore to shore. Just above Buenos Aires the river is divided into a number of forks, which form an extensive delta through which the great branches run and a number of islands have been created. The principal branches of this river in Argentina are the Paraná, Uruguay and Paraguay. The Uruguay River rises in Brazil, less than one hundred miles from the Atlantic Ocean, and has a length of one thousand miles. The Paraguay and Paraná Rivers also have their sources in Brazil, near the centre of the continent, and the former has a length of seventeen hundred miles before its waters mingle with the latter. It has two tributaries, the Pilcomayo and Bermejo, which are navigable for small craft. Each of these rivers is more than five hundred miles long, but they are exceedingly tortuous, so that navigation is rather difficult and uncertain. The Paraná River reaches way up into Brazil. It has its source only a few miles from one of the principal tributaries of the Amazon, over a stretch of swampy ground of which a part of the water flows into one river and part into the other. All of these rivers carry down immense quantities of mud. In places the deposit on the river bottom is from thirteen to twenty-five feet deep, and it has many banks and shoals. The problem of keeping channels open to Buenos Aires is a big one, and many dredges are kept constantly at work. It is generally believed that the interior of Argentina was at one time a vast inland sea, and that the flat plains have been formed by the soil which has been deposited by these rivers during the prehistoric geological ages. The waters of the Atlantic are coloured by this mud long before the mouth of the river is reached. The water in the bath-tub looks almost like thin pea soup.

ON THE UPPER PARANÁ RIVER

The range of temperature and climatic conditions is very great. In the extreme northern provinces the temperature is similar to that of Mexico and Florida. On the central pampas the summer heat is connatural with that of Southern California and Tennessee, while the winter temperature resembles that of the Ohio Valley. The thermometric range between the extremes of heat and cold, however, is much less than in the corresponding latitudes of the northern hemisphere. In general the climate of the central pampas may be said to correspond roughly with that of the great cereal producing sections of North America, although the yearly average is rather higher and the fluctuations are somewhat less violent. It is better adapted for the growth of grain and raising of stock then the newly opened provinces of Canada and is more habitable for man. In fact the name of Buenos Aires (good airs), applied to a city and province, is not a misnomer. North of Buenos Aires snow is rare and frost unusual, except in the higher altitudes. South of there it grows progressively colder as one travels towards Cape Horn.

In the matter of rainfall, also, there are great variations in different sections. The zonal distribution of rainfall runs in belts from east to west.

This is due to the prevailing winds. The great agricultural district receives from twenty to forty inches annually, or about the same as the region around the Great Lakes of the United States. West of this is a narrow strip that receives only about half of this amount of rain, and then along the slopes of the Andes is a belt which does not receive to exceed ten inches. This would favourably compare with New Mexico and Arizona. In Patagonia the conditions are reversed and the arid belt is along the Atlantic coast, while the districts near the Andes receive a fair amount of rainfall. This distribution of rainfall is of utmost importance in the development of the country. As agriculture extends it occupies the watered area, and the pastoral industry is driven little by little farther into the more arid sections. Sheep and cattle are gradually moving west and southwest into the semi-arid districts. The province of Buenos Aires, which a few years ago was the pastoral centre, is now one of the most important agricultural sections. As the process continues it will become increasingly necessary to open up more southerly ports for the shipment of animal products, while the northerly ports will remain the chief exporters of grain.

There are at least a half billion acres of fertile arable land in Argentina, that can be turned to the cultivation of products for the sustenance of man. All of this land is easily accessible to the Atlantic. There are no natural barriers such as transverse ranges of mountains. The northern provinces can reach Rosario or Buenos Aires by the La Plata system of waterways, while the rest of the country can, by the simplest railway construction, be joined up with one of those ports, or with Bahia Blanca, or one of the new ports in Patagonia. At present these three ports are the only ones needed, or that will be until Patagonia has undergone greater development. Only the upper edge of the country is within the tropics. From there as far south as Buenos Aires the climate is almost that of the Gulf States, while that city has a climate very similar to Los Angeles. The heat in summer is sometimes oppressive, but not more so than in New York or Chicago. It is doubtful whether there are so many of those oppressive humid days in the southern as in the northern metropolis. It is never so cold in winter as to prevent out-of-door life. Even in Tierra del Fuego the winter climate is no more severe than that of Northern Michigan. The pampas of middle Argentina probably have less rain than our own middle west. Water is, however, not far below the surface, and wells are easy to construct for the windmills, which form so prominent a feature of the landscape on the *estancias*. In Misiones the landscape is Brazilian, and in parts of Patagonia it resembles Arizona, only they do not have such extreme drouths. Anything that can be successfully raised in the United States can be grown in Argentina, and generally much cheaper. The country, however, lacks our great mineral wealth. Iron is scarcer than gold, and coal is imported by the millions of tons each year. Great discoveries may be made in the future, but Argentina will never be a great competitor of the United States in mineral products.

Argentina is a land of big things. Farms are reckoned by the square league, consisting of nearly six thousand acres, instead of by the paltry acre. All grains are measured and sold by the metric ton of twenty-two hundred and five pounds, instead of by the diminutive bushel. That country is now the greatest flax-producing country in the world, and ranks third in wheat and second in corn. It has more horses than any country except Russia and the United States, more sheep than any country except Australia, and is exceeded in the number of cattle only by the United States. If all the sheep in Argentina were marched across the United States two abreast they would form a solid column reaching from Sandy Hook to the Golden Gate. Argentina contains within her borders the largest city in the southern hemisphere, and the second Latin city in the world. She probably exports more foodstuffs than any nation on the globe, if you include both meat and grains. And yet the real resources of the country have only been scratched on the surface. It is predicted by good authority that the United States will have to import meat from foreign markets before a not very distant day. There is no other country that can be looked to except Argentina with her millions of sheep and cattle and thousands of fertile leagues that invite development. A brilliant future certainly awaits this great republic on South American soil, and North Americans may well inform themselves upon the country, its people and resources.

Argentina might be divided into two parts, Buenos Aires and the Camp—the name given to the country. Buenos Aires is at once the London, New York and Paris of the republic and dominates the country as no other capital of the world does. It is the largest Spanish-speaking city in the world, being more than twice as large as Madrid. In the sixteenth and seventeenth centuries Asuncion, the capital of Paraguay, was a far more important place. It contains most of the factories of the country, receives the greater part of the foreign trade, does the banking of the nation through its great moneyed institutions, and is the social and business centre where the money made by those in the interior of the republic is spent. It is growing at the rate of nearly one hundred thousand persons each year. The large admixture of foreigners coming in keep this city, as well as the nation, up to date. New ideas are thus brought in from everywhere, and the latest inventions and improvements follow. The Spanish type has been considerably modified by the foreign commingling so that this capital is now as cosmopolitan as any in the world.

Most people are accustomed to think of all the South American republics as *opera bouffe* affairs. Unfortunately there has been too much foundation for that reputation in the past. This has probably been the greatest obstacle to advancement hitherto. Paraguay is still in that condition, and Uruguay has its almost annual struggle between the *blancos* (whites) and *colorados* (reds). These uprisings are generally trivial affairs and do not deserve the importance given them. There are, as a rule, no great principles involved, and the struggle is primarily for the control of the government between different leaders. They are usually of short duration and attended with little bloodshed. They are due to that mediæval idea so strongly intrenched in the Spanish character that changes can only be brought about by fighting. The idea of settling these questions at the ballot box has not been fully developed. The writer was in Uruguay during one of these revolutions, and Montevideo was as quiet as one could expect to find a city of that size. A great many young men had fled for fear of conscription in the army. The only way in which he was discommoded was by the necessity of going to the authorities to get a permit to leave the city, as no one could embark on a steamer without this government passport. This revolution was the most severe one that they had had for five years. There had been several conflicts in the interior between the *blancos* and *colorados*, and some blood shed. Argentina was blamed by the press for the trouble, as it was alleged that Argentina wanted to create disorder and then seize the country on the plea that only in that way could property interests be protected.

Argentina in times past went through the same performances. Revolution followed revolution and dictator followed dictator; but that time has passed. The principal reminder left is the despotic and arbitrary rule of the prevailing party. The "elections" are controlled and manipulated by the party in power. It is always easy to foretell who will be the successful candidate by looking at his support. A political campaign was in progress during the writer's visit, so that he had an opportunity to observe the trend. The billboards and fences were covered with proclamations of the candidates and announcements of their policies, mass meetings were held in the Plaza de Mayo, and other public places, but the administration had selected its own successor and there never was the slightest doubt as to the result. Although these high-handed methods still prevail, it is daily growing less possible for serious disturbances to arise. The building of railroads and telegraphs has brought the different sections into touch with each other. The great investment of foreign capital has had a steadying influence toward more stable conditions, and has compelled the leaders to appreciate the necessity for improved political conditions because of the country's need for additional foreign gold in developing its natural resources. They realize that such aid can only be secured by carefully safeguarding the financial, commercial and industrial interests, and they have set themselves at work to provide the necessary guarantees of good behaviour.

The Argentine Republic consists of fourteen provinces, ten territories and the Federal District. The provinces are autonomous in their interior government, while the territories are ruled by a governor who is appointed by the President. The Federal District, which includes Buenos Aires, is administered by an *intendente,* or mayor, appointed by the President, and assisted by a municipal council elected by the people. The Argentine Republic has established the federal idea of a union of states as its form of government. The constitution, which was adopted in 1860, is modelled closely after that of the United States. The only changes since that time have been some amplifications of the original articles. The legislative power is invested in a National Congress which consists of the Senate and Chamber of Deputies. There are thirty senators and one hundred and twenty deputies. They receive a salary of eighteen thousand dollars per year in paper money. Senators are elected by the legislatures of the provinces, which are really states, for a term of nine years, and to be eligible for election the candidate must be thirty years of age and have an annual income of two thousand dollars. Each state and the Federal District is entitled to two senators. One-third of the Senate is elected every three years. Deputies are elected for a term of four years by direct popular vote in the proportion of one to every thirty-three thousand inhabitants, and one-half are elected every two years. They must be twenty-five years of age and have been citizens of the republic for four years. The President is elected by electors who are chosen by the people for a term of six years. Neither the President, nor Vice-President are eligible to succeed themselves without one term intervening. The President is assisted by a cabinet of eight members, who are designated as follows: Interior, Foreign Affairs and Worship, Finance, Justice and Public Instruction, War, Marine, Public Works, and Agriculture. The Vice-President is also president of the Senate. Each province has its own courts, but there are national courts of appeal and first instance as well. The Supreme Court consists of five judges, who are appointed for life by the President.

The centralization, or nationalization, of the nation has gone ahead rapidly in recent years. The forcible separation of the city of Buenos Aires from the province of the same name was one of the best things ever done by the government. In removing the preponderance of Buenos Aires the constant friction between that province, on the one hand, and all the other provinces, on the other, was removed. Railroads have been subsidized and immigration encouraged by the national government, in the effort to develop the country. The post-office has been brought to great efficiency, and its service is rapid and trustworthy. The telegraph lines are nearly all controlled by the government, although private ownership is not prohibited. Of the thirty-five thousand miles of telegraph wires, enough to go around the globe once and a quarter times, perhaps one-half are owned by the national government and one-fourth by the provinces. The greater part of the income is from customs receipts, and the national government also contributes toward the support of the provinces and territories in order to equalize taxation. The government has learned lessons from former experiences in the fluctuation of money values, so that the paper dollar, or peso, has been officially fixed at forty-four cents gold. Exchange does not vary more than a fraction of a cent from that rate at the present time.

The first European navigator to discover the Rio de la Plata was Juan de Solis, a Spanish captain, in the year 1508, while in search of a passage to the Pacific Ocean. Magellan did not visit these shores until 1520. A chronicler who was with Magellan says that the "gigantic natives called canibali ate de Solis and sixty men who had gone to discover land, and trusted too much to them." The first settlement was established at Buenos Aires in 1536 by Pedro de Mendoza, who has been termed a freebooter, and who was made governor by the Spanish Crown. This settlement was destroyed shortly afterward by the hostile Indians, and no permanent settlement was established on the mud flats of the "river of silver" until nearly forty years later.

During the succeeding centuries the Spaniards did all that they could to exploit this country and check all advancement. The only aborigines were wild and nomadic Indians. Argentina was for a long time subject to the vice-regency of Peru, and many of the settlements were made by explorers who came across the Andes. In this way Tucuman was founded in 1565, Cordoba in 1573 and Santa Fé in the same year. The Jesuits spread their settlements along the rivers far up into Paraguay and Brazil, and laid the foundation of that mighty power which lasted for two centuries. They subdued the Indians and turned them into peons or labourers, but otherwise treated them kindly. For a long while the history of Argentina is merely a record of the internecine struggles of a loosely connected province. The settlements were wide apart and there was no homogeneity. Portugal and Spain fought with each other for supremacy and the settlement of the lines of demarkation. It was not until the time of our own declaration of independence that Spain finally realized the importance of this colony and made it a vice-regency, Dom Pedro de Cevallos being named as the first viceroy. The Jesuits were expelled and much of their property confiscated. Some good grew out of this change, as a number of the viceroys were men of ability and integrity. The spirit of independence, however, grew and the feeling of revolt steadily increased.

In 1805 Great Britain, then at war with Spain, attempted to capture the city of Buenos Aires, which had already become an important trade centre, but was repulsed on several occasions. This was done by the provincials with scarcely any help from Spain, and success gave them confidence in themselves. On the 25th of May, 1810, independence from Spain was formally declared, and this patriotic movement did not cease until actual independence was achieved several years later. The first Congress was summoned in 1816, and the United Provinces of the La Plata River were formally organized. The first president was elected in 1825, and Don Bernardo Rivadavia was chosen to that position. Uruguay was at one time forcibly annexed by Brazil, and this action precipitated a war with Brazil. Argentina championed the smaller state, as a result of which the independence of Uruguay was guaranteed. Internal wars and revolutions were numerous in the early days of the republic, for ambitious leaders were everywhere fighting each other. In 1820 there were a dozen changes of government. The services of several progressive and able presidents brought order out of chaos, established the country's credit and set the country onward toward the era of progress and prosperity which she has now enjoyed for a number of years.

From this it will be seen that the early history of the Argentine Republic is permeated with the smell of blood, and that there has been much human sacrifice. After studying the history of the many wars and conditions one can readily read the disappointment and sadness of heart contained in the political document left by General Bolivar, which concludes with the words, "I have ploughed in the sea." Europe at one time went through similar conditions, but it is doubtful whether in their worst stage the middle ages equalled the first half-century of the history of the Latin-American republics. Out of the troublous times of the fifteenth and sixteenth centuries in Europe emerged nations which had been strengthened by the lessons of adversity learned in the internecine struggles of that period, in which principle was opposed to oppression in every form. The iniquitous policy of the Inquisition superimposed upon excessive taxation brought about revolt among the Spanish colonies. In their struggles the colonists have our deepest sympathies, for it was a revolt against tyranny in its worst form. After freedom, however, the colonists were still Spaniards, and a turbulent nature had been inherited.

To this inherited trait can be traced the revolutions, civil wars and political turmoils that have followed. To this fact can be attributed the tardy economic development of many of the South American republics, and even of Argentina until the last quarter of a century. This spirit has now been almost eliminated in Argentina, which has probably progressed farther in this respect than any of her sister republics. The signs that the old Spanish character is losing its baneful grip on this country are multiplying each day. It has been a long and hard lesson for the Argentinians to learn that political freedom does not mean unrestrained license, but it is being more clearly interpreted each year. The conditions are better understood when compared with Uruguay, Paraguay or Venezuela, where political conditions are still as they were in Argentina a half-century ago. Travel is safe, investments are secure, and perhaps the most severe criticism that one can make is that so great a dependence is placed upon a material prosperity.

CHAPTER II
THE METROPOLIS OF THE SOUTHERN HEMISPHERE

"What is the Camp?" I asked of a Buenos Airean one day.

"Everything outside of Buenos Aires," was his reply.

"Is Rosario a part of the Camp?" I questioned, for Rosario is the second municipality in the Argentine Republic, and is a city approaching two hundred thousand inhabitants.

"Yes, but we would not say so in Rosario."

This little conversation reveals the pride of all *Porteños*, as they call themselves, in their city, for the term Camp is used as country is with us. Buenos Aires contains the wealth and culture of the republic, and is the centre of the political as well as national life. One-fifth of the entire population dwell there, for the head has outgrown the body. "Paris is France," says the Parisian, but the importance of that capital to France is outclassed by the significance of Buenos Aires to Argentina.

Buenos Aires is a wonderful city, and its inhabitants are a remarkable people. Italians and Spanish abound there in great numbers; thousands of French, British and Germans have found a haven on the low bank of the Rio de la Plata, and it would be difficult to find a race in Asia or Africa that has not its representatives in that cosmopolitan metropolis. On the street almost any tongue may be heard, and nearly every European language is represented by its own newspaper. It is not a tropical city, such as Rio de Janeiro, nor an indolent one, but a city of business and enterprise with a great deal of the Latin love of pleasure in evidence. Women have become open competitors of men in the offices and stores, and the old conservatism of Spain has been compelled to yield to a broader cosmopolitanism.

"There is nothing in any other city that cannot be found here," is the boast of the *Porteño*. In a general sense the claim is true. The skyscraper, the elevated railway and the "tube" are missing, but there are few conveniences or luxuries that cannot be purchased, if one only has the price. The price is usually high, for Buenos Aires is a very expensive city in which to live. Nearly all articles pass through the custom house and have a certain percentage added to the original cost in the foreign markets.

There are almost a million and a quarter of these busy people who make their homes in Buenos Aires. In the New World it is exceeded in population by only three cities of the United States. It is as cosmopolitan as New York, and is the hub and centre of the whole republic. On the vast pampas grow the grain and meat which sustain the energies of the factory workers of Europe, who, in turn, send to Argentina the product of their looms and machine shops. It is upon the fertility of these broad leagues, which produce such great quantities of cereals, meat, wool and hides, that the people live. There is little manufacturing in the city and the absence of smoke-stacks is the most striking aspect, when viewed from a height by an American.

"GIANT CRANES ARE SWINGING"

It is only necessary to go down to the immense docks of Buenos Aires to get a vivid idea of the vast commerce of this city. It is a scene that cannot be duplicated even in New York with its far greater traffic. All you can see along those docks is the lofty bow of an ocean greyhound heaving up now and then above the dock-shed, as the tide ebbs and flows, and each one looks very much like the other. Here in Buenos Aires they stretch along the edges of the basins, funnel behind funnel, bridge behind bridge, as far as one can see, until the vision is lost in a veritable sea of masts. A splendid freighter just in from Europe and loaded with champagne, automobiles and other luxuries may lie next to a river boat just in from Paraguay and loaded with oranges and bananas. Giant cranes are swinging, heaped-up trucks are constantly on the move and men are carrying loads backward and forward. Here are vessels from all the carrying nations of the world, flying the flags of Germany, Italy, France, Great Britain, Spain and Austria, but the flag of the United States is not visible. Out of the thousands of vessels which entered this port last year, there were only four small ships that sailed under the stars and stripes of Uncle Sam. Out in the river dozens of boats may be seen anchored, for the freighters are oftentimes obliged to wait three or four weeks before they can enter one of the basins and discharge their cargo. Outside the vast warehouses, which are always packed clear to the roofs, are scores of trucks and drays busily loading or unloading, and conveying freight to and from the railroad freight depots and the commission houses. And just beyond the line of drays is the dock railroad, where the switch engines are busily engaged in shoving cars backward and forward.

These immense docks, built only a few years ago, are already too small, so rapidly has Buenos Aires grown. Although almost four hundred years old, this city is as new as Chicago. For generations it remained only a miserable collection of mud huts, with lots three miles deep that could be purchased for an old, broken-down horse, or a second-hand suit of clothes. When our Declaration of Independence was given to the world only three thousand people lived on these mud flats now built up with great structures. Then it began to grow slowly, until a half-century ago it had reached a population of seventy-five thousand. Its greatest growth, however, has been in the last twenty years. A quarter of a century ago there was only a flat mudbar along the waterfront of Buenos Aires. Ships were compelled to anchor several miles out in the river. Boxes, bales and passengers were conveyed ashore in lighters and row-boats. High-wheeled carts were then pushed out into the water so that passengers could land without getting wet. Plans for a system of docks were then prepared by an English engineer, which were completed at a cost of forty millions of dollars. Five great basins were constructed which extended along the river front for three miles. At that time, however, the tonnage of this port was less than a million. Now it has reached ten millions, and additional basins are absolutely necessary. A magnificent and commodious custom house is now being built at a cost of a million and a half of dollars to provide room for the large working force necessary to care for this immense export and import trade.

It is as a town of pleasure, however, that the native Argentinian loves to think of his capital. "Paris," says he, "why, Paris and Buenos Aires should not be mentioned in the same breath." In his opinion Buenos Aires has Paris beat to a "frazzle," although that particular word has not yet entered his vocabulary. This is the feature of the city that almost any inhabitant will dwell upon whenever you meet him. In his opinion the theatres cannot be equalled. He will tell you of the Casino, where the best vaudeville acts of all Europe are played; and of La Escala, where the singers follow each other in melancholy procession, each one dressed in the same strapless bodice and stiff, bespangled skirt. One may sing in French, another in Italian and still another in Spanish, but each one wriggles her powdered shoulders and presses her hands to her heart in the same pathetic way. The men smoke and stare, seldom applauding, and the Argentine ladies—they give La Escala a wide berth.

"THEY FILE AROUND AND AROUND BETWEEN THE PALMS"

Then there is the Jockey Club, with an entrance fee and annual dues higher than any club in New York. Only native Argentinians can belong to it, although the diplomats and a few other favoured foreigners are given an honorary membership. There is an English Club which is rather an exclusive organization, and a German Club which occupies a fine new building. The Club de Residentes Estranjeros, or, as it is generally called, the Strangers' Club, is the one that appeals most to the visitor, however, for a stranger will be given the courtesies of the club for one month upon a simple introduction by a member. There are at least fifty similar social organizations in Buenos Aires, for the *Porteños* are a hospitable and sociable people and love to mingle together socially. The races are held on

Sunday afternoons from twelve o'clock to three. Outside the race track may be seen a long line of carriages and automobiles drawn up along the curb. The instant the races are over this line melts away and every vehicle wends its way toward beautiful Palermo Park, where, joined by hundreds of other similar vehicles, they file around and around between the palms and indulge themselves in the passion of staring at everyone else. At five o'clock on a Sunday afternoon, or on feast days, of which there are more than thirty in the course of a year, the crowds are at their greatest. The parade of vehicles is oftentimes three deep and would stretch out many miles if placed one behind the other in a straight line. There are no dark mantillas and no closed carriages to conceal the female occupants, and it is a sight for the men. It is a procession of human upholstery with expensive trappings, huge Parisian hats, expensive gowns and an abundance of cosmetics. Side by side with rich turnouts plated with silver and gold, magnificent horses and footmen as well as coachmen in rich livery, may be seen men just in from the Camp dressed in their less sophisticated clothes and riding in hired victorias, and the music-hall singers with their overdressed air and ravishing smiles, which they bestow with a generous freedom.

Calle Florida is the fashionable shopping street. In the late hours of the afternoon the street is crowded with the shoppers and idlers, and all traffic is excluded from the thoroughfare during those hours. Mamma and her daughters, Juanita and Carmencita, are out to look at the pretty things, the latter in their freshly starched skirts and bright-coloured ribbons. Others, who have no shopping to do, invent some excuse for being on Florida at that hour, and the young dandies stand on the corners, twirling moustaches that turn up at an angle of forty-five degrees and smoking the inevitable cigarette. When the witching hours of night have come the crowds again appear. Calles Florida, Cangallo, Esmeralda, Cuyo, Maipu and many others are brilliantly illuminated, for the theatres and cafés are in that section, as well as the best restaurants, and rathskellers, and these people certainly love to eat. There are many good restaurants, of which the Sportsman is probably the most popular. Here you may partake of almost any European dish—to say nothing of native ones. In addition to music a free moving picture show is provided. To obtain a seat at certain hours it is necessary to make arrangements beforehand, for diners linger long at the table. The meal usually begins with a dish of cold meats. Then comes a salad or the soup, together with the appetizers. Fish and three or four kinds of meat then follow, ending with a pastry or *dulce* (sweet) of some kind. It is surprising to see what a meal a thin Spaniard will put himself on the outside of, together with a choice assortment of liquors, and seem no worse for the effort.

During my visit the "Merry Widow" was being played in three different languages, French, Italian and Spanish, in as many different theatres. The Teatro Colon is the largest opera house in South America and the very best of opera is given there, a government subsidy being granted. There are few of the world's great artists who have not appeared here at some time in their career. In no country in the world can better Italian opera be heard. It will seat thousands of people, and it is always a fashionably dressed audience. A thousand dollars for a season box is readily paid by the nabob of Buenos Aires. Low-necked gowns for the women and evening dress for the men predominate, and jewels by the peck may be seen sparkling all over the audience. Nowhere can wealth and beauty be seen in greater abundance.

There are almost as many Italians as those of Spanish birth in Buenos Aires. If all the Italians in the city were gathered together into one quarter they would make up a town as large as Genoa. Likewise the "Spaniards from Spain," who now live in Buenos Aires, would populate a city larger than old Toledo. The British colony is probably next in numbers, with the German a close rival and France following in the rear. Americans do not cut much of a figure in numbers, for the North American Society, recently organized, had great difficulty in locating three hundred who claimed allegiance to the Stars and Stripes. And yet this small but enthusiastic body agreed to furnish a statue of George Washington, the father of liberty not only in our own land but in all the Americas, to be erected in that city. The city government has generously granted a site in one of the finest locations in the city. It will be a pleasure to future visitors from the United States to see the familiar likeness of our honoured hero gazing down at them with his benevolent manner in this Latin city.

Buenos Aires is very much unlike our American cities. In the first place there are no skyscrapers that lift their lofty roofs upward. The highest building does not exceed six or seven stories in height. Then there are miles upon miles of streets with buildings of one story predominating. It is laid out in rectangular blocks, averaging about four hundred feet on each side. The streets are narrow, and even in the residence sections they are generally built clear up to the street line. These narrow streets are a relic of the old days when this city was small and dormant. Narrow thoroughfares then meant shaded walks, but shade at that time was a more valuable asset than it is now in a hustling city. The principal business streets, such as Florida, Cuyo, Cangallo, Bartolomé Mitre, San Martin, 25th of May, etc., are only thirty-three feet wide, and you will wonder how the traffic is managed. It is done in this wise. Street cars and vehicles are only allowed to move one way. On the adjoining street they will move in the opposite direction. It is surprising how this plan helps to solve a serious problem of congestion. Cabs and automobiles dash along with seeming disregard of human life, and yet few accidents result. A uniformed policeman is stationed at each street intersection where traffic is congested, and assists in the protection of foot passengers and drivers. This police force made up of men with Indian blood in their veins impresses the visitor as most efficient. There is now a law in effect that no street shall be opened up in the future that is less than sixty feet in width.

"THE BROAD AND IMPOSING AVENIDA DE MAYO"

THE AVENIDA ALVEAR

There is one exception to the narrow streets, and that is the broad and imposing Avenida de Mayo, near the centre of the city. This street, with its wide pavements and rows of trees, lined on either side by hotels, fine stores and office buildings, reminds one of the famous avenues of Paris. The open-air cafés, which line the broad sidewalks of this avenue, only emphasize this resemblance and testify to the fact that the old-world spirit is still alive in Buenos Aires. At one end of the street is the Plaza de Mayo, at the far side of which is the government building in which are the administration offices; and at the other terminus, a mile away, is the Palace of Congress, which has just been completed after thirteen years of building, and at a cost of eight million dollars. With its great dome it gives a prospect very much like that of the Capitol at the end of Pennsylvania Avenue in Washington. The cross streets all begin and end at Calle Rivadavia, just one block from this avenue, for they have a different name on the two ends. One of the streets in the city is called Estados Unidos, which is the Spanish for United States. The Avenida Alvear, which leads out to Palermo, is another striking street. The mansions which line it are interspersed with gardens and plazas, and this broad avenue gains in beauty by this wealth of verdure and flowers.

The people of this southern metropolis may put off until "to-morrow" many things, after the manner of the Spanish people, but they do not idle to-day. Everywhere it is work, work, work, and the people earn their bread by the actual sweat of the brow. That is, all except the wealthy *estancieros*, or plantation owners, who became wealthy by the marvellous rise in the value of their lands. Many men bought a square league of pampa land fifteen or twenty years ago for a few thousand dollars, and it is now worth fifty dollars an acre. This enables them to live in Buenos Aires in idleness and comparative luxury. Greater opportunities, another climate and the virgin soil have instilled a new life into bodies and brains. It is a mingling of the spirit of the old world and the new which shapes the daily life of this city. The term "effete," so often applied to Latin nations, and the "proverbial laziness" of Spaniard and Italian, so often referred to by writers, does not apply here. From the shipping sections where boats, barges and tugs throng in endless procession, from the flats on the river where hundreds of acres have been reclaimed in recent years, to the business section and the wide tree-planted avenues where the electric cars rush out into the residence section, the traveller will observe nothing but movement and effort, unceasing work and activity. In fact, were it not for the difference in architecture, a warmer shade in the complexion of the people, the sonorous consonants of the Castilian tongue, and the fact that the passer-by who jostles you never fails to lift his hat and apologize, the traveller might imagine himself in some unfamiliar part of New York or Philadelphia. There are the same workmen laying asphalt streets, the same gangs of builders and labourers tearing down buildings and laying foundations for great business structures, or demolishing rows of houses to make way for new avenues or squares. Everywhere the city is expanding. It already covers an area four times as large as Manhattan Island, three times larger than Berlin and more than twice that of Paris.

The Spanish people love the beautiful, and that same trait is observed in Argentina. There are many beautiful plazas in Buenos Aires, as well as several free public parks and gardens. In all there are seventy-two of these artistic recreation spaces where the "good airs" of the city can be enjoyed by the population. The finest park is magnificent Palmermo with its rich vegetation, which is a half-hour's ride from the centre of the city. This park is a breathing-place and recreation-ground of which any city might be proud. Although it is below the tropics, yet some species of the palm thrive here, and the vegetation is more luxuriant and much different from that of the latitude of New York or Chicago. The principal sporting and play grounds are all near this park. Through it runs a broad boulevard which leads out to Belgrano, the fashionable suburb of the capital. In this suburb, as well as in the city proper, there are many magnificent private homes, which are veritable palaces. In the older part of the city the courtyard, or *patio,* so typical of Spanish architecture, may be seen. The glimpse of the foliage and blossom that it reveals is decidedly refreshing. In the later buildings, sad to say, the *patio* has disappeared, for the increased value of space seems to forbid this luxury. The network of bars at the windows has likewise vanished.

ONE OF THE PALATIAL HOMES OF BUENOS AIRES

The city offers a prize each year for the handsomest structure that is erected, the awarding of which is in the hands of a regularly organized commission. In addition to the reward, which goes to the architect, the owner is exempted from taxes for a certain period, and is reimbursed out of the city's funds for whatever sums he has expended in creating a street front of artistic character. Buenos Aires owes very little of its beauty to nature. Lest some inharmonious advertising should mar the scene the municipality has taken control of all out-of-door display advertising. No poster can be placed on wall or fence unless it passes muster with the official in charge of this work. The height of a building must have a fixed relation to the width of the street, in order to preserve the light and air. Less than two decades ago the space occupied by the docks was a marshy strip of ground. Now a broad park called the Paseo Cristobal Colon (Columbus) has been laid out and planted with trees and shrubbery. Built upon a site with no natural beauty, so much more credit is due the landscape artists who have transformed this dreary spot.

The markets of Buenos Aires are interesting places to visit. The best hour to visit them is very early in the morning, for everything is astir at that time and all the supplies may be seen in their abundance. As early as four o'clock all is bustle and life. The throng is so great that it is oftentimes with difficulty that one can thread his way through the busy crowd of buyers, sellers and porters. The markets are not especially beautiful but they have a wholesome cleanliness. The most striking feature is the overflowing quantities of everything. Eggs are there by the thousands of dozens, vegetables by the van-load, meat by the ton and fruit by the car-load. The contents of a whole orchard may be seen at a glance. One could fill his house with the fine peaches and pears and scarcely see any diminution in the supply. These two fruits, together with the Mendoza grape, are the finest kinds. It used to be that one could buy a week's supply of vegetables for a small sum, and meat for almost a song, but prices, except for meats, are now almost as high as in our own city markets. A noisy, bustling, motley crowd of people of all sizes and colours fill the aisles. Buxom cooks, pretty Italian girls and vendors with their enormous baskets jostle against each other. To watch the bantering is a source of endless amusement.

"COWS ARE BROUGHT TO THE DOOR"

"You are a thief, as every one knows," says the market woman. "Oh, Señora, only an angel like you could say such things," replies the merchant. And thus they go on passing similar compliments without either one losing his or her temper until a bargain is finally struck. The vendors, however, do not unduly urge, and apparently do not seem to care whether you buy or not. There seems to be no standard of value. In the late afternoon meat may be purchased very cheap, as the law requires all meat to be sold the same day on which it is killed. The butchers go out to the municipal slaughtering houses very early in the morning and kill as many animals as they think they can sell that day.

Those who do not find it convenient to come to the market are supplied by the vendors, who carry fruits and vegetables from door to door. Their supplies are carried in baskets which are suspended on poles swung across the shoulders. The air is filled with the cries of these picturesque peripatetic merchants, of the scissors-grinders and the dealer in notions, most of whom are Italians. In the morning and evening cows are brought to the door and milk drawn direct from nature's reservoirs in any quantity desired. The tinkle of a bell is the herald of the milkman's approach, and the doors open as the good housewife or maid appears with pitcher in hand. Donkey's milk is also delivered in the same way, and its use is often preferred for the feeding of infants.

The capital of Argentina is more like an American city than any other city of South America. The architecture is entirely dissimilar, but the movement on the streets, the arrangement of the stores, and the general bearing of the people bears a marked resemblance. They like to be called the Yankees of South America, for that term signifies energy, resourcefulness and progressiveness. They are deserving of the term too. They are less strenuous than Americans, for they love holidays and enter heartily into the holiday spirit whenever the occasion permits. In that way they seem to get a great deal of pleasure out of life, perhaps more than many of our intensely absorbed, overworked business men.

THE RICOLETA CEMETERY

It is not a city one need hesitate to visit. All the creature comforts may be had. There are good physicians, good hospitals, good schools and the other advantages of populated centres in either the United States or Europe. There are no less than sixteen hospitals in the city, most of which are maintained either by the municipal or federal government. The British Hospital is an admirable institution, and is the one generally patronized by the Americans, for it has a staff of very able physicians. There are also numerous asylums for various unfortunates, foundlings' homes, orphanages, etc., of a very high character. Electric street cars, which carried one hundred and twenty-five million passengers last year, run in every direction, and splendid trains convey passengers to almost every part of the republic. Carriages of all kinds and taxicabs remind one of New York and London. Hotels and restaurants abound on every hand. A visit to this southern metropolis opens one's eyes to the fact that South America is forging ahead at a much more rapid pace than we have ever dreamed.

One of the finest cemeteries of the world is the Ricoleta Cemetery, the fashionable burying place of Buenos Aires. As one enters its appearance is that of a marble and granite city, with small palaces on either side, and narrow streets which are paved the same as the streets of a city. These small palaces are vaults within which the mortal remains of the departed are buried. They are of all sizes and conditions, from small to massive, and from the grand to the unpretentious. Some are the palaces of the rich and others the humble tenements of the poor. A few of these vaults contain hundreds of bodies. All have but one room that can be seen as you enter, and this room is rather furnished as a chapel of the dead, and is not, as a rule, very large. The entrance to the tomb is by a door almost at the level of the street. Sometimes a marble slab in this room may contain the sarcophagus of some distinguished member of the family, but in general this small room is only the entrance to the vault underneath, which contains the bodies. One will generally find this small room filled with flowers, real or artificial, and bouquets are oftentimes placed there at intervals of only a few days. The outside doors of this mausoleum are often of plate glass, furnished with locks, and many of them have lace curtains and gratings of iron curiously wrought. In the vault underneath the coffins are placed on shelves, one above another in niches which have been provided and then cemented in. Although this cemetery is not large it contains, so it is said, about two hundred and fifty thousand inhabitants.

One of the oddest customs in Buenos Aires is that relating to funerals and the burial of the dead. In this city funerals are great functions and the average burial is a very expensive affair. The undertakers advertise their business much as merchants advertise their dry goods. Each one will state how much more he will furnish for his money than his competitor, and praise the caskets which he will furnish and style in which he will conduct the funeral. These are provided in first, second and third class. A first-class funeral is a very imposing occasion. The hearses provided are the most ornate I have ever seen. They are always black, drawn by black horses, and the woodwork is made of carved ebony in very intricate design. Coachmen and footmen, both in the same sombre black livery, are provided, and many coaches follow the hearse, also provided with a coachman in mourning dress. Then again the newspapers will be filled with advertisements of families giving an invitation to their friends to be present at the funeral, also announcing the masses which are given from year to year on the anniversary of the funeral, and inviting their friends to be present at this solemn service. At the church servants will be posted at the door to receive the cards of those who go in, or those who send their regrets, the same as they would at any other social occasion. By scanning the papers the Argentinians keep track of the masses said for their friends. The Argentinians are very respectful toward funerals, and every one will reverently bare his head as a cortege passes by.

The expense of conducting the business of this great city runs into big figures. For the year 1909 the total sum was about thirty million dollars, but the resources were in excess of this amount. In addition to some property tax there are many special imposts, such as tax on advertising permits, building permits, slaughterhouses, markets, cemeteries, street cars, carriages, etc. The national lottery pays a certain proportion of its receipts into the municipal coffers, and the race courses also contribute. The liquor license is small, and as a result the number of such establishments where intoxicants are sold is very large, although saloons or bars after the American or English fashion are found only in the business districts. *Lecherias*, or milk shops, are very numerous, and thousands of gallons of milk are sold over the counters by the glass. Frozen milk takes the place of ice cream at these establishments, which are very neat and cleanly. The police force numbers nearly five thousand, or about one to every two hundred and forty persons. The fire department has numerous stations and is well organized. There are both a national and a municipal department of hygiene, which have control over all municipal sanitation. The efficient work of these organizations has brought down the death rate to where it will compare very favourably with the other large cities of the world.

The water supply and sewer system of the capital are likewise under the direction of the national government. Few cities of the world have a better service. The water is taken from the La Plata River far enough up to avoid any chance of pollution. It is obtained from wells which are driven beneath the bottom of the river, and the water is pumped through tunnels to a central station. Here it is filtered and then distributed to all sections of the city. The central reservoir, called the Aguas Corrientes, is in the heart of the city. With its imposing brick and terra cotta facing on every side, it looks like a magnificent palace, and so I thought it at first sight. Inside, however, it consists only of immense tanks from which the water gravitates over the city. This shell constructed for the water tanks cost the municipality almost a million dollars, and it is all done for the sole purpose of adding to the artistic beauty of the capital.

CHAPTER III
THE CAMP

The flat pampas, or plains, which constitute almost ninety per cent. of the Argentine Republic that is suitable for agriculture and pasture, are generally called the Camp. The name is derived from the Spanish word *campo*, which means country. The Camp is the mainspring of Argentine prosperity. The marble palace of the millionaire, as well as the mud hovel of the immigrant, has to thank this rich soil of the *campo* for its foundation. It is upon this land that the republic has grown and prospered. Its eccentricities and its products are watched with all the anxiety usually lavished upon a baby by anxious parents; and it is a pretty big infant, for the Camp comprises millions upon millions of fertile acres.

The Camp is a vast plain. It spreads its smooth, unbroken surface for hundreds of miles, with no natural hillock higher than those which the termite ants have erected, and no depression more marked than those which the huge cart-wheels have cut in the loose surface soil. It can best be characterized as an ocean of land, spreading out like an unruffled sea from horizon to horizon. Here and there, in the distance, objects may seem to arise out of this vast expanse like little islands at sea, and the illusion at times seems almost perfect. A nearer approach, however, shows them to be the buildings of an *estancia*, or a grove of trees. Even the groves did not exist before the hand of man altered the landscape, for the plains of Argentina were unblessed by any forest growth whatsoever—with the single exception of the rare ombu tree, specimens of which might be met with at intervals of several miles. Spots, which at a distance appear as dark lumps, finally shape themselves into humble structures of black mud, which are the homes of colonists. Their sombre and unattractive exterior may be relieved by the flaming red or vivid blue dress of an Italian girl, which makes a welcome bit of colour under the circumstances. The dust clouds in the distance will be found to be floating behind horses' hoofs, or the wheels of a cumbersome wagon drawn by several yokes of oxen. These clouds move onward across the pampa much as the black smoke trails behind a slow-moving steamer.

These vast stretches of level land may produce a certain sense of irritation upon one newly arrived in Argentina. He may ride for league upon league on his horse, or travel for hour after hour by train, awaiting that change of scenery, which his experience leads him to believe will inevitably occur. He might start in the centre of the republic and travel for scores of leagues east, west, north or south, and find the same unending monotony. But there is, nevertheless, a certain fascination about this very vastness of the Camp which grows upon one; in these leagues upon leagues of rich soil, which here spread themselves in readiness to receive the seed from the hand of the farmer, and to yield forth an abounding harvest in return for the labour bestowed. Upon these plains one may watch the herds of cattle and the flocks of the sheep which are scattered clear to the limit of one's vision, a distance so great that the largest animals stand out as mere specks against the sky. One may travel through miles of the golden grain ready for the sickles of the reaper, and then will come upon an equal stretch of flax in flower, which gives the fields a bluish tint. Interspersed with the wheat and flax may be seen the green corn and the purple of the alfalfa blossom. These broad patches follow one another in almost endless succession. Although one's horizon is at all times limited, he knows that, in whatever direction he looks, that which lies beyond is an exact repetition of what is stretched out before his eyes.

"AGRICULTURE HAS SPREAD FAR AND WIDE"

Agriculture has spread far and wide in Argentina in the last two decades. Its forces are moving ever westward and southward, driving the "squatter" ever farther and farther afield. It has already crossed the boundaries of what was once known as Patagonia, no man's land. Wire fences now enclose the lands which once were the scenes of settlers' battles and boundary disputes. Grains and alfalfa have replaced the coarse natural grass, which was indigenous to these plains. Groves of willow, eucalyptus and poplar have been planted in the older sections of the Camp and make a diversion in the landscape. The picturesque windmill, made in the United States, is a familiar landmark on the horizon almost everywhere, for it is necessary to pump all the water during the greater part of the year.

The Camp has never been divided into homesteads. The most of it is owned by the *estancieros*, whose holdings are estimated by the square league, almost six thousand acres. A man with only one square league is a small farmer, and there are many estates of five and ten square leagues. Many of these were purchased for a mere pittance twenty years ago, and the rise in value has made the owner a wealthy man, so that he can live in

Buenos Aires a part of the year in luxury, or take a trip to Europe each year, as many of them do.

Formerly Argentina was almost entirely a pastoral country. Millions of cattle and sheep wandered over these plains and fed on the rich herbage. The amount of land devoted to stock grazing has been reduced, but the quick-growing alfalfa furnishes more pasture to the acre. At the present time there are thirty million cattle, sixty-seven million sheep, seven million, five hundred thousand horses and mules in the republic, which is a very respectable showing, and places Argentina as one of the most important stock-raising countries in the world. They are very fine stock too. It was the care of the stock that gave rise to the "gaucho," the cowboy of South America, and it was this character that gave romance and local colour to the Camp.

THRESHING GRAIN ON AN ESTANCIA

As a grain-raising country Argentina has advanced by leaps and bounds. At the present time it is the greatest flax-raising country in the world, and our own linseed oil mills have been obliged to import seed from there during the past two years. It is second only to the United States and Russia in the production of wheat, and in some years has exported more than our own land. At the stations one will sometimes see mountains of wheat bags awaiting shipment to the ports, where hundreds of vessels are ready to carry this grain to the hungering millions of Europe. The threshing outfits move ponderously from one *estancia* to another, doing the entire work of harvesting on a percentage basis, usually one sack out of every three. Some of them are pulled by oxen or mules, and others are run by traction power. These processions move across the plains in imposing fashion. The huge stacks commence to rise in twos and threes like giant mushrooms, until the landscape is dotted with them. Then strings of wagons, laden to the brim, carry the wheat to the warehouses, which open wide their doors to receive this valuable product of the soil. The stacks must be made very secure, for the winds sweep over these plains with almost incredible velocity.

"NOT A HANDSOME STRUCTURE, BUT ... RATHER STRIKING"

Italians have flocked to Argentina by the hundreds of thousands. They have become the most important asset of the agriculturist. The colonist is usually allotted a certain number of acres, which he cultivates on a fixed share. Perhaps the landlord reserves as his portion one bag out of every ten of grain. The colonist is given the bare land, and must provide his own dwelling. But that is a simple matter. Rough boards are made into a mould, similar to that prepared for the pouring of cement, into which mud mixed with straw is placed. When this has dried the boards are removed, and the wall of the house is finished. Spaces for doors and windows are then cut out, a roof placed over it, and the house is ready for occupancy. Or this mud may be cut into bricks, which are allowed to dry in the sun and then laid up into walls. A roof of thatch made of coarse grasses is generally used. From an artistic standpoint the result is not a handsome structure, but it is rather striking. The black mud walls are sombre and commonplace, and even the best of them is scarcely more than a hovel. There is reason, however, for this economy in the construction of a house, as the colonist may be obliged to move to another section of the plantation in two or three years, or even to another plantation, when it will be necessary to build another home. The frugal Italian during these years is no doubt sending money back to Italy, or depositing it in a bank in a neighbouring town. Many of them, after a few years, tiring of the mud walls and ceaseless work, go back to their beloved Italy, where the few thousands saved make them veritable capitalists among their friends and neighbours.

The *estanciero's* life is a rather lonely one, for his neighbours are few and far between. If he is an Englishman or Scotchman, as many of them are, you will find the British atmosphere all about. There will be tennis courts, cricket grounds, and, perhaps, a golf course where the family and their friends will find recreation. Pheasant hatcheries are sometimes maintained, and these birds and the long-eared rabbits, which are very plentiful, furnish the shooting so popular with the British sportsman. The Camp store, however, is the centre of life on the *estancia*. It is the post office and the general place of rendezvous. There are heaps of padlocks and nails, stacks of lamps and coils of wire. Beside quaintly carved native saddles will be fierce-looking knives a foot or more in length, which peacefully repose in bright new leather sheaths. Boots that might have graced a cavalier of old jostle against bottles of patent medicine guaranteed to cure every ill to which human flesh is heir. Business is never done in haste. The gaucho measures time by the progress of the sun, and an odd half hour or so never bothers him. There is always a little time for gossip before and after the purchase has been made, and then there must be a drink for friendship's sake.

Drouths come sometimes, and the locusts, to break in upon the prosperity of both colonist and *estanciero*. But there is seldom an absolute failure. The locusts are present almost every year, and it is a constantly recurring fight against the scourge of these pests.

The real development of the live stock industry in Argentina began with the discovery that meat could be frozen and shipped any distance. Since that time the growth has been almost phenomenal. It used to be that long-horned, rakish, bony *criollos* (native stock) wandered over the pampas feeding on the succulent grasses, and dying by the thousands during a season of drouth. Now the sleek short-horned stock have taken their places, and they fatten upon the rich alfalfa pastures which have been sown by the planter. This plant roots so deep that it will remain green in drouths that would cause the native grass to become dry and dead. Fine sheep have superseded the scrubby animals that once stalked the plains; and even the horse has acquired finer legs and shoulders, and developed a more graceful arch to his neck. Indeed, it may be said that the average stock in Argentina will compare favourably with those of any other nation on the globe. The change has been brought about by the importation of the very best breeding stock from Europe, which have formed the nuclei for the present herds.

The Durham, Hereford and polled Angus are the chief grades of cattle that one will find. In one section of the country one breed will predominate, and a few leagues away another will prevail almost exclusively. Cattle are always sold at so much a head, and never by weight. "Do you never weigh them?" I asked of an *estanciero*. "Oh, yes, we weigh a few so that we have an idea of the general average." In the transaction, however, between him and the buyer, weight is never mentioned. The buyer will look over the bunch for sale and offer a stated figure, which may or may not be accepted. They are then delivered to him at a given point, and shipped to the stockyards in Buenos Aires, or to one of the many slaughterhouses in the republic. The number of stock to be kept is a serious problem for the proprietor. More than one *estanciero* has been ruined by overstocking his *estancia*, and then, either locusts or the drouth coming, he was left without feed for his animals.

The cattle dip is a very necessary adjunct to every stock farm. The idea was adopted from Australia, where the cattle raisers had similar experience with the tick fever. It consists of a wide yard which gradually narrows into a lane wide enough for only one animal. When the animal is driven forward it faces a lengthy tank which it is necessary to ford. This tank is filled with a medicated solution and, as the animal swims through it, men with poles push them entirely under. The animal does not enjoy swimming through this nauseous, badly-tasting mixture, but he has no option, so, shutting his mouth tightly, he flounders through in the best way possible. It is rather a sorry looking creature, however, that emerges on the other side. Another form of dipping cattle is a cage into which an animal is driven, and this is submerged in a tank filled with this medicated solution. Either method accomplishes the desired result, which is to give the cattle a thorough saturation that will kill the tick.

Second in importance comes sheep. Although they abound all over the republic they are found in greatest numbers in the southern provinces. The development of these animals has been studied a great deal lately and scientific methods have been introduced. The finest of rams have been imported in order to improve the breed and the former coarse wool is now being replaced by a much finer quality. The Argentine merinos will now rank with those from any part of the world. One will find Leicesters, Oxfords, Black-faced Downs and all the other fine breeds. A number of New Zealand ranchers have come to Argentina in recent years, and they have been especially successful in sheep raising. The breeds have been bettered, and foot-rot as well as other diseases combated with so that the results have been very beneficial to the industry.

Sheep farming in Argentina is an old industry. The number of sheep has grown until there are now at least ten for each man, woman and child in the republic. How many sheep the pampas can support is hardly known, but it would be several times the present number. Where there is plenty of rain an acre will support three or four head, and at other places it would be safer to keep three or four acres for each sheep. In the Buenos Aires province the best ranchers place about six hundred sheep to each square mile. The sheep farming is all conducted on a big scale, and there are few small flocks. The most of the flocks range from ten thousand to seventy-five thousand, with some possibly several times the latter number. The sheep are watched on the open pampas by shepherds on horseback, each having the care of a fixed number. It is the shepherd's duty to see that the flocks do not mingle, and to keep them free from disease. For this work they receive a stated sum monthly, which would not be considered large in the United States.

Formerly the sheep were raised for the wool, pelts and tallow only. Even then they were profitable. The carcasses were even used for fuel. Now, with the development of the frozen meat industry, this meat feeds the mutton-eaters of England. Hundreds and thousands of tons of frozen mutton are shipped down the La Plata every month. It is frozen so stiff that it will keep for months and be as palatable as freshly slaughtered meat. The slaughtering establishments are mostly located along the Paraná River, between Buenos Aires and Rosario. Acres upon acres are covered with sheep pens, slaughtering houses and freezing establishments. The frozen carcass is sewed up in fine white muslin cloths, and then laid away to await the next steamer, whose hold will be filled with these ghostly bundles. The wool is sent to the great wool market in Buenos Aires. Each man's wool is placed in a pile by itself, all unwashed, and so brings a low price because of the weight of the grease in it, for wool will lose almost half its weight in washing. The Argentine farmer prefers to sell it at the lower rate and allow the European or American buyers to clean it.

The lambing and shearing seasons are the two busiest and most anxious seasons for the sheep raiser. A good lambing season will almost double the flock, so prolific do they become. Sheep shearing used to be done almost entirely by hand, but nearly all the big ranches now have sheep-shearing machines driven by steam or gasoline power. Still, whether done by hand in the old way or by machines in the modern way, sheep shearing is arduous work. The shearers often go about in bands from ranch to ranch. The quickness and skill of some of the shearers borders almost on the marvellous. One hundred sheep daily is a fair average for good shearers, but some exceptionally expert operators can double that score. A great deal of care has to be exercised to clip the wool as close as possible, and still leave the animal uninjured. A shearer who could not practise his business without badly cutting the sheep would soon be discharged as incompetent. The poor animals have to put up with a few scratches and cuts, but it is seldom that one is severely injured. The amount of wool and mutton sent out from these sheep ranches is almost incredible. An especially fine quality of wool is produced on the great ranches of Patagonia, one of which is larger than the state of Rhode Island.

A HERD OF HALF-WILD HORSES

Horses are also raised in great numbers in Argentina. One who sees the fine draught horses in Buenos Aires need not be told that Argentine horses are of good breed and quality. The average Argentinian thinks that he knows more about a horse than anything else. Pedigreed stallions have been imported by the hundreds, and the very best blood has been brought in. One will find as good horses in Argentina as anywhere. They are generally well taken care of, too, for lean and skinny horses are very rare. During the Boer-English war fortunes were made out of horses, for the British government bought thousands of head and paid fancy prices. They were beaten, too, in many a bargain by the shrewd *estancieros*. Pig breeding has not been developed much as yet, although considerable stride has been made in some sections, but the export of pork does not amount to any considerable sum. Great hopes are, however, entertained by the Argentinians for this industry also.

All agriculture is on a gigantic scale. The rapid development has been a surprise to even the most hopeful *estanciero*. Railways have, in many instances, been almost unable to cope with some of the crops, and trains have been run night and day to carry the grain to the exporting centres. The wheat accumulates at the shipping points until vast stacks are piled up at the various stations in the wheat lands. One company's cars cannot run over another company's tracks, and this further adds to the congestion. The wheat is carried to the stations on huge carts with wheels eight feet high and drawn by from ten to a dozen oxen. A load of several tons may be balanced between these two lofty wheels. As the carts move forward they are accompanied by an awful screeching noise which is ear-splitting. The carter does not care to use grease, as he says that the noise encourages the oxen. The cry goes up each year for more labourers to care for the crops, and the need still exists. Because of the lack of elevators and granaries the grain must be quickly gathered and threshed. Women and girls, men and boys all work from early morning until late at night for the few harvest weeks. The grains are generally more profitable than stock, and in some districts have crowded the latter out. Corn is one of the most profitable crops at the present time.

"THE HARVESTING MACHINES ARE USUALLY PROPELLED FROM THE REAR"

During the harvest time the Camp is a busy place. Clouds of dust all over the horizon denote activity in the grain fields. Managers and overseers are kept busy riding from one group to another. Thousands of Italians come over for the harvests and then return to their native land. The harvesting machines are usually propelled from the rear, either by steam power or animals. Attached to the side of the "strippers," which simply cut off the heads of the grain, is a large harvest cart into which the grain drops. Four roads will be cut from a central point at right angles to each other, which run to the outer edge of the wheat field. In the central point the oblong stacks are formed. By this system the fields of golden grain rapidly disappear before the onslaughts of the cutting machines.

Thirty years ago Argentina was a wheat-importing nation. Some of the knowing ones said wheat could not be successfully grown on the pampas. Since then the grain-producing area has been increased each year and the beginning of the end is not yet in sight. At first it was thought that only the land between the Paraná and Uruguay Rivers was available, but now it has spread south into Patagonia and west to the Andes. The available wheat land has been estimated at more than 200,000,000 acres, of which only a small per cent. is at present under cultivation. This wheat land is mostly a rich black loam, from a few inches to three feet or more deep, surmounting a subsoil of clay.

There are few rivers or lakes on the Camp and there is little surface water. The old-fashioned wells sunk very deep in the ground, in which the buckets are raised by horse power, are still quite common. Windmills of American make add a picturesqueness to the landscape. Ponds are banked up into which the water is pumped, and from them the troughs are filled. These wells seldom go dry even in the severe drouths in that land.

The midday siesta is almost universal in the Camp, for the sun beats down unmercifully hot for a few hours. The languor of these hours is all-pervading. Stock huddle together and put their heads in the shadow of the bodies of the others. The mosquito is very much at home on the Camp and sometimes makes the nights unappreciated.

A GAUCHO AND HIS WIFE ON AN OUTING

One fearful disease is the anthrax, which is taken from cattle. The first symptom is a red mark on the skin, which is irritating. If unattended to this will develop into a blue boil surrounded by little blisters. After a while the sensitiveness disappears and no pain is felt. The blue is more pronounced and a full-fledged case of anthrax is developed. Something must be done promptly. The common treatment, when no surgeon is near, is to heat a wire red hot and burn out the infected spot clean from the surrounding flesh. This is a decidedly painful operation when performed without anæsthetics, and requires a remarkable degree of stoicism. The affected spot is absolutely without feeling. If this or another effective operation is not performed by the third day the chance of recovery is very slight, it is said. The gauchos are the principal sufferers.

Like his counterpart, the cowboy of the western plains, the gaucho is a unique character, and his individuality is probably the result of his environment and the life he has led. The freedom of the plains and lack of refining society have made him a man with a rough exterior which, however, oftentimes clothes a tender human heart. The gaucho of Argentina is generally of mixed blood. The blood may have become mixed centuries back, when the first Spaniards came to this country, but it still shows in his swarthy features. For centuries these people have lived an easy-going, care-free existence on the great plains of that republic. If there is one thing the gaucho loves, it is his freedom, and it is difficult to accustom him to the restraint that becomes necessary as development and private ownership proceed. In the centuries past the gauchos have always been engaged in the wars and revolutions which were common. The side they fought on did not matter much, for it was victory only that was sought. When there were no public disturbances to furnish excitement, they got up feuds on their own account, and fought each other. The Camp is full of tales of the gauchos and their deeds or misdeeds, many of which savour of real knight-errantry. It is these tales that has given the Argentinian plains an individuality. The old-time lawless gaucho has generally disappeared in the march of civilization, but the modified character remains and works for the ranch owner. Many of them have intermarried with the Italian and Spanish colonists who have migrated there. The railroad has perhaps been the greatest enemy of the gaucho, just as it was of the cowboy on our own western plains, because settlers have everywhere followed the iron horse.

The costume of the gaucho has not changed. It still consists of a broad sombrero, a shirt and the *bombachos*—wide Turkish trousers that range in colour from black to snow-white, and which fall to just above the ankle, where they are enclosed in a pair of tight-fitting boots. The *poncho*, a blanket which is placed over the shoulders in cool weather, varies from the most sombre hues to the boldest colours—brown and black to brilliant scarlet or purple. The effect of such a brilliantly-clothed apparition coming upon you unawares in a remote district can better be imagined than described. A great broad knife is almost invariably stuck in the belt, many of them a foot in length and of fantastic pattern. It is generally encased in a leathern, but sometimes in a metal, scabbard. This knife is intended not only for defence, but it is his principal aid in eating lunches out on the Camp. His favourite food is *asado con cuero,* beef roasted over the fire without removing the hide, and he is an expert in preparing this luxury. Dressed in all his finery, and mounted upon a saddle inlaid and ornamented with silver as many are, with fancy stirrups and huge clanking spurs, the South American gaucho is a sight worthy to behold.

The gaucho is a born horseman. From earliest childhood he has been accustomed to a horse's back. Before his legs are long enough to reach the stirrups of a saddle the gaucho rides bareback, and an occasional tumble does not seem to be minded, for they are determined to ride. Caution or fear concerning horses is not known among them—such sentiments are altogether incomprehensible to their understanding. I have seen contests between the gauchos and American cowboys in Buenos Aires, and, although the latter are quicker in saddling and mounting a pony, they cannot stick on a bucking broncho any better than the former.

GAUCHOS BRANDING CATTLE

The gaucho is a rather taciturn individual, and is not given to many words. At the same time he is easily offended if any sense of superiority is shown. He may not show resentment on the surface, but a volcano may rage underneath a placid and immobile countenance. If there is, in his opinion, sufficient provocation, he will probably bide his time for revenge and await it patiently. It is not always done in the open, either, since he does not want a chance for failure. If he likes his employer his devotion is admirable, and he will serve with a commendable faithfulness. When roused by liquor the gaucho is often very troublesome, and then it is that he starts out to avenge real or fancied slights, and he sometimes commits serious crimes. Money does not appeal to the gaucho in a strong sense, and crimes as a rule are not committed for that purpose, but they are to avenge slights or real wrongs for which he thinks personal reprisal is the only adequate remedy. To requite a wrong with him is a point of honour. The gauchos are natural gamblers and, besides ordinary games of the Camp, there is scarcely anything that is not made the subject of wagering, and the average gaucho's money soon disappears. It is doubtful whether education will make the gaucho a more efficient ranch hand, though it will make him a better and more intelligent citizen of a republic.

The work of the gaucho is generally confined to the care of stock, of which such vast herds swarm the pampas in almost every direction. The mustering of cattle in Argentina is called a "rodeo." Viewed from a distance, one will see a line strongly marked wind its way over the level plain, with a dust cloud hanging over it, which is visible long before the animals come in view. As the armies of red, white and dun animals approach nearer one will see the picturesque gauchos riding here and there like officers of an army bearing commands.

When the place of rendezvous has been reached the cattle are kept tramping around a central point, as they are not near so likely to get frightened or stampeded if kept on the move. When the inspection or count is ended, the different herds are gradually separated by the gauchos and driven back to the feeding grounds. If a count is intended a line is formed through which the cattle are driven, and the cattle are numbered as they pass through the line. This is sometimes a difficult operation, and especially is it so if they aim to divide the herd into two or more bodies. One animal is driven to the right, another to the left and so on. This sometimes leads to a great deal of excitement and confusion among the cattle, and stampedes are easy to happen under such circumstances. Stockyards have been built on many ranches, where a narrow passage is constructed through which only one animal is able to pass at a time. This greatly simplifies the counting or dividing process. Furthermore, there is less danger of the animals injuring each other in their excitement. The gauchos are clever with the lasso, but cannot equal the American cowboy with that rope. Altogether the gaucho is a very useful and a very necessary man on the cattle *estancias* of Argentina, and his services are generally appreciated.

CHAPTER IV
THE RIVER OF SILVER

The Rio de la Plata, the "river of silver," is one of the great river systems of the world. That name is properly applied only to the month of the system, which reaches just a little above the city of Buenos Aires, a distance of a couple of hundred miles from the Atlantic. From there it receives the name of the Paraná, which has its source in the wilds of Brazil. Where it pours its waters into the ocean this wonderful river is one hundred and eighty miles in width, and at Montevideo it has narrowed down to sixty-five miles. Opposite Buenos Aires it is still twenty-eight miles from shore to shore. The La Plata, as it is generally called, discharges the water from a basin much larger than the Mississippi, and the volume of water brought down by it is said to be exceeded only by the Amazon. It drains the greater part of the fertile pampas, reaches up into the coffee lands of Brazil, and carries down to the Atlantic the melted snows of the loftiest peaks of the Andes. The basin is in the shape of an immense horseshoe, and includes, besides the two above counties, all of Paraguay and parts of Bolivia and Uruguay.

The Uruguay River, which flows into the La Plata almost opposite Buenos Aires, is one thousand miles long and is navigable for several hundred miles, the Paraná for almost two thousand miles, and the Paraguay, from its junction with the latter stream, floats boats of shallow draft for fifteen hundred miles farther. Altogether these various streams furnish thousands of miles of navigable waters on which regular communication is furnished by large and commodious steamers. Nicolas Mihanovitch is the undisputed king of this river traffic, and dozens of vessels plying on these rivers bear the white letter M. with a black background on the funnel. They furnish a nightly service between Montevideo and Buenos Aires, and weekly or semi-weekly service up the Paraná and Uruguay Rivers.

Vessels drawing sixteen feet of water can proceed as far as Rosario, but ocean-going steamers seldom ascend any farther, as the water becomes shallower beyond that city. Boats of twelve feet draught can proceed as far as Asuncion, the capital of Paraguay, eight hundred miles farther inland. The waters carry much mud, and the channel sometimes changes its course by the formation of mud banks. Hundreds of islands have formed, some of which probably started from a submerged tree, about which the sediment was deposited. In truth the Paraná plays with islands and sand banks as a lesser stream does with pebbles. A recent scientific writer has given some interesting facts concerning its eccentricities. Says he: "A schooner which sank nine years ago off La Paz swiftly developed at its tail an island a mile long, now crowned by willows. My photograph of the old port of Paraná town in 1902 shows an island eight hundred and eighty yards long by four hundred and ninety feet wide fronting it; in December, 1907, only one hundred and sixty feet of the island remained. Thirty years ago a market gardener made a shallow ditch cut-off opposite Ibicuy River (Lower Paraná), to take his produce down the river. The Paraná elected to take his work in hand, and now ocean steamers pass through this channel on their way down from Rosario."

In the rainy season the Paraná spreads out for dozens of miles over the level land and forms an inland sea so wide that the banks are almost invisible. This flood season lasts for three months in the year, generally from March to June. At this season the Paraguay pours a mass of water twenty miles wide and twenty feet deep into the Paraná. Added to this is the water of the Alta Paraná, and the Lower Paraná then spreads itself out over the low lands of the western bank.

> "Shallow, disreputable, vast,
> It sprawls across the western plains,"

to use the words of Kipling. Because of the slight fall it takes three weeks for the flood waters to flow from Asuncion, a thousand miles upstream but only two hundred and three feet above sea level, to Buenos Aires. It is estimated that this river brings down a cubic mile of soil in twenty-two years. This soil is deposited on the western shore of the La Plata, and, were it not for the work of man, would soon convert Buenos Aires into a landlocked harbour. As it is, the dredging charges entailed by this yearly increasing mass of deposit are very large.

In places the banks of the Paraná are lined with reeds and willows, but farther up the trees become larger, and there is a forest growth. In one place may be seen gigantic reeds twenty feet high, then a solitary palm tree with a crest of fan-like leaves, and again a dense forest of various growths may crown the bank. Gnarled trees with clusters of beautiful crimson flowers occasionally add a contrast of colouring. Masses of weeds and grass are continually floating by. One cannot help but think of the voyage of Sebastian Cabot up this unexplored stream, in 1526. In a small vessel of only a few hundred tons he ploughed through these waters, avoided destruction on the islands, and ascended to a point above the site of Asuncion. He was months in accomplishing that voyage, which is now made twice a week in five days. It is not a hard trip, except that the scenery becomes rather monotonous. Otherwise the accommodation is quite good, the fare is cheap, and, as a rule, the cabins are comfortable and are kept very clean.

By steamer it is nearly three hundred miles from Buenos Aires to Rosario, the second city in the republic, and takes just about a whole day. The great delta of the Paraná, just above the metropolis, is very interesting, for it is studded with numerous islands. There are several ports on the left bank where large *frigorificos*, meat-freezing plants, are located, where vessels may be seen at the docks at all times waiting for their loads of beef and mutton. The largest of these is at Campaña, only fifty-one miles from Buenos Aires, where the River Plate Meat Co. has its freezing works. At Zarate is the freezing plant of the Las Palmas Produce Co., and at San Nicolas is another large *frigorifico*. At last Rosario, which used to be an unimportant place, is reached, but that designation would not answer for the hustling city of to-day.

Soon after leaving Rosario the river passes through the rich wheat belt, with the province of Entre Rios on one side of the bank and Santa Fé on the other. For a distance the banks of the Paraná are quite high on one side, but they gradually become lower. At length the town of Paraná, a city of twenty-five thousand inhabitants, and the capital of the province of Entre Rios, is reached. It is the distributing point for quite a large section of country and a shipping port for the products as well.

Opposite Paraná is the city of Santa Fé, capital of the province of the same name, which is of about the same importance as its rival on the other side of the river. The river leads up past La Paz and Esquma, at which latter place the province of Corrientes is entered. The city of Corrientes contains a population of about twenty thousand, and is a distributing and shipping point for that province. It is not a pretty city at all and has nothing to distinguish it. Here a change must be made to boats of lighter draught, for there are rapids between this city and Posadas that will not permit a draught of more than three feet in the dry season. It is only about twenty miles to the junction of the Paraguay River, and is two hundred and twenty-five miles from Corrientes to Posadas, the capital of the territory of Misiones. It is the collecting depot for the up-river trade above this point, and is a thriving little city of about six thousand inhabitants.

The Paraná becomes grander and more picturesque the farther up one ascends it. Its quiet picturesqueness grows upon the traveller. It is hemmed in between the hills of Paraguay, on one side, and those of Misiones on the other. Its width, hitherto anywhere from two to five miles, suddenly shrinks to two-thirds of a mile, and its depth increases. The well-wooded ranges of hills slope to a current running five knots an hour. A graceful line of waving bamboo marks the mean height of the river and is only broken by the many streams which come tumbling down. You are travelling toward the equator, and the vegetation changes. The trees become still larger, and the grass is more luxuriant. Many varieties of palms make their appearance. A thousand miles from Rosario is the junction with the Iguassú River, and a few miles from its mouth are the famous falls of the same name. They are on the boundary line between Brazil and Argentina, and only a few miles away from the border of Paraguay. At some imaginary point on the broad Paraná, in the midst of these vast solitudes, these three republics meet.

The Falls of the Iguassú, which here lie half concealed by the crowding forests, are a worthy rival of Niagara. The scenery surrounding is, in its lone loveliness, in harmony with the solemn grandeur of the cataract. The roar of the waterfall is all the more impressive because of the solitude that reigns in these primeval forests. These falls cover a wide area, as they are nearly two miles in length. They are so great that they must be viewed from several points before their full magnitude dawns upon the traveller. They plunge out of the hidden recesses of the forest in many places, for numerous islands have been formed which are now densely wooded. Nature here seems to have revelled in perfect abandon in producing this wonderful spectacle. It is like another Niagara set out in the midst of a wilderness, where the hand of man has done nothing to add to or detract from what nature has here prepared for the delectation of mankind.

The falls may be divided into two sections, the Argentine and Brazilian cascades. The Iguassú River is very wide just above the falls where it takes a very sharp turn prior to making the first plunge. It makes a series of three leaps, the last being a drop exceeding two hundred feet. The unequal erosion of the rock has given the falls a horseshoe shape very similar to Niagara. Below the falls the water passes through a narrow gorge where the depth is so great that a hundred fathom line has failed to sound it. The natives call it bottomless. In 1905, during an unusually severe rainy season, the water rose so high here, because of the narrowness of the gorge, that for five days it was backed up to the total height of the lowest falls, two hundred and ten feet.

Ascending the Alta Paraná, another one hundred and twenty-five miles, one reaches the smoking cataracts of La Guayra. So scored are the river's banks on either side by cascade and torrents that it might be called "waterfall land." The Falls of La Guayra are another series of mighty cascades on the border between Paraguay and Brazil. Above the falls is a great lake all of the waters of which must pass over these precipices and through a narrow gorge. At one point it is only two hundred feet from cliff to cliff. The current piles up in the centre with a corkscrew motion which forms a maelstrom, with which the famous Whirlpool Rapids are a quiet pool. The total plunge of these falls is three hundred and ten feet. Above the La Guayra the Alta Paraná widens out and the hills retreat. At a distance of four hundred miles, or a total distance of one thousand six hundred and forty miles from Buenos Aires, are the Uberaponga Falls, another frantic water power awaiting the harnessing by man. One can follow this stream on up to its source in a flat, swampy section, which is also the source of one of the principal affluents of the Amazon. It drains a very large section of Brazil, for, because of the range of mountains which follows the coast line in Brazil, water falling within a few miles of the Atlantic turns its back on the blue waters of the ocean and journeys from fifteen hundred to two thousand miles before entering salt water by means of the La Plata.

The route up the Uruguay River is much more picturesque than that up the Paraná. This majestic stream is about six miles wide at its junction with the latter river. It is somewhat less obstructed by islands here, so that both banks can usually be seen. And yet this great stream has moods, as well as other rivers. The current in its main channel will oftentimes change. It will encroach here and recede there, submerge an island in one place and form a new one in another. After a long drouth navigation must be conducted with caution, but the normal depth is generally sufficient for all purposes. During times of flood all kinds of strange small animals and vegetation are brought down by the Uruguay. The water is decidedly clay coloured. On one side is the flat Argentine plain, and on the other the undulating shores of Uruguay, for this river is the international boundary line between these two republics. Small topsail schooners may be seen coming down the river loaded with timber or fruit, and bound either for Montevideo or Buenos Aires. Farther up the stream contracts and one gets a more intimate acquaintance with the country. The banks shrink back and reveal a glimpse of flowering shrubs, willow trees, and an occasional palm. A stretch of bright, sandy beach may occasionally unfold itself. It is sometimes difficult to distinguish shore from island. Buoys mark the channel, which is very much zigzag. The sunsets on these broad waters and flat pampas are really wonderful. They paint the clouds in every colour and shade of rosy pink and brilliant red, and the waters become of a bluish hue. The cliffs on the Uruguay side are tinted in many colours, while the Argentine bank is nothing but a straight, black line.

The boats stop on either side. One hundred and thirty miles from Buenos Aires, and on the Uruguay side, is the town of Fray Bentos, where the great Liebig's Extract Factory is located. On the opposite side and a little further up is Concepcion del Uruguay, which is an interesting little town. The busiest and most important town of Argentina on the Uruguay River is Concordia, two hundred and seventy miles from the metropolis. It is a town of perhaps fifteen thousand inhabitants, and has railway communication as well. Because of a falls and rapids at this point the large river steamers cannot proceed beyond Concordia, although light draught boats can ascend considerably farther.

Between the Paraná and Uruguay Rivers lie the two goodly-sized provinces of Entre Rios and Corrientes, and the territory of Misiones. The two provinces are each about the size of Indiana, and are rich in agricultural lands. Wheat was first successfully cultivated in Entre Rios, and these provinces still produce large quantities of grain as well as much stock. Each one has a population of about a third of a million and it is increasing each year. A number of colonies have been established there which have been quite successful. Corrientes contains several swampy lakes which cover many hundreds of square miles. A part of the year the greater part of these lakes is dry and then furnishes excellent pasturage. Their worst feature is that they are the breeding places of the tick and other pests to stock. A good system of drainage might make these lands invaluable. It also possesses one large body of water, called Lake Ibera.

Misiones is a little larger than Massachusetts, and has a population not exceeding thirty-five thousand. Its lands are fertile, but the climate is more tropical and it has not been developed so rapidly as the other sections of the country. It is the only province in Argentina that shares the tropical conditions of Southern Brazil. The name was derived from its settlement by the Jesuits after they were expelled from Brazil. For a time their colonies were very prosperous and thousands of Indians were gathered together at Apostoles, Santa Ana and San Ignacio. The work was all done by the Indians under the direction of the priests. The ruins of San Ignacio, which was established in the sixteenth century, and which can still be traced in the forest growth, show the solidity with which the place was built. Many ruins of the houses can still be seen, each one with a niche in which was placed the statue of a saint. New settlements of Russians and Poles have recently been established in this territory which give promise of success. There is much rich virgin land awaiting development in forest-covered Misiones. *Yerba maté*, tobacco, mandioca and sugar-cane grow in great abundance.

Proceeding up the Paraguay River from its junction with the Alta Paraná it is about two hundred miles to Asuncion. The river twists around over its wide bed in a very capricious manner, and in flood times spreads over thousands of square miles of the *llanos*, or plains. One can travel several hundred miles farther by small steamers up into the great state of Matto Grosso, Brazil, which is twice as large as Texas, and perhaps of equal fertility. The unoccupied grazing lands of that state will, some day, support millions of cattle that will be demanded by earth's teeming millions.

Flowing into the Paraguay River from the west in Argentina are two rivers, the Bermejo and Pilcomayo, the latter of which is the international boundary line with Paraguay for a long distance. Each of these rivers is more than five hundred miles in length. The Bermejo River is entirely within Argentine territory. It is exceedingly tortuous and its actual length is about three times as great as the real distance between its source and its mouth. Small steamers can navigate it for at least half of its length.

Between these two rivers and extending across the Paraguay River into Paraguay lies what is known as the Gran Chaco. This is a broad plain, alternating with forest, which includes thousands of square miles of territory. It is the least known of Argentine territory, because of the difficulties of travel, and also because of the fact that wild and savage Indians who lead a nomadic existence are still to be found in certain sections. It was a mysterious and strange country to the early explorers. Into this wilderness the natives fled, and both fancy and imagination peopled it with all manner of strange wild beasts. The territorial boundaries were never definitely settled, until President Hayes, acting as arbitrator, fixed the boundaries between Paraguay and Argentina. These vast leagues are now divided into two territories, Formosa and Chaco. The former is almost as large as Ohio and the latter equals Illinois. In the two territories the reported population is about one person to each five square miles. There are many curious phenomena in the Chaco. The edges between plain and woodland are as clearly cut and as straight as if a surveyor had done the work. In fact the line of demarkation is drawn with remarkable exactitude. On one side will be a forest, and on the other the smooth plain stretches out with not a tree upon it to break the severity of the contrast. In other places there will be only palm trees, with not a single specimen of another species for variety. It is a land of strange watercourses. Broad streams that have ploughed all the way from the Andes in the full light of day burrow beneath the ground in the Chaco and continue their course underground. During heavy rainfalls it is claimed that small fish descend from the clouds. Fish eight or ten inches in length will be found in pools after showers, where there had been no water, and the ground had been in a parched condition for months. Do they lie imbedded in the earth like frogs? Are these fish amphibious? These questions have not yet been answered. It is a fact that there are many odd phases of nature in this little known section of Argentina; the same character is found in a goodly part of Paraguay, and it even extends up into Brazil.

A FOREST IN THE GRAN CHACO

The forest section of the Chaco is not a dense growth like the tropical forests. The trees do not stand close together; and the spaces between are not impenetrable, although some underbrush and tall grasses impede the way. Yet a man on horseback can easily thread his way through them. The only inhabitants are the Indians and half-breeds, the latter of whom are only partially civilized. Their homes are mud huts of a single room where the entire household, irrespective of age and sex, lodge. The Chaco abounds in game of many kinds. Partridges, wood-pigeons and snipe are very plentiful, and almost every species of water fowl in addition. A species of wild turkey is also to be met with, which affords most excellent sport as well as eating. The osprey, whose plumes are so much in demand, is a native of this land. The tapir, ant-eater, wild pig, jaguar and the lone wolf—a creature that has never been known to live in captivity—are found here in their native wilds. Poisonous snakes are very common, and huge pythons are occasionally encountered in the swamps. It is the innumerable insects, however, that make life almost unbearable for the white man, for he is subjected to both diurnal and nocturnal torture by the hordes of these pests.

At the present time this section is chiefly exploited for the quebracho wood. This is a very hard, fine-grained and tough wood. It was so named from the words *quiebra-hacha*, the axe-breaker, and was well named, for it does defy ordinary axes and saws. It is a tree found only in the Chaco. There are two varieties, the *colorado* (red) and *blanco* (white), of which the former is the most valuable. From this tree are made railroad ties which will last for thirty years, and it is the richest in tannin extract of any tree yet discovered.

The quebracho tree usually stands out by itself and is easily discernible at a distance, both from the character of its bark and the peculiar formation of its branches. Four or five trees to the acre is about the average yield. The tree is tall, two or three feet in diameter, and is crowned by a rather thin, oval mass of branches and leaves. The leaves are oval, smooth and shiny, and it is only partially deciduous. It lives to a great age, but also grows quite rapidly, so that it can be cultivated in the future as necessity demands. Formerly this tree was sought only by the railroads for their sleepers. About fifteen years ago it was found to be full of tannin, and, as oak bark was becoming scarce, this demand was rapidly developed and now forms the principal use for quebracho. Not only the bark yields tannin, but the sap and wood as well. The bark contains about eight per cent. of tannin, the sap three or four per cent., and the heart of the tree will yield as high as twenty-five per cent. of this essence so necessary to the tanner. It is a difficult and expensive product to market because of the remoteness of the forests and scattered character of the trees. In many places narrow gauged railroads and spurs have been run out through these trackless wastes in order to bring the logs to the mills or rivers. Otherwise it would be slow work, for during a large part of the year the roads are almost impassable and oxen suffer much from the climate and insects. These light railways have been found to be by far the most economical means of getting the logs to market. One company owns four million acres of the Chaco, and is prepared to cut logs into sleepers, make fence posts, or prepare it into tannin extract, whichever offers the most profit. There is a big and constantly increasing demand for all. The increase in construction of the Argentine railways makes a demand for sleepers, and failure of other sources of supply gives an ever widening market for the tannin extract.

Some of the railways in the Chaco end at the rivers, where the logs are loaded on boats and taken down to Rosario or Buenos Aires. Small sawmills are now found way out in the Chaco far from civilization. Other companies have their factories in the Chaco district, where the whole work is done and the extract prepared for shipment. This substance is known in the markets as "Quebracho Extract." It is easily manufactured where the proper machinery has been installed. The wood is passed through a machine which cuts it into shavings and the smallest possible chips. These are collected into immense kettles, where it is treated by chemical processes until all the tannin has been removed. After this the fluid is reduced by evaporation to a thick, jelly-like mass which is poured into sacks, where it is finally dried into the substance sold in commerce. Some of the companies engaged in this business have been capitalized for very large sums, and considerable towns have grown up around their establishments. Civilization and development have followed the construction of the railroads here as everywhere.

AN INDIAN WOMAN OF THE GRAN CHACO

In 1895 the first exportation of quebracho extract is recorded from the River Plate. In that year it was four hundred tons only. By 1902 it had reached nine thousand tons, and now the annual export exceeds thirty thousand tons. Of this enormous export the United States takes fully sixty-five per cent.

There are several thousand Indians who live in the Gran Chaco, and they comprise a number of tribes, all of whom, however, have the same general characteristics. These Indians are absolutely unlettered, and they have developed no civilization or institution of their own. Furthermore, they have the reputation of being treacherous and cruel, and many small parties of whites have been treacherously murdered. They are perhaps the most barbarous of any Indians in South America. Others of the same tribes inhabit the Chaco of Paraguay. It is said by those who have made a study of them that these Chaco aborigines are more ignorant and much less tractable than any of the natives of Patagonia.

They dwell along the rivers in this great wilderness in the simplest kind of abodes, and away from the settlements wear practically no clothing whatever. One distinguishing feature is the habit of tattooing the skin, which is very common. Not only the warriors, but the women as well, indulge in this custom, which, in their opinion, beautifies them. At first glance these tattoo marks oftentimes resemble the markings of smallpox, but a closer inspection shows that it is all in geometrical design. It is effected by pricking the skin with a big thorn, dipped in an acrid milky substance obtained from a plant that grows near there, and which leaves an indelible mark wherever it touches. It is absorbed by the epidermic tissue. This juice is obtained by breaking off the clusters of flowers of the plant, called the *iguoqui*, and this milky substance then exudes from the stem. It is used as it comes out of the stem, for it must be fresh. The Indians are also almost hairless on the face and body, due to the habit of depilation of the skin. This latter characteristic is in common with our American red men, and the tattooing takes the place of paint.

Horrible tales are told of these Chaco Indians and their murder of travellers. On the other hand numerous instances are known where they have saved the lives of white men and tenderly ministered to their wants. They have been accused of being cannibals, and probably were in the past. "I have seen them drink the blood of animals killed for our use with avidity," says an Argentine writer. They do not live exclusively on meat, but also eat roots and wild fruits, and the wild honey which is found in abundance. From fruits and honey they also make fermented drinks, of which they are very fond. They are nomadic, and wander from one place to another in quest of game and fruit. They have few domesticated animals, such as the dog and horse. They neither understand nor practise agriculture, although they sometimes plant little patches of corn or sugar-cane, which they have learned from the priests. They barter a little among themselves, but of trade in general they know nothing, and so they beg of travellers whom they meet instead of offering to trade. It is said they cannot even count above four. In medicine they resort to sorcery and incantations rather than to any curative herbs.

Polygamy is permitted among these Indians, but is not commonly practised. The portion of women is very much as with the red men, for to them falls the hard work of the home. If her husband dies the wife mourns for a year, and it is not proper for her to marry again during that time. She even refuses to converse and walks apart from all the others. The dead are burned by some tribes and buried by others. Those tribes who bury always place a gourd of water by the grave. This is both for the deceased and his friends, who come to visit the grave, and is probably due to a fraternal and hospitable idea in this land where a drink of refreshing water is sometimes more welcome than food.

CHAPTER V
THE GARDEN OF THE REPUBLIC

The second city in Argentina is Rosario de Santa Fé. It is the Chicago of Argentina, for it is the chief wheat market, and is about as far inland as Pittsburg. It is connected with Buenos Aires by two branches of the Central Railway, as well as river communication. Rosario is to a great extent a replica of the national capital on a much smaller scale. The streets all cross each other at right angles. One-storied buildings predominate everywhere, and I do not believe that there is a structure which exceeds three stories in the city. Even in the business section one story is the general rule. In the way of municipal improvement Rosario is up to date, and contains all the advantages of the metropolis except population. There are a number of plazas after the usual style, and a beautiful park adorns one section of the city. Electric light and cars serve the entire city, so that in physical comforts Rosario is not behind similar cities in Europe, or North America. There is quite a considerable foreign colony and each one boasts its club where the members can meet, eat, drink and be merry. Although Rosario is almost two centuries old, it was an obscure little village up to a generation ago. In the past ten years it has doubled its population.

As a commercial centre Rosario is of great importance. Tapping the greater portion of the rich provinces of Cordoba and Santa Fé, it receives enormous quantities of wheat and other cereals as well as live stock. It is accessible to ocean-going steamers, and hundreds of vessels leave it each year loaded with food for the millions of Europe. The Paraná River at this point is nearly a mile wide, and is an imposing, if not beautiful, stream of water. The river has cut its channel down into the soil to such a depth that the bluffs upon which Rosario is built stand about sixty feet high. Warehouses line these bluffs, and the wheat is transferred to the waiting vessels below by gravity. Each warehouse has a long chute running down to the river bank through which the grain is poured. It has been bagged on the *estancias* and is shipped in the same bags to Europe. As soon as a bag touches the chute it speeds down the inclined plane into the waiting vessel.

The bags follow one another in quick succession. At harvest time the wheat often becomes congested at this port.

Large port works have been constructed so that the docks have accommodation for a goodly number of boats, although not comparing at all with Buenos Aires in extent. From here the river lines carry passengers up and down the Paraná for hundreds of miles, and then they branch off to the Paraguay and Alta Paraná. Quite a network of railway lines also converge at Rosario, and altogether it is a hustling and busy place.

The large and rich province of Santa Fé is second in importance only to that of Buenos Aires. It is long and narrow, being several hundred miles in length from its northern to its southern boundary, and is almost as large as England. The capital of the province is the city of Santa Fé. For a long time this little city was an unimportant place, even though it was the provincial capital. To-day it is, after almost three hundred and fifty years of existence, a place of about twenty-five thousand inhabitants. It is proposed to deepen the channel so that ocean-going steamers can reach this port, but this project will not be done before "to-morrow." The northern part of this province partakes of the character of the Chaco and is undeveloped. At least three-fourths of the state, however, is rich land, well suited for the cultivation of cereals, which form the principal product, and have contributed most to the wealth. There is usually sufficient rain in this province, but its nearness to the Chaco makes it subject to a visitation which is almost equal in its destructive qualities to that of the drouth.

The farmer everywhere thinks that he has his full share of troubles. But the American farmer has never had to contend with the locusts to the extent that frequently befalls the Argentinian. One who has never seen a plague of locusts can scarcely appreciate the troubles undergone by Pharaoh when the clouds of locusts appeared as a punishment for his disobedience. The farmer in Argentina, however, can heartily sympathize with the Egyptian king, and, like him, would be willing to do or promise almost anything to secure relief from this enemy to his peace and prosperity. During the past season these abominable insects destroyed millions of dollars' worth of grain in that republic, and roused the people to greater efforts than ever to find some means of exterminating them. In travelling across the country last winter, which is their summer, I saw thousands of acres of corn absolutely stripped of all the leaves, and millions upon millions of the winged locusts were visible from the train, so thick in places as to almost cast a shadow.

The locust is blessed, or cursed, with a voracious and unquenchable appetite. This appetite is perhaps equalled in extent only by the hatred with which it is regarded by the farmer. Prior to 1905 Argentina had not had a scourge of locusts for several years, but since that time they have come almost every year. The first intimation of their approach is usually in October, when a few flying locusts will appear coming from the north. These seem to be the advance guard, for in a few days they are followed by increasing hordes, until the clouds of insects are so thick that they obscure the sun like passing clouds. Although these locusts are so numerous they do not do so much damage, as they are migrating and do not stay in one place long. A farmer may wake up some nice morning and find his beautiful shade trees stripped almost bare by the locusts that have alighted during the night. But in a day or two these will be gone, although others may follow. Future trouble has been laid up for him, however, for eggs have been laid by the millions. These are usually deposited in a small hole which has been bored down in a bare space of ground.

With the advent of the young locusts about six weeks later the real troubles of the farmer have begun, and matters begin to wear a serious aspect. The little gaudy-coloured creatures, with their yellow, green and black bodies and red legs, are shaped very much like grasshoppers. They cannot yet fly, and for that reason remain as the guests of the landowner for several weeks while they are awaiting their final development. They pass slowly along, jumping in grasshopper fashion from stem to stem, or leaf to leaf. They cling in clusters to each leaf and stem like a devouring army, and stay there until it is absolutely bare. The extent of the damage which they are able to inflict can be seen by inspecting a corn field after their visit. The transformation is as marvellous as it is tragic. Every shred of the rich, luxuriant leaves and tassels has disappeared, and only the thin, bare stalks, shivering and desolate, remain. Even the houses will be invaded by these unpleasant creatures (beasts, the Englishman would say), and to say that they are unwelcome but mildly expresses the real feeling of the farmer who sees the fruit of his toil thus disappearing before the hordes with insatiable appetites. The only vegetable growth that will not be touched, except as a last resort, is the Paraiso tree. They will eat everything else first, and only fall back upon the leaves and bark of this tree when all other food has failed.

In about six weeks the wings have developed and the "hoppers" become "fliers." Their bodies have waxed fatter, but their colouring has become sobered. Then flights will again become noticeable. A swarm will sometimes resemble a vast smoke-cloud from a burning city or straw stack. They will oftentimes settle on the boughs of limbs in such quantities as to cause the limbs to bend and crack beneath their weight. Carriages, trucks and the fronts of locomotives will be thickly coated with the fragments of the bodies of the insects, which they have killed. In such armies, where numbers are countless, casualties go for nothing. A trifling loss of a few thousand or a few millions is only a drop in the ocean. You might as well try to stop a cloud passing across the sky by shooting at it as a swarm of these insects.

One newspaper account, which I saw, reported: "The north and centre of Entre Rios are simply covered with locusts both in the hopper and flying stages. The city of Paraná was invaded by a swarm calculated to be nine miles in front and several miles in depth, and so thick that the sun was partially obscured. Other cities are hurriedly being enclosed with screens in order to keep the locusts at bay. In places they have completely devastated the vineyards, orchards and maize. In many places a cry of desperation is heard. In the province of Santa Fé swarms of fliers passed Santa Isabel bearing east; enormous swarms passed General Lopez proceeding west; Monte Vera reports the passage of fliers towards the north and south. The work of destruction goes on successfully. To-day between Zarate, Pilar and Campaña were destroyed sixty-eight thousand kilos (more than seventy-four tons) of saltona (hoppers)."

The farmer is in a quandary what to do. If he had only a hundred acres to look after it would not be so difficult, but none of them have fewer than thousands of acres. How to secure the labour to drive these locusts is a difficult problem.

The government has passed laws requiring each landowner to maintain men to fight the locusts, on the basis of about one to each thousand acres. If this is not done the owner is fined. The general method is to dig pitfalls three or four feet deep, the outer edge of which is protected by overlapping sheets of corrugated iron. These traps run out for some distance. The locusts, while still in the hopping stage, are driven towards this trap until these pits are oftentimes nearly filled up with their bodies. They are then covered up with a coating of earth, and they die very quickly. If this work is thoroughly done it is quite efficacious, but it is oftentimes difficult to get sufficient labour, for it is unpleasant work because of the nauseating odour from the bodies of the crushed locusts. Unless the work is systematically and thoroughly done, however, it does not have much effect, for a few millions will not be missed. If one man does his work well, and his neighbour is indifferent to his duty, then his work is for naught, as they will soon swarm over his land again from his neighbour's fields. United effort alone is efficacious, and that is what the government is endeavouring to either induce or compel the people to do. It has a commission at work studying this and other insect pests, and the best way to exterminate them.

The source of these insects is not positively known. They come from the north, in what is known as the Chaco, which is a vast wilderness little known, and covering tens of thousands of square miles. Some think that they come from the state of Matto Grosso, in Brazil, which is an empire in itself just north of the Chaco. Accurate knowledge of the location of their hatcheries is yet wanting. The insect is fortunate in having chosen the wild and unexplored portion of the country for its home. The wisest and surest method of getting rid of these locusts, in my opinion, would be to search out this place and destroy them there. In that way it might be possible within a very few years to absolutely rid the country from this scourge of locusts as it is to-day.

AMONG THE HILLS OF CORDOBA

No one knows any good purpose that the locust serves unless a chastening against pride and vain glory. They are relished by the ostriches and poultry, who devour them greedily. Chickens will enjoy a hearty meal upon them, but the result is that the eggs are ruined for edible purposes. The interior becomes dark, almost a wine colour, and they are given a fishy flavour, which is altogether unpalatable. Thus the malice of the locust towards man holds fast even in death, and makes him useless as food for the fowls which frequent every barn-yard. It is little wonder that the far-reaching cry comes up from Argentina for help and deliverance from this awful pest.

Adjoining Santa Fé on the west is the still larger province of Cordoba. The eastern part of this province is level, but the surface begins to rise and is broken here and there by ridges and hills. During the summer season many seek the hills of Cordoba to escape the heat of the summer. There is a fine train service from Buenos Aires to Cordoba. This city is about two hundred and forty-six miles beyond Rosario. The Central Argentine runs through trains and makes the trip in about sixteen hours. The railway reaches the hills quite a while before the city of Cordoba is sighted, and there are a couple of little branches that run to Alta Gracia and Rio Segundo respectively, each of which boasts a summer colony. The former is quite noted as a health resort.

The city of Cordoba is the capital of the province of the same name, and one of the most important commercial towns of the republic. It is situated at an elevation of fourteen hundred feet and has a population of almost fifty thousand. It lies in a hollow, and can hardly be seen by the incoming traveller until almost upon the town itself. The woods and hills, with the Rio Primero (first river), in the foreground, make a very pretty picture. Cordoba has always been noted for its university, which was granting learned degrees long before our own universities were even thought of; and it has been granting them continuously ever since. It is also a strong centre of Catholicism, and has more priests in proportion to the population than any other city of Argentina. The public buildings are all very creditable, of which the University, Cathedral, National College, Normal School and government buildings are the principal. There is quite a noted observatory located on a nearby height, which is under the control of the national government. Its first director was a North American. The work accomplished by this observatory has received high praise from both Europe and America, and has aided much in the work of studying the southern heavens. There are several pretty squares and promenades. The many hotels are filled with a well dressed crowd of people in summer, and much of the fashion of the capital is transferred to this place for a few weeks.

From Cordoba the Cordoba Central Railway conveys the traveller through a not very thickly settled country and across some salty marshes to the fair city of Tucuman, which is situated in what is called the garden spot of the republic. This city is about the same elevation and has about the same temperature as Cordoba. "Have you seen Tucuman?" is a question usually asked of the foreigner, for the Argentinians look upon this city and district with a pardonable pride. Here is the effusive description of a native writer, who becomes poetic in dwelling upon the beauties of this favoured city.

"O Tucuman! thou the most beautiful among thy sisters, all hail to thee! Whether I contemplate the level plain or lift up my eyes to the lofty mountains encircling thee on the side of the Circola Massimo or the Occaso, my soul is thrilled with delight and admiration. Nature, who has been somewhat niggardly to thy companions, has lavished her gifts on thee, her favoured one, because thou wert beautiful and beloved! To thee she has given the vast plain of the Pampa, and bounded it with a semicircle of hills so as to welcome the Alisian winds, that in return for thy hospitality, enrich thee with the life-giving elements gathered in their wanderings over numberless Alpine heights, and fraternize with thy river, called by thee the Fondo, but changing its name over and over again, according to the caprice of the friendly lands whose bosoms it fertilizes. And if the sun shines on thee with burning rays, his heat is tempered by the moisture dropping from the clouds as they are rent by electricity, with sudden explosion, or prolonged thunder.

"Hence thy soil is verdant in the winter, and in spring is adorned with innumerable flowers—a treasure-house of exotics—giving place one to the other for thy embellishment during half the year; and in the summer and autumn thou gatherest abundantly the fruits of a few growths."

The city is laid out in the usual checkerboard fashion, with extremely narrow streets. In a public hall here the declaration of independence was signed on the 9th of July, 1816. There are a number of large churches, a cathedral and several schools. The spiritual welfare of the people is not neglected through lack of opportunity to attend service. There is a public library, a theatre, etc. It is an ancient town, having been founded in what was then a remote district, in 1585. It is in sight of some very high peaks of the Andes, although a considerable distance away. Tucuman is in the centre of a rich sugar district, there being about thirty sugar factories at work. Almost one hundred thousand tons of sugar have been produced in a single year, in addition to large quantities of alcohol. Rice growing is also quite a feature of this district. The soil is carefully cultivated and irrigation is resorted to by many of the planters, for an abundance of water is easily obtained. The climate is what might be termed semi-tropical. Tucuman is the last city of any size or great importance in the northwestern provinces.

North of Tucuman are the provinces of Salta and Jujuy, both of which reach to the borders of Bolivia. To the west of Tucuman lie the provinces of Rioja and Catamarca, as well as the territory of Los Andes, all of which border Chile. These are all mountainous states, but they are neither small nor unimportant. The smallest one is as large as Massachusetts, Rhode Island and Maryland, and the largest one, Salta, is nearly as large as all of

New England. The altitude of the towns varies from Rioja, the capital of the province of the same name, at an altitude of only seventeen hundred feet, to Jujuy, capital of that province, which lies four thousand two hundred and seventy feet above sea level, and is the highest city in the republic. Jujuy is distant just about one thousand miles from Buenos Aires by railroad, and is at the foot of the spurs of the range of mountains that reach up into Bolivia. Although so near the Tropic of Capricorn yet the elevation prevents the extreme heat that prevails in the lowlands during the summer, while the freezing point is never reached in winter. The scenery in the neighbourhood of this city is really beautiful, for hill and valley, wood and plain all contribute to make up an enchanting landscape. When the connection with the Bolivian railway is completed this city will be on another transcontinental line from the Atlantic to the Pacific. The territory of Los Andes, in the extreme northwestern corner of the country, is the most mountainous section and is very little known.

The provinces of Cordoba and Santa Fé are the home of many beautiful birds. One of the most gorgeous of humming-birds is to be found here. Its body is green streaked with gold, with a vivid scarlet tail. A common song bird is the *bien te veo* (I see you well), so named because its song is supposed to represent those words. The call, which is an extremely musical one, is repeated over and over again. It is brightly coloured and is a species of thrush. The oven-bird is a favourite bird and is looked upon much as the robin with us. It is chiefly remarkable for its nest, which is built of mud and is entered by a doorway. The nests are usually built upon any convenient post, and in places one will find half of the telephone and telegraph posts surmounted by one of these nests. It is a common saying that the oven-bird will not, under any consideration, build its nest on a Sunday.

There are many birds of the vulture tribe in Argentina. Patagonia is especially a wonderful country for these birds of prey. Of these the chinango is a small carrion-hawk of a brown-gray colour. Another is the carancho, which is very common throughout the Camp. This bird is a dark brown with a light band across the wings. These two birds prefer carrion, but will attack enfeebled and helpless small animals such as hares or lambs.

> "Next comes the condor, awful bird,
> On the mountains' highest tops,

Has been known to eat up boys and girls
And then to lick its chops."

Thus runs the nursery rhyme about the chief of the larger army of the vulture tribe, which is common in the states adjacent to the Andes. Seen against the pale blue of the sky, swerving in graceful circles at a great height amidst the inner solitudes of the Andine peaks, its stately flight and grand spread of motionless wing make it seem like a noble bird. On a nearer view it shares the repulsive appearance of all birds that feed on dead animal flesh. Eagles are scarce in the Andes, and the condors take their place. They are difficult to approach unless they are gorged so that they cannot fly. Their size is enormous. One writer tells of killing one in Patagonia that measured nine feet, three inches across the outstretched pinions, and some of even greater size are reported. They are sometimes four feet long from tip of beak to tail. They hatch their young amid the snow-covered crags at an altitude of twenty thousand feet, so it is said, for they can endure a temperature which renders human existence impossible.

These birds, which fly so high that they become mere specks on the intense blue of the skies, exceed the vulture in their ability to discover a dead carcass. It has been said that they will follow a mule train a long distance waiting for a disabled animal to be left behind. If a sick animal, large or small, is found they will immediately pluck out the eyes, and then wait for the animal to die before eating it. They fly so high that it is impossible to shoot them, and the only way to kill the condor is to place a dead animal as a decoy and then lay in ambush until the birds appear. It is one thing to admire these birds wheeling in graceful circles on quiescent wing, but it would be quite another for the lonely and helpless traveller out among the hills where no help was near. Long before aid could come this powerful and unscrupulous bird might discover the helpless one. These gigantic birds have been tamed when captured at a sufficiently early age. Some have found them interesting pets, but their immense size soon makes their presence very undesirable around the house and farmyard.

Argentina is undoubtedly rich in mineral deposits which have as yet scarcely been touched. All along the Andes, from Bolivia, herself extremely rich in the precious metals, to Tierra del Fuego, traces of silver, gold and copper have been found. The indifference to the exploitation of this mineral wealth may be due to the lack of available capital, the difficulties of transportation of the ore and the scarcity of fuel in the mineral zones of the country. The exports of all minerals do not reach half a million dollars yearly, of which copper is one of the principal items. The early history of the country records a story of marvellous wealth dug from the earth. The future may have a still greater story to tell. The workings of many of these earlier mines have been absolutely lost. The locations of mines from which fabulous wealth was wrung are unknown to-day. Some of these mines date back to the early conquerors, and others to the Incas themselves, who overran this section of the country. Ancient bronze instruments of that race have been found here, giving indisputable evidence of that fact, although it is doubtful if they ever had a permanent abode in these mountains. The Indians used to bring tributes of gold to the priests, but would not reveal the site of the hidden mines.

The principal mines of Argentina, that are being worked to-day, are in the provinces of Rioja and Catamarca, in the northwestern part of the republic, and in Mendoza. The most important are undoubtedly the Famatima copper mines of Rioja. The government has recently constructed a wonderful aerial wire ropeway here which is really a marvel and has greatly aided in transporting the metals. The main ropeway is nearly twenty-five miles in length, with its highest terminal nearly fourteen thousand feet above sea level. Power is available for control and to assist the upward traffic. One span of this wonderful ropeway is half a mile in length where it cuts across a deep valley.

Argentina possesses some fine marble quarries and their production has been gradually increasing. The production of gold and silver is comparatively small. Within the past year petroleum has been found near Mendoza, and a number of good wells have been sunk. If this valuable oil can be found in large quantities it will go a long ways toward solving the problem of cheaper fuel. Nearly three million tons of coal are imported annually to supply the need of fuel. Nearly all of this coal is imported from England, the shipments from the United States in 1909 being only a few thousand tons, but petroleum products are nearly all imported from North America. The value of the products of the mines of Argentina will average nearly a million dollars a year.

CHAPTER VI
THE PROVINCE OF GOOD AIRS

"You must see La Plata."

I heard this from so many Argentinians that it led me to visit this made-to-order city of which they are so proud. It is an hour's ride—thirty-five miles—from Buenos Aires to La Plata. After leaving the suburbs the train crosses the dead level of the pampas in a line as direct as the crow would fly. Through great *estancias*, with their immense herds of cattle and flocks of sheep, the line passes, after escaping from the suburbs of the metropolis, with a half dozen small and unimportant towns along the route, in which the one-storied buildings are ever built in monotonous lines with the front wall a little higher than the rest in order to give it a fictitious height. One explanation given me for this high front is that it acted as a protection in street fighting. Whether built for that purpose or not, this parapet has frequently been used by both civilians and troops as a protection in the revolutionary scrimmages which have been so frequent in the past. At last the train runs into an imposing station that would be a credit to almost any city, with a façade which is really an architectural gem. This is La Plata, the wonderful.

When the national government appropriated the city of Buenos Aires as the national capital the inhabitants of the province of the same name, which had hitherto dominated the country, were highly indignant. Unable to change the official edict they set to work to create a rival city. At that time there was not even a settlement at La Plata, and only a few mud huts denoted its location. A site down the river was chosen in order to secure a deeper natural channel, and avoid the necessity of so much dredging to keep the channel free from mud. A new port, called Enseñada, was constructed, with commodious docks, the new capital having been located five miles back from the water front. To complete this stupendous undertaking the province assumed a bonded debtedness of $70,000,000, most of which was obtained in Europe, and not until then was the vanity of these provincials appeased. It was one of the greatest follies that the Argentinians have ever engaged in.

It was in 1881 that the government decided to build this new capital for the province of Buenos Aires. It was to be a model city, and worthy of its rank as the chief city of the wealthiest province of an opulent republic. To this end the finest architectural raiment for a corporate body that could possibly be conceived was erected, with all the ostentation possible in a Latin nation. Magnificent public buildings, palatial law courts, a great cathedral and stately edifices of every kind—all were comprised in the scheme. Broad avenues paved and planted with rows of trees, stretching their long lengths between the imposing facades, were traced upon paper by the architects, and builders were set at work to reproduce these plans out of brick, stone and mortar, and the resulting city of La Plata stands to-day as their monument.

The city was laid out with an astonishing degree of boldness and originality, and upon an ambitious scale. It was hoped by the builders that its splendour would bring to mind those pictured conceptions of the perfect town. Each edifice was to be so placed as to lend its own proper proportion of dignity. In this model town there was to be no crowding together of palaces, as had heretofore been common in Spanish cities, nor were rows of squalid little one-storied houses to be permitted to jostle with their imposing fronts the walls of stately palaces. No, not in La Plata. To accomplish this result the resplendent palaces were planted at regular intervals about the city, each in its own garden and faced by its own boulevard and plaza, and separated from the next one by a becoming row of private houses. There was to be no confusion or congestion as a result of buildings crowded together, and no vulgar hustling. In justice to the builders it may be said that there never has been anything of the latter quality, for the strenuous life has never yet found lodgment in La Plata.

"A SOMNOLENT ATMOSPHERE SEEMS TO PREVAIL"

The first impression upon the visitor is very peculiar, for a somnolent atmosphere seems to prevail. As one emerges from the station two broad thoroughfares open up before him. These broad streets, which are still designated by numbers, with their extensive sweep of carriageway, were designed to resound to the hoofs of horses and the noise of wheels; their broad pavements were intended to ring with the tramp of multitudinous feet —but they do not. The founders of La Plata reckoned without their host. One may gaze down the entire length of a street and not see a single figure; one might stroll through any of the little parks set out with trees and palms and find every bench unoccupied. The vast white palaces are practically empty. Occasionally one will see an electric car sweep leisurely around the corner, or a cabman lazily waiting for a "fare," but the car does not hurry and the cab driver does not worry over his inactivity. One wonders where the inhabitants are. The fact is that the few who do live here fill so little of the space that they are seldom seen. It has never succeeded in becoming a residential city in spite of the beauty of the parks, the low rentals and other advantages. The grass is abundant everywhere. In fact some people are so unfeeling as to assert that the green grass grows all round, round, round, as the song has it. As it is, the green tufts thrust themselves upward in many places through the pavements and around the rough cobble-stones of the driveways. In some of the suburban streets a little more grass would make a solid lawn. It sprouts from crevices of neglected walls and roofs, and even from the uncompleted walls of the great cathedral, which lies in neglect. This structure, great in plan, is oppressively desolate in its abandonment and the silence that broods over it. The sparrows build their nests within its yawning walls and are undisturbed, and one wonders how long such a condition will remain.

THE LEGISLATIVE PALACE, LA PLATA

Magnificent buildings have been built and are in use. The Government Palace is a beautiful building set facing a great and imposing plaza. The Legislative Palace, Municipal Building, Law Courts, Bank of the Province of Buenos Aires and other palaces are all splendid buildings, worthy the capital of one of our own states. In them some life is visible, and one will find a number of clerks busy over the books in which the records of the provincial business are kept. The officials prefer to live in Buenos Aires and make the trip back and forth each day, spending only a few hours in La Plata. A university, one of three in the republic, has been built with beautiful buildings adapted to its purposes, and a number of students are enrolled on its roster. There is a beautiful park with a fine zoological garden where the roar of the lion and the trumpet of the elephant disturb the silence of the groves. It contains one of the finest avenues of trees that I have ever seen. In the centre of this park has been built a large museum, which is a treasure-house of curios of the native tribes of South America. When the public offices close after five or six hours of opened doors, and the evening train pulls out for Buenos Aires, La Plata sinks into repose until another day breaks.

There was a time when La Plata was a livelier place. The docks at Ensenada were much used before the new docks were constructed at the larger capital. Now the great boats, flying the flags of Great Britain, France and Germany, steam majestically by this sleepy port and unload their passengers and freight at Argentina's metropolis. Nevertheless this city with its palatial buildings and broad streets, overspread with silent gloom, is still the official capital of a province. There are those who say that La Plata is only sleeping, merely in a state of coma from which it will emerge one day and surprise the world with its great and wonderful doings. Perhaps—maybe; that is for the future to decide. If it has a great future it probably lies in the docks at Ensenada, although a large slaughtering house has recently been built here by an American firm. At the present time it is enjoying a prolonged siesta from which nothing seems to awaken it. Built for a hundred thousand people there are not more than half of that number that live there.

The province of Buenos Aires is the richest and most populous province in Argentina. Including the federal capital, it contains one-third of the entire population. On several occasions this province seriously considered secession from the rest of the republic—but that was before it lost the metropolis. In area it is more than twice the size of Illinois, and resembles that state very much in its physical characteristics. It contains a number of towns of fair size, and a trip across the province to Bahia Blanca, about three hundred miles distant, is a very interesting journey.

There are two or three different routes, but the most interesting one is that via Tandil. Passing out through the English suburb of Temperly, the main line heads out for the level pampa with scarcely a turn for mile after mile. The fields are thickly dotted with cattle and sheep, for this is one of the best stock countries in the republic. Although a number of small stations are passed it is not until Dolores is reached, after a run of more than a hundred miles, that there is a town of any size. This is a city of probably eight thousand, with the usual plaza and church of the Camp towns, and is a junction point for several branches of the Great Southern. It is the seat of the courts of justice for the southern portion of the province, and has a prison of considerable size. At Maipu is the branch for Mar del Plata, the seaside resort, but the main line turns westward. This passes through a fine pastoral district where Scotch landowners are very numerous and prosperous. Soon afterwards the railroad enters the only transverse range of hills in Argentina, some of the peaks of which reach an elevation of from three to four thousand feet and furnish a pleasing variation to the monotony of the horizontal landscape. Tandil, which is distant from Buenos Aires more than two hundred miles, is picturesquely located among these hills and has a population of several thousand. About three miles from the town is the famous rocking stone, which is an irregular flattened cone about thirteen feet in height and sixteen feet in diameter at its base, and is so beautifully poised on the edge of a slope that it sometimes moves even in a slight breeze. And yet the combined strength of several teams of horses has been unable to move it from its base. There are many other picturesque spots and curiosities in this neighbourhood, and there is a very pretty waterfall formed by a stream which comes down among the hills. Juarez and Tres Arroyos are the only other towns of any importance until the thriving new port of Bahia Blanca is reached, at the mouth of the Naportá Grande.

PUERTO GALVAN, BAHIA BLANCA

Bahia Blanca, the "white bay," is a thriving place. It is a name the significance of which is not yet wholly appreciated in the United States, or the world at large, for its importance has not yet been fully grasped. The growth of this city has been phenomenal, mushroom-like, and yet its development has been substantial. As a port its strategic value cannot well be overestimated. It is the only safe naval harbour for the big battleships, and the government has built an arsenal and docks on the eastern side of the estuary, called the Puerto Militar. It is a natural outlet for one of the richest agricultural sections of the republic. The wheat which was formerly shipped to Buenos Aires, and exported from that port, is now loaded on ocean liners from Bahia Blanca, and forwarded to Europe. The railroads are pushing out their lines west and south, and opening up new wheat and grazing lands each year, so that the shipments from this port are jumping by leaps and bounds. Not very long ago this site was nothing but a sandy waste, with an unimportant settlement at which only coasting vessels stopped. Now there are electric tramways and lights, great elevators and a good system of docks. The value of the land has increased and a few far-sighted individuals have reaped fortunes. The "boom," if such it can be called, is still on as development progresses. The Great Southern Railway at first had a monopoly on the business of this port, but the Buenos Aires and Pacific has built into it, and now claims a share. The port works of the Great Southern form an addition by themselves and are called Ingeniero White, in honour of the engineer who built them. Several moles and elevators with an enormous capacity and which cost a million and a half of dollars have been constructed at these terminals. Puerto Galvan is the name of the Pacific Railroad terminals. To what extent Bahia Blanca will become a rival to Buenos Aires is uncertain, but it seems to me that there is room for both and to spare. It now ranks next after Rosario. Three hundred miles is a goodly distance, and each town ought to continue to grow rapidly, and neither necessarily at the expense of the other. Bahia Blanca is bound to expand, as she has the great undeveloped western pampas and the fertile part of Northern Patagonia right at her very doors. At the present time Bahia Blanca has a population in the neighbourhood of fifty thousand inhabitants.

Between Bahia Blanca and the Andes lie three rich territories, all of them of goodly size. The most important one at present is La Pampa, which is directly west of the southern half of the province of Buenos Aires. It is about the size of Iowa and is rapidly being populated and stocked. A few years ago this territory was entirely undeveloped, and the gaucho in charge of wandering herds of sheep held full sway. Railway extensions brought private ownership, however, and now this territory bids fair to become one of the richest sections of the republic. The Western and Southern Railways are both continually pushing extensions across the fertile plains, and material prosperity everywhere follows. It now has a population of about one person to each square mile. According to statistics it is third in the number of sheep of all the territorial divisions, which is a good showing for a new country. Wheat and flax culture is also being rapidly developed. Toay and General Acha are the only towns of any importance, the latter of which is the capital.

The territory of Rio Negro lies directly to the south of La Pampa and stretches from the Atlantic Ocean to the Andes. It lies between the Colorado and Chubut Rivers, and is watered by the Negro River as well. Along these rivers there are a number of *estancias* already located, most of which are owned by companies and many by foreign landowners. A new branch of the Southern Railway has been constructed across this territory, following the

Rio Colorado, the red river, for some distance, then cutting across to and following the Rio Negro, the black river, as far as the town of Neuquen. This has led to the establishment of other *estancias* along those streams. All three of these rivers carry an abundance of water, and it will not be long until the question of irrigation will be taken up on the same lines as in our own western states; then there will be a development take place that will make this land blossom as the rose. The possibilities are there and the great demands for grains will sooner or later lead to this action. There is no doubt that those lands are fully as rich as any part of Colorado or California, and that is saying a good deal. The Rio Negro and Rio Chubut are both navigable for vessels of light draught for a considerable distance.

Neuquen is another large territory, as large as Ohio, lying right at the base of the Andes. It is mostly mountainous and as yet very little is known about this province, as few have visited it. Its population does not exceed fifteen or twenty thousand, many or most of whom are Indians. The rainfall is not abundant, but it is well watered by the streams which are formed by the melting snows. It is possible that it could be cultivated just as profitably as the province of Mendoza, which joins it on the north, and which partakes of much of the same character of soil and physical configuration as Neuquen. Chos Malal, a small town in the mountains, is the capital, but it is difficult of access. A railroad extension, however, is now headed in that direction.

The slopes of the Andes here and in many parts of the republic are covered with valuable timbers. If these timbers were near the markets or easy transport they would be worth fabulous sums. As it is Argentina imports nearly all her building lumber at high prices, with an undeveloped wealth of timber within her own borders. Most of these forest lands have scarcely been explored, and it would be impossible to give even a faint estimate of their real value, but it is undoubtedly very great.

CHAPTER VII
THE MYSTERIOUS LAND OF THE PATA-GOAS

Patagonia has always been a land of mystery. Only a few years ago the geographers labelled it "no man's land," because no nation seemed interested in it. Later Chile and Argentina, longing to expand, cast envious eyes upon this great territory immediately adjoining their borders, and parcelled it out between themselves. The Andes was made the general boundary line, and this gave to Argentina by far the greatest share of the territory. Even Tierra del Fuego, the Land of Fire, was thus divided, so that each nation has a share in that large island which is the last inhabited land on the way to the Antarctic continent.

Patagonia impresses the traveller as vast and elemental. Its natural configuration is stamped with these characteristics. From its northern boundary it tapers gradually to the Straits of Magellan. The Argentine section naturally divides itself into three divisions, running north and south. Along the Atlantic shores lie the pampas, the flat and level plains. These plains rise in gently graduated terraces toward the west, one level plain above another. Then follows a network of lagoons and lakes, some connected by rivers and others by channels, many of which shift and alter under the climatic influences. On the western side the Andes range of the Cordilleras stand out against the sky like a mighty barrier. They are a tumult of mountains ever climbing upwards, their lofty gorges choked with glaciers, their hollows holding great lakes of ice-cold blue waters, and about their bases stretch thousands of miles of forests of which only the mere edge has been explored. Thus it is that the vast extent of Patagonia offers the most extreme and the most abrupt contrasts. Flat pampa, with hardly an undulation in sight, stands in sight of mountains almost inaccessible in their steep escarpments. Side by side these contrasts lie, mountain against plain, forest against thorn-scrub. The wind is the only element common to both. For a thousand miles the Atlantic coast is a low-lying, level, treeless series of bleak and brown downs, with few bays that offer protection to shipping; the Pacific coast, in Chile, is dented and notched with fiords, and the shores are covered with dense forests due to the excessive rainfall.

Patagonia is a land of big distances. On the Atlantic coastland it is often a ride of three or four days from one farm to another. The holdings are measured by the square league and not by the quarter-section. There is one farm that covers five hundred square leagues, or more than two million acres of land, and is larger than the state of Rhode Island. No wonder the distances seem almost appalling to the traveller. One accustomed only to cities would indeed feel very forlorn here. As one travels into the interior, a white face becomes more and more rare; empty leagues upon leagues surround you on every side. One seems to stand alone with only the wind, the mirages and the limitless distances, and the blue sky above for a canopy. This wild land appears, according to geologists, to have been the last habitation of the greater beasts of preceding ages. It is now one of the last to be occupied by civilized man, and receive its proper share of the human population.

The discovery of Patagonia dates from 1520, when that intrepid explorer, Ferdinand Magellan, forced his way down the east coast of South America in the face of continuous storms. With his little fleet of five vessels he pushed on in the hope of finding a strait which connected the two oceans. He was compelled to winter one season along the coast of Patagonia. A mutiny broke out among his captains and only one remained loyal. Two of the others were executed, and one was marooned upon the shore. For months no signs of life appeared on shore, although expeditions were sent a short distance into the interior; but one day a painted savage, very tall, appeared. One of the crew wrote, "So tall was this man that we came up to the level of his waist-belt. He was well enough made and had a broad face, painted red, with yellow circles around his eyes, and two heart-shaped spots on his cheeks." Thus was the report of giants inhabiting Patagonia first carried back to civilization. They were named Pata-goas, big feet, and that name has since clung to the country. Sir Francis Drake visited these shores a half-century later with a small squadron, and during the succeeding hundred years a number of navigators skirted along the coast. Several of them brought back tales of the giants, but these have since been found erroneous, as the Indians are not much taller than the North American Indians, whom they strongly resemble in physical characteristics. Darwin visited this country early in the last century and gave the first detailed account of the country and people, and his report dwelt strongly upon the desolate character of the land. Since then it has become better known, and a number of travellers as well as scientists have visited Patagonia and recorded their impressions. The Chilean and Argentine boundary commissions have also been at work for several years, establishing the international boundaries, and their reports have contained much valuable information.

On the eastern coast there are a number of settlements, such as Santa Cruz, San Julian and Gallegos, at the mouths of the half-dozen rivers which pour their icy waters across the wind-swept plains. Gallegos is the name given by the Spaniards to the strong west wind, so this name was given to a river, and, finally, to the little settlement at its mouth. This village of corrugated iron is a Mecca for the sheep-men and Indians who dwell in the vicinity. From it a few highways may be traced out on the pampas, where they disappear. The Welsh have founded settlements at Dawson, Gaimon and Trelew, which have grown into thriving colonies, and there are a few smaller ones in the interior. The Welsh settlements are made up of good sturdy folk, who are excellent pioneers for an undeveloped country.

The sheep ranchers on these lonely pampas are interesting studies. Some of them own hundreds of thousands of these useful little animals, and there is one company that possesses more than two millions which are kept on their several ranches. These are usually divided into herds of a couple of thousand each. Each flock has several square miles of pasture allotted to it. The shepherd has a number of dogs who aid him in controlling the recalcitrant ones, and they understand their masters' orders very well. These herders are Scotchmen, Germans and half-breeds. The animals feed all the year around on the pastures. The successful ranch in Patagonia must possess both a winter camp and summer camp. The winter camp is land available for pasturage which is protected from the fierce winds and where the snow does not fall too deep for the sheep to get at the grass, as no provender is put up for them. The summer camp is any other grazing land which is so exposed that sheep could not feed on it during the winter. From this it may easily be seen that the number of sheep that can be maintained is determined not by the total acreage, but by the extent of winter camp. Even under the best conditions an unusually severe winter greatly decimates a flock. At the end of winter the shepherds always go out over the ranch, taking the pelts off the bodies of the animals that have perished during the winter. Another feature to be sought is accessibility for the bringing in of supplies and taking out of the wool. For this reason most of the ranches are located near the rivers so that boats can be used. From some places in the interior it is a trip occupying days and weeks for the ranchman to transport the wool to market.

A SHEEP DIP

The *estancia* buildings are usually insignificant affairs, for all the material has to be brought long distances. One of the most distinctive features is a large square corral into which the stock can be driven, and the miles upon miles of wire fencing which spread out across the plains in a thin line. Every farm has its own store, where the men get their supplies at good prices. The "scab" is one of the enemies of the sheep here, as elsewhere, and the ranchers constantly fight it. The "dip" is usually employed, in which the sheep are washed several times each year. It is expensive to keep the sheep free from this troublesome little parasite, which spreads so rapidly, but it must be done, for it will eat into the flesh and the sheep will frequently die before many days after infection. The dip fluid is placed in large vats so deep that the sheep must swim in order to get through it, and they are then driven into it at one end and emerge on a dripping board at the other side, where they are allowed to remain for a few minutes for the "dip" to drip and run back into the pool. The cost of running a sheep ranch in Patagonia is comparatively small because of the low value of the land and low wages paid.

It is not difficult to leave civilization behind in Patagonia. For hundreds of miles in the interior there are few pioneers and only an occasional tribe of wandering Indians. Otherwise it is absolutely unpeopled. Near the Cordilleras it is practically houseless; scarcely a human inhabitant can be found, and little animal life flourishes under the snow peaks and in the unmeasured spaces of virgin forest. There are hundreds of square miles of forest land, gorges, open slopes and terraced hollows, on which the eye of a white man has never yet fallen.

For the traveller across this vast land it is necessary to take a supply of food and an entire camp outfit, including a reliable guide. A man alone seems very puny within this vast setting. The wind-blown grass stretches out as far as the eye can see, with the thorn and a green shrub called "poison-bush" for variety. In other places the surface undulates in graceful monotony, and occasionally a swift-flowing river cuts across the plains on its impatient way to the sea. Mirages like lakes or squadrons of cavalry will often be seen near the horizon. Many long reaches are almost desert wastes and are known as the "land without water." Over the sterile wastes the cold winds from the Andes sweep and raise great dust and sand storms which are almost blinding and suffocating.

Herds of wild cattle are found in some places, although not in such numbers as the stories that are sometimes heard down in that region would lead one to believe. The guanaco is the principal game animal, and helps out the traveller in the way of food. This animal is very much like a wild llama and they are found by the thousands, although generally in small herds. They look very picturesque when seen in an attentive attitude, with their long sleek necks stretched out in inquiry or curiosity. Wild ostriches may also be found in many parts, while duck and geese are generally plentiful where there is water. Of the wild animals the puma is the most dangerous, and will sometimes attack a man. He is a terrible foe to the sheep farmer, levying heavy toll upon his flocks before strychnine or a bullet puts an end to his career. The wolf is another enemy of the farmer. The curious armadillo is quite common, and is considered very good eating by the hunter.

Lake Buenos Aires is one of the big lakes of Patagonia. One writer, who spent several weeks in that vicinity, says: "Lake Buenos Aires is certainly the very heart of the wind's domain. While we were there the wind never died down; it blew all the time, often lifting sand and gravel, and sometimes a great piece of our camp fire, sheltered as that was. It raged on most days, blowing so hard that most people in England would not have cared to venture out of doors." This lake is the largest of a chain of lakes which lie in the foothills of the great Andes system. It is fully seventy-five miles in length from north to south, and its waters are in perpetual motion from the action of the winds. Near the lake is a stretch of arid land that is the very picture of desolation. There is a very horror of bareness about it that almost makes the eyes sick to look upon it. Right near it is one of those sudden contrasts that one will find in Patagonia, fine and fertile land where sweet flowers bloom in profusion. Lake Argentine is another large lake to the south of the other. It is a great sheet of blue water, is higher up, and the peaks of the Cordilleras are nearer. This lake and those farther south are often filled with small icebergs, for the climate is getting colder all the way.

At almost the southernmost point of the mainland lies the little city of Punta Arenas. It is situated on the Straits of Magellan, and is sheltered from the worst storms by the many islands which lie between it and the Antarctic seas. Punta Arenas is the most southerly city in the world, several hundred miles farther south than the Cape of Good Hope. There is plenty of building space left in this city, but a few years ago, when the boom was on, the people had visions of a southern Chicago. Fabulous prices were asked for building lots and real estate agents were almost as plentiful as the Indians. That time has passed and the town has dwindled. Its latitude is about that of Labrador, but it is much more equable and is not so severe as many imagine. Perhaps fifteen thousand people live here and seem to be contented. It is a very mixed population. You can hear Spanish, English, German, Italian, Russian and even the Chinese mingled with the guttural tongues of the Indians. The Scotch are probably the most thrifty of the inhabitants and many of them have lived there two or three generations. There are many rough characters, some even who have drifted from the mining camps of our western states. The loafing places are the bars, where many brawls occur during the long winters. There are clubs, however, where the well-to-do gather and have their games and drink their favourite drinks just as they do the world over. Most of the buildings are cheap one-story affairs, frequently built of the corrugated iron so common in this land. Punta Arenas is a free port, and this makes it a great supply station for vessels passing through the straits. All the vessels passing through the straits call there for supplies and coal, and this business, together with the trade in whaling products, wool and furs, furnish the inhabitants with employment. It is one of the great wool-exporting ports of the world, having shipped more than sixteen million pounds of that commodity in a single season, and four hundred thousand pelts. It is a beautiful ride through the Straits of Magellan, with their many narrow channels, and the icebergs, which are always in view.

NATIVE INDIANS OF PATAGONIA

Out upon the pampas the traveller will occasionally stumble upon the *toldos* (huts) of the Tehuelche Indians. These are simply made huts of the skins of the guanaco sewn loosely together at the edges, and supported squarely upon awkward-looking props or posts forked at the top to admit the ridge poles. The skins are fastened to the earth by wooden pegs. The Tehuelches are the native Indians of Patagonia—the so-called giants—and are well built specimens of manhood. These Indians live almost as their ancestors did hundreds of years ago. They are still nomads and exist entirely by the chase. They do not cultivate anything whatever, but sometimes own a few cattle. In general they still dress in skins, although some of them have purchased store clothes at the settlements. As a rule they are mild mannered, when sober, and do not deserve the name of being bloodthirsty savages. Their numbers have greatly decreased since the first discovery of Patagonia through dissipation and disease, and some have estimated that the total number yet remaining will not exceed a few hundred. They still hunt with bows and arrows and the *bolas*. This consists of three thongs of rawhide fastened together at one end, with stones or bits of iron on the free end to give them weight. The Indian throws the *bolas* with marvellous accuracy at any animal he may be pursuing, and the thongs wind themselves around the legs of the animal, thus entangling it. The principal game animal is the guanaco, which furnishes them food, raiment and shelter, and skins which they can barter with the trader for fire-water or other luxuries.

They are an ignorant and superstitious race. A death will invariably cause them to shift their camp, for to their superstitious minds the place must be accursed. Sickness is always the work of the evil spirit and is driven away by incantations. With them there are good spirits and bad devils. The dominant spirit of evil is called Gualicho. He is an ever-present terror, and they spend a good portion of the time in either fleeing from his wrath or propitiating it. They believe in a future life which will be much the same as the earthly one, except that there will always be plenty of food with an abundance of grease.

There are practically no tribal laws, as the Tehuelches are usually peaceable. Quarrels and fights occur only as a result of drink. Polygamy is permitted but is uncommon. The women are well treated, although they have the bulk of the work to do as among all primitive tribes. The men practically live on their horses and a Tehuelche is lost without a steed. The women are not at all overburdened with beauty. Progress does not appeal to the Tehuelche. As his forefathers were, so is he content to be—a human atom with a movable home, passing hither and thither upon the waste and dreary spaces of his native land. He is silent when in the presence of strangers, dignified at all times; unobtrusive as well as inoffensive, and very lazy. He does not particularly care to mingle with white people, but will not run away from them.

USELESS BAY, TIERRA DEL FUEGO

The Fuegian Archipelago, that little known group of islands at the southern extremity of South America, covers a goodly territory. It contains as much land as Nebraska, and is several hundred miles long from east to west. A perfect labyrinth of tortuous, wind-swept waterways separate the hundreds of islands which form this group. They are no doubt formed by the submerging of the lower end of the Andes Mountains. When the land sank these stormy waters beat through the valleys and chiselled the shores into incongruous shapes and labyrinths. They are not all a desolate mass of ice and snow, however, but contain plains which are covered with succulent grasses and slopes which are thickly wooded. The largest island, called Tierra del Fuego, is half as large as Illinois. It is divided longitudinally between Chile and Argentina, by far the largest portion belonging to the former nation, and the best part of it too. This name was originally given to the entire group of islands by Magellan when he saw the trails of smoke made by the camp and signal fires of the natives who dwelt on them.

Thirty years ago this entire island was roamed and hunted over by the aborigines. The fact that the northern part consisted of open country, with few ranges of hills, caused the white man to look upon it with envious eyes, as pasturage for sheep. Then began a warfare against the Indians which almost resulted in their extermination. Thousands of sheep now quietly graze in the rich valleys and on the verdant plains, and thrive very well indeed. Very little of the land is cultivated, although perhaps susceptible of cultivation, but the marketing of the products would be a difficult feature at the present time, and the season is short. Its latitude is about that of Labrador but the climate is probably milder, and its longitude is that of Boston. In the summer the grass is green, but in the winter the chilly winds change it to a rich brown. The ground rats are a terrible nuisance to the farmer, as they burrow in the fields so much that they destroy half the usefulness of a good meadow. The mountain slopes are covered with a thick growth of trees, ferns and mosses up to a height of a thousand feet or more, due to the great amount of rainfall, but above that distance the growth is very stunted. It seems strange to see green trees and green grasses amid snows and glaciers, but such is the contrast offered by this "land of the fire." The trees are mostly evergreen, not very high, but very close together. A deep bed of moss, into which a man may sink knee-deep, generally surrounds them, and large ferns with leaves a yard long grow in places otherwise bare. Even bright flowers make this sombre landscape seem almost gay when the sun shines on a summer day.

Desolation Island, on the Chilean side, is a bleak and barren island well indicated by its name, while others are Clarence, St. Inas, and Navarin. There are many others, from islands twenty miles in length to some so small that a good base-ball pitcher could toss a stone clear over them. Cape Horn is a monster rock which thrusts its jagged outline into the Antarctic seas. It is a couple of hundred miles south of the Straits of Magellan, and more than a thousand miles south of the Cape of Good Hope. It is surrounded by waters that are tossed by terrific storms which mariners fear. The hulks of wrecked vessels can be seen on every hand as reminders of the terrible tribute which has been here levied. Even in the Straits of Magellan the glaciers are always in sight, and masses of ice hundreds of feet high are frequently seen, seeming to threaten the venturesome mariner for invading those beautiful waters. It is sometimes impossible for vessels to force their way through the Smythe Channel, which is the most picturesque route through the Straits, but is least used. There is not much animal life except seals, with occasionally a whale, but wild ducks and geese are generally plentiful.

Midway on the southern coast of Tierra del Fuego, and on the Argentine side, is a bleak and inhospitable coast upon which the government has established a prison. This place, named Ushuaia, is the southernmost settlement in the world. The barriers created by nature are impassable without the massive and forbidding walls erected by man. To the south is the unknown Antarctic, to the north the impassable barrier of snow-clad peaks, and in all other directions the fathomless channels separating, it from the other islands. With the exception of the irregular trip of a small steamer from Punta Arenas and an occasional visit from an Argentine warship, this little settlement is unvisited, and not even a telephone or telegraph wire keeps it in communication with the world. There are two prisons here—one for military and one for civil prisoners. In one are the offenders of the Argentine army, and in the other several hundred criminals, many of whom are the very dregs of humanity sent down here from Buenos Aires. Here in this unknown quarter of the globe, guarded by a few score of armed men, these unfortunates work on the roads, dress stone for new and stronger walls, or make the coarse garments worn by the prisoners. Few attempt to escape, and fewer still succeed, for the loneliness and desolation alone would keep a prisoner where human companionship might be found. There is little danger of a prisoner escaping if he attempts, as there would be no means of a wanderer supporting himself.

There are two races of Indians who inhabit these inhospitable islands, the Yahgans and the Onas, both of whom are very low in intelligence. Even though the climate is very cold a part of the year, these savages formerly wore very little clothing, but greased their bodies with fish oil that keeps out the cold. In recent years, however, they have begun to wear warmer garments. They are very treacherous, and many murders have been traced to them. They will mingle very little with white people, but always hold themselves aloof. Their houses are of the most primitive character and are frequently little more than a hole in the ground or side of a hill, or a rude construction of brush on a skeleton of sticks stuck in the ground. Sometimes they are made of guanaco skins sewn together, from which the hair has been removed. They are not particular about food, as to whether it is very fresh or not. They live entirely by the chase and fishing, and in every way are as near to primitive savages as it would be possible to find in the Americas. There is frequently a dearth of food, and then it is that they are driven to eat the flesh of a stranded whale or of an animal found dead. Ground rats and the fishy-flavoured penguin are included on their regular bill of fare. As usual among savage tribes, the women do the most of the work, and assist in the hunting and fishing as well as prepare the meat after it has once been caught.

The Yahgans are short and muscular and below medium height. Their lower limbs seem rather stunted, but above the waist they are heavily built. The Onas are better built and will average above the American in stature. They are strong and well built specimens of the human race. The struggle for existence has made them inexpressive in feature and stoical in actions. Good fortune or ill fortune is met in much the same way. Their settlements are now usually found in the regions which have not attracted the white men. On these islands and the southern part of the largest island where it is not rock, there is generally bog or impenetrable forest, and here these pristine people dwell.

CHAPTER VIII
CROSSING THE CONTINENT

At Retiro station in Buenos Aires one takes the tri-weekly transcontinental train for the ride across the continent. "B. A. P." upon the coaches stands for Buenos Aires and Pacific, which is the line that carries the traveller to the limits of Argentine territory. The gong strikes, the Argentinians who have gathered to see their friends away on this long journey wave their adieus and the train slowly pulls out without the clanging of an engine bell, with which these British locomotives are not provided. The passengers are all leisurely in their preparations for the journey, and one will seldom see the spectacle of a woman grabbing a box in one hand and a struggling child in the other and rushing frantically for her car. There is usually plenty of room, and whether there is or not the passenger takes his own time.

The trains on this line are very comfortable, although one misses the luxurious Pullmans of the United States. All the passenger coaches are compartment sleepers, and one diner is attached. There is no smoking or observation car, so that the solitary traveller oftentimes finds it lonesome, but smoking is permitted everywhere except in the dining-car, where gentlemen are requested not to smoke "when the *señoras* are present." Some of the passengers gather in the diner after the tables have been cleared and talk or play games. The diner has good service and the only trouble is to keep the dust out of your food. A good meal of several courses is furnished in this *comedor* for two Argentine pesos. All of the diners of course have a bar, so that no one need to go thirsty, whatever his needs or demands may be.

The passengers on this train are always a mixed crowd. One will find tourists from many countries, English or German engineers, Chilean business men, Argentine *estancieros*, half-breed gauchos in their picturesque trappings, etc., etc. A half-dozen languages will greet one's ears in the corridors. This feature is, however, one of the pleasures of such a trip. One will begin to speculate about his fellow passengers, and then as he meets them he will learn how far his conjectures come true. He will also learn that this is one of the meeting places of the four quarters of the globe.

One of the chief discomforts in riding across these plains is the dust which sifts in through the windows and doors at times until it is almost stifling. Then again a baby *pampero* may come up and blow almost with the force of a hurricane. A Kansas blizzard is hardly equal to it in force and velocity. The dust at times comes in such clouds that it makes difficult work for the section-hands, for it must be removed from the track. I have heard stories of the real, simon-pure *pampero*, which comes up from the Patagonia plains, blowing cars off the track, and the propelling of cars by means of a sail hoisted up on the car. One thing is sure, it is decidedly unpleasant and will so fill your mouth with dust that you feel you are continually chewing sand.

The real *pampero* generally follows a drouth and is preceded by a few days of extreme heat. At last a cloud appears on the pampas which looks like a great woolly ball set in a frame of gold. The dust of the road begins to fly and whirl about in little eddies. Bird and beast seek shelter and the people may be seen scurrying in every direction. Millions of insects scud past in the clouds of fine dust. The lightning flashes in sheets and forks, and the thunder seems to shake the very earth. Then comes the welcome rain, not in drops but in sheets, and mingled with it hailstones big as nuts. A few minutes after the rain ceases and the sun shines in a tranquil, cloudless sky. The atmosphere is so transparent that one can see almost incredible distances. The people breathe in deep draughts of the delicious air, the blood circulates freely and one feels as though he had renewed his lease on life.

One could scarcely imagine an easier country through which to build a railroad than across these pampas. Not only is it level but a shallow excavation gives a solid road-bed which needs little ballast. The work has mostly been done by Italian gangs who are employed by contractors. One can see their camps in many places. They live in small "A" tents and a car fitted out as commissary wagon is labelled the *provideria*. It is really a small department store on wheels, where almost anything can be purchased at reasonable prices.

The line from Buenos Aires to Mendoza, six hundred and fifty-five miles in length, is built on the broad gauge so common in Argentina. For several hundred miles after leaving Buenos Aires the country is as level as a barn floor, and the train traverses fertile fields in which wheat, corn and grazing lands alternate. One will pass through corn fields miles in length and then wheat fields still larger; and following these the alfalfa pasture will extend clear to the horizon, with immense herds of cattle dotting it until, in the distance, where earth and sky meet, the largest animals appear as mere specks on the landscape.

One is impressed with the great agricultural resources of Argentina, for only a small portion of this part of the republic is uncultivated. All of it is owned in large *estancias* that are measured by the square league, which comprises almost six thousand acres. The man with only one square league is a small farmer, and many of the *estancias* measure ten square leagues, or even more. Statistics show that among the one hundred thousand reported landowners there is an average holding of six square miles. The locusts are a terrible curse for the farmer, and they were very bad last season. I saw millions of them in crossing the pampas. It costs these ranch men thousands of dollars each year to fight this scourge of locusts, and as yet no permanent remedy has been discovered.

The road runs nearly due west. An insane asylum called "The Open Door" is passed about forty miles out from the metropolis. A number of Camp towns, such as Mercedes, Chacabuco and Vedia, are passed, but none of them are attractive places. At the latter place the province of Santa Fé is entered, and a number of small towns are passed before the province of Cordoba is reached. Several branch lines shoot off to the south, which are feeders thus thrust out for freight, and branches of other lines run in from the north. Villa Mercedes, four hundred and thirty-two miles from Buenos Aires, is the first large town. The land has begun to rise and this town is sixteen hundred feet above sea level, although the aspect is still that of plains. It is situated on the Rio Quinto, and is a place of perhaps ten thousand people. This used to be the terminus of this line until it absorbed the Great Western a few years ago, which continued the westward route. It is one of the concentration camps for the instruction of conscripts drafted into the artillery regiments.

The broad pampas are perhaps not so lonely as they seem, for there is generally an abundance of bird life. Flamingoes haunt the lagoons, and long-tailed hawks sit like silent sentinels on the fence posts. The largest bird is the ostrich, of which there are tens of thousands scattered over these broad leagues, which have not yet been broken up by agriculture. In the entire republic it is estimated that there are more than four hundred thousand ostriches. They will feed among the stock, but the agriculturist soon makes them disappear. These long-necked and long-legged birds form a very pretty addition to the landscape. The South American ostrich is smaller than the South African species, and its feathers are not nearly so valuable. They are extremely abundant, however, and bring in a pleasing revenue for the farmer. The feather gatherers bargain with the *estanciero* to pay him so much for each bird found and picked on his *estancia*. Many of the ostriches are very tame, for the owners do not allow them to be hunted, but they roam at will, easily getting over the low fences that hedge in the fields. In some places the South African ostriches have been introduced and are raised for the commercial value of their plumes.

The next place of importance is San Luis, capital of the province of that name, at a still higher elevation. The dead level aspect has now changed to gentle undulations. The long gray shadows on the horizon are the peaks of the Andes, at a distance of one hundred and fifty miles. In this city there has recently been located an observatory by the Carnegie Institution of Washington. The purpose of this observatory is to observe the motion of all stars of the seventh magnitude in the southern heavens, and several American scientists are in charge of the work. A few miles beyond San Luis is an artesian well two thousand feet deep, which was sunk by the government and yields an immense supply of water. The pampa grass now stands in clumps and bare spots become more frequent. The railroad changes its direction time and again instead of taking a bee-line for some distant point. The stony character of the soil increases, but at last a land of vines and tall poplars is entered, and it is not long until the train rolls into the station at Mendoza.

"Hotel Grande."

This was the instruction I gave to my cab driver at the station in Mendoza after my baggage had been deposited in the vehicle by a *portero*.

"No hay," he answered, meaning that there was no such hotel.

I then told him to take me to the best hotel in the city. When we arrived at the hotel selected by him I saw an imposing building on the opposite side of the plaza with "Hotel Grande" upon it in large letters, and instructed my Jehu to drive me over to it. The secret of the matter is that the other hotel paid the driver a peso for each guest. There is only one good thing to be said about the cabs in Mendoza, and that is, the fares are cheap—if you know the established rates. A few years ago a tramway company laid tracks and began operations. Enraged at this intrusion upon their rights the cab owners began a war of fares. They lowered their charges to the level of the rates of the tram line, and announced that they would carry passengers to their very doors for the same price as the street car line would deposit them at the nearest corner, which might be blocks away. The deserted and abandoned rails which one may see in a few places proclaim the glorious victory of the cab owners. Although the fares have advanced somewhat since the abandonment of the street railroad they are still remarkably low.

A GLIMPSE OF THE ANDES FROM MENDOZA

Mendoza is one of the most picturesque cities in Argentina. It is an oasis in the midst of a stony desert. There is hardly a drier climate in the world, and, where the rainfall alone is depended upon, nothing will grow. Lying at the very foot of the lofty Andes range, it is the westernmost city of the republic. The streets are quite wide and the buildings are almost without exception of one story. The reason for this is the earthquake. The greatest disaster of that kind happened in 1861, and the inhabitants have been haunted ever since by fear of a return of such a holocaust. The tremors which occasionally occur are a constant reminder of the dangers; and the ruins of the great cathedral, whose walls crashed down upon the crowd of supplicants who had gathered within for protection, still stand as a warning. Reports vary greatly concerning that disaster. The most generally credited figures are that of a population of twenty thousand no less than twelve thousand met with death. It is difficult to believe, in the face of similar modern disasters, that any such proportion of fatalities occurred either from the earthquake, the fires that followed or the lawlessness which prevailed in the confusion of the next few days. It is said that many fell victims to the assassin's knife when they were trying to escape with their few earthly belongings. The new houses have all been built of mud bricks with an extra amount of straw or cane mixed in, and the one-storied walls are made very thick. The result is an elasticity that is considerable of a safeguard against the earth's tremblings.

The old ruined town lies about a mile from the new town and is a mass of ruins, scarcely a single house remaining intact. There is something sadly depressing about these heaps of fallen stones, broken arches and sightless windows—relics of the old Spanish-Moorish architecture. The old city covered about two hundred acres and contained seven churches and three convents. The first shocks levelled almost every building to the ground. They are a place of frequent pilgrimage and one may still find burning candles in nooks and corners, placed there by devout relatives of those who were hurled unshriven into the beyond. Surely purgatory cannot long retain the souls of those who were overtaken by death while at worship, even though they were unprepared to leave this world.

The centre of the town is the broad Avenue de San Martin, the alameda, with its double row of trees and the stream of water that runs on either side of the roadway. Were it not for this shade and the running water, the streets of Mendoza would be pretty hot in the middle of the day. Down this wide, cobblestoned street the Mendozians have their *corso*, or carriage drive, and one will see victorias with bells on the tongue wedged in with two-wheeled country carts, and all other kinds of vehicles. Happy farmers and the distinguished citizens of Mendoza mingle together on this occasion. There is a certain kind of provincial good humour about this little city so near the lonely Andes. Small boys armed with buckets on long poles dip the water from the canals and fling it across the thoroughfare. On Monday morning, or following a *fiesta*, this battle with the dust is conducted by a lot of shame-faced men who are not volunteers or employees of the city, but are working out a fine for the previous day's debauch. The city also possesses a very pretty park besides a number of plazas. There is considerable street life in the city, and the cafés afford evidence of this, for they are wont to spread their tables far out under the trees in this genial climate.

Mendoza is not a temperance resort, for it is a great wine centre. This is the country of the grape, and it is this fruit that has brought wealth to Mendoza. All about the city are vineyards and meadows, and the outlines of the farms are marked by rows upon rows of graceful poplars. Millions of those poplars have beautified this country, which at one time was a barren waste, and would still be so were it not that man has harnessed the streams formed from the melting snows which rush down from the snow-clad peaks. Irrigation was first established by the Spaniards several hundred years ago, but it has been extended and systematized by the grape growers in recent years. Dams have been built across the rivers and the waters forced through artificial channels, until now there are more than twelve hundred miles of these channels, which water a district of approximately one thousand square miles.

As soon as you leave the city you will see the grapevines growing. Some are trained upon a low prop, as in France or Germany, others climb a staff and look like hops, while many vines creep up the poplar trees and stretch their tendrils across to the next tree, so that the tree trunks are all connected and form a cool, vine-covered lane for hundreds of rods. The vines are thus trained to form cool drives for the owners, and they are especially seductive when the great bunches of ripe fruit hang just high enough out of reach to be tantalizing. Little canals trickle here, there and everywhere among the fields of vines, and thus keep the roots ever moist. The prosperity of

Mendoza is bound up in these tiny little streams, which give life to the grape, the onion and potato, for it seldom rains here. The day of my visit the sky became overcast with dark, foreboding clouds, as though a terrific storm was threatening. I hesitated to venture forth. The landlord said, "It looks this way nearly every day but it never rains." I found out this statement was true and that rain is a rare event.

The development of the wine industry in the Mendoza district has been almost phenomenal. The greater part of the wine produced is not of a high quality, so that it appeals only to the masses and not to the connoisseur. The wealthier classes are satisfied with nothing less than the finest of European wines and champagnes. The quality of the grapes produced is of the finest, and the very best European varieties have been imported. The profits in some years are almost fabulous, for a few acres will bring in a handsome return. Some of the wine-manufacturing establishments are quite large and produce great quantities of that liquor so popular in all Spanish countries. The presses, vats, casks and everything in them is of the latest design. One will find wines leaving these establishments with Bordeaux, Burgundy, Moselle and Muscatel labels. It is shipped in both cask and bottle, and one will see high ox-carts and cumbersome wagons loaded with large casks on their way to the railroad station on almost any road leading to Mendoza. Thousands of tons of the grapes are shipped each year in the fruit form, for it is a peculiarly luscious growth and the bunches attain enormous size. Other fruits have been found to grow equally well at Mendoza and fruit canning is becoming quite an industry there. Peaches, pears and plums grow to good size and of good flavour, while apples, quinces and cherries do very well. The fruit culture is spread over a wide area of country and the culture is rapidly increasing. It is the boast of the Argentinian that the country is capable of producing every conceivable species of fruit, and it is not an idle boast. If the same care was taken that they give that industry in California they could flood the markets of Europe with their fruits. The general trouble is that the trees grow so easily that they are practically unaided, so that the fruit is oftentimes full of flaws and will not pass for prime quality in the markets. Grapes are about the only fruit to which scientific methods of culture have as yet been applied.

At Mendoza a change is made to the less comfortable narrow-gauge train, which conveys the traveller through the fastnesses of the Andes. The mountains are now plainly visible and the snow peaks can easily be distinguished from the dark background. The route leads first through grape and peach orchards, but these soon give place to the cactus and scrub growth which cling to the foothills. The Mendoza River, fed by the melting snows, tumbles along on its way down from the mountains and is crossed and recrossed many times. An occasional station is a somewhat forlorn outpost of human life. It consists principally of a water-tank and pile of fuel. The sole occupants visible are usually a woman, some children and a few goats, for the master of the house is probably at work. The solitudes are broken only by the shrill whistle of the locomotive. One enters a land of torrents, chasms, precipices and other freaky outbursts of nature.

At a distance of about one hundred miles from Mendoza is the Puente del Inca, Bridge of the Incas, one of the famous natural bridges of the world, and near it are some mineral springs and a hotel. This bridge is of limestone formation, the span being about one hundred and fifty feet in length, with a width of one hundred and twenty feet, and is about sixty feet above the Mendoza River, which flows beneath. There are many legends and tales which are told about this curious bridge, so named because it is said to have been on an old trail used by those ancient people.

CROSSING THE ANDES

A little further on is the station of Las Cuevas, the last stop in Argentine territory and the entrance to the tunnel under the mountain. The elevation at this place is in excess of ten thousand feet. There is a certain weird fascination about this spot so high up and seemingly so remote from all the hustle and bustle of the twentieth century. It is a place of contrariety. The contrast between light and shade and the different colours is very marked. There is no delicate and gentle shading of tints. There may be a black wall surmounted by the clear white snow; near by will be other rock walls, pinnacles or spires of green, violet, pink, blue or yellow. It is as though nature had set up a great kaleidoscope between the sun and the bulwark of rocks in order to flood this valley with colour.

When I crossed the Andes it was just a few weeks before the tunnel was opened to traffic. In early days this intervening distance between railhead was covered on foot or in the saddle. Later came the broad, white-covered four-horse coaches which conveyed our party. Five hundred horses and mules, many carriages and baggage wagons and a considerable force of men were maintained for this service. Four times the air-line distance is covered in reaching the highest point on either side. Extra riders with a hitch rope to assist a stalled vehicle follow the carriages. The manager, who was an American, and his guards, took short cuts and appeared in the most unexpected places. Scrambling, twisting and turning, the cavalcade mounted higher and higher, and the air became so cold that a heavy wrap felt comfortable. The air was wonderfully clear, and the distant mountain peaks were clearly outlined against the turquoise blue of the heavens. As the long line of carriages winding their way up the zigzag trail neared the summit, a sharp turn in the road suddenly revealed a striking statue outlined against the sky, and a feeling almost of awe fell upon us. While the carriages were stopped for the driver to examine the harness preparatory to the descent, the passengers gazed in silent admiration upon this monument. Lofty peaks lifted up their weird masses of black basaltic rock and dazzling snow into the clear blue of the Andean sky, among which were Aconcagua and Tupungato, which were clearly visible if one had a sharp and quick eye.

"Sooner shall these mountains crumble into dust than the people of Argentina and Chile break the peace to which they have pledged themselves at the feet of Christ the Redeemer."

"THE CHRIST OF THE ANDES"

This is the inscription that appears on one of the tablets placed on the monument known as "The Christ of the Andes." I know of no other monument, except the statue of Liberty enlightening the World, in the New York harbour, that is so imposing or impressive as this colossal statue, which is placed on a gigantic column in a pass almost thirteen thousand feet above the level of the sea. The silence and grandeur on all sides make it doubly impressive. The figure of Christ is twenty-six feet in height. In one hand it holds a cross, while the other is extended in a blessing, and as if uttering the one magic word "peace." It was erected as a symbol of perpetual peace between the two nations, and was cast in bronze from the melted cannon of the two nations. Its location is on the international boundary line, which had just been established by arbitration, after war between these two countries seemed inevitable. A boundary standard has been set up right near it with the word "CHILE" on one side and "ARGENTINA" on the other. When this monument was dedicated, on the 13th of March, 1904, more than three thousand persons witnessed the ceremonies in this wild region. The appalling silence was broken by the roar of cannon and the music of bands. After these sounds had died away in the distance, there came the words of the Bishop of Ancud: "Not only to Argentina and Chile do we dedicate this monument, but to the world, that from this it may learn the lesson of universal peace." Now that the railroad is completed these sturdy little animals have made their last trip, and fewer people will gaze upon this striking monument. The peon with a mail bag strapped on his back has tramped his way for the last time down the rocky trail in the winter snows. *El Christo* stands among the lonely crags, deserted, isolated and storm-swept, but ever with a noble dignity befitting the character.

The Chilean terminus of the tunnel is at Caracoles. From here another railroad of metre gauge, called the Trasandino Chileno, carries the traveller to the station of Los Andes. It has been found necessary to construct snow-sheds in many places in order to protect the track from snow-slides, which are likely to occur in August and September. From Los Andes to Valparaiso the route is over the Chilean State Railroad, which is of standard gauge, and passes through some rich and fertile valleys on its way towards the Pacific.

The scenery on the Chilean side is grandly picturesque and affords some magnificent views of mountain scenery. There are one hundred and eighteen bridges, an average of more than two bridges to the mile, from Caracoles to Los Andes. At El Portillo is the rock-bordered Inca Lake, on whose surface is reflected the mountains which slope abruptly into its waters. Masses of rock seem poised on ledges ready to project themselves down into the valleys with destruction in their path. One of the most wonderful sights is a narrow gorge, very deep, which forms the bed of a swift stream. At one place the overhanging rocks nearly meet, and this is called the Salto del Soldado, the Soldier's Leap. It received this name because it is said that, during the early struggles for independence, a Chilean soldier, pursued by the enemy, escaped by leaping his horse over this chasm. How true the tale is I do not know, but it is a striking freak of nature, and is plainly visible from the train. There are in all one hundred and forty miles of the sublime in nature on the transandine railways, which will compare with any mountain railroad in the world, although the most sublime part, hitherto crossed by wagons or mules, will not be visible from the international express.

The Cordilleras of the Andes are formed of three distinct ranges running north and south. The western range forms the watershed and is the boundary line between Argentina and Chile, while the central range contains the highest peaks, Aconcagua, Mercedario and Tupungato. The eastern range is divided from the central one by a wide plain or plateau, several miles broad, known as the Uspallata, which is some six thousand feet above sea level and is one hundred and fifty miles long from Mendoza north. Without lakes or trees, this plain is one of the most desolate and uninteresting spots imaginable, but the varied colouring of the stratification is marvellous. This lower range conceals the higher peaks from view as one approaches from the Argentine side.

As one proceeds from Mendoza the upper valley begins to close in and the track pierces the main range of the Cordilleras between walls of porphyry and granite. To the north one gets at last a glimpse of Aconcagua some twenty-three thousand and eighty feet above sea level, and higher than any peak outside of the Himalayas. It is more than ninety miles from the Pacific and can be seen on a clear day from Valparaiso, for its lofty head is lifted up above its neighbours. It is on the Argentine side, and all the melted ice and snow from its slopes pours down over the pampas of that country. It is surrounded by winding valleys, by rugged and precipitous spurs and ridges which are difficult of access. One of the best views is from the Puente del Inca where the Horcones Valley opens out into the Cuevas Valley. It has been termed a volcano, but there are no signs of a crater and few traces of scoriæ. To the north of Aconcagua lies the Mercaderio, over twenty-two thousand feet, and to the south Tupungato, just a few feet lower. On the Chilean side, near the Cumbre, is Juncal (19,500 feet), and near it are the peaks of Pollera, Navarro, Maipo and the great volcano of San José.

The most striking aspect of these Andean solitudes is their terribly bleak and desolate appearance. Trees there are none, but only a few shrubs and blades of grass growing in the clefts of rocks here and there; nothing but a huge expanse of yellow sand and stone, with peaks rising on every hand whose extraordinary stratification presents many-coloured hues which are almost bewildering to the eye. Great torrents flow down their sides whose waters are of a dull, brackish colour. These are exceedingly rapid and full of dangerous holes, so that the fording of them is perilous. The line of perpetual snow is about seventeen thousand feet, although this varies. In the spring there is a very curious phenomenon at times on the glaciers and snow slopes. It consists of huge fields composed of cones, or pyramids, of frozen snow, some four or five feet high, placed close beside each other. These cones are called the *nieve penitente*, or penitent snow, because of its semblance to the cowled Penitent Friars. This effect is caused by the combined action of the sun and wind upon the frozen masses.

Aconcagua is distant about a dozen miles from the Inca or Cuevas. The weather, however, is uncertain even in summer, and a terrible wind usually prevails after sunrise. These render exploration work difficult and even dangerous. In the winter the snowfall is excessive. In the summer there is no snowfall and the wind blows the dust from the desert-like valleys in stifling clouds, which are oftentimes almost unendurable. Storms which are almost blizzards spring up as by magic on the high altitudes. The lightning is especially vivid and dangerous.

The pass of the Cumbre is one of the most dangerous passes because of its fearful storms. Every few miles there are the dome-shaped *casuchas*, which have been built for shelter, with their doorways perched up high above the ground as a precaution against being snowed under. In one of the most dangerous parts is a little graveyard by the roadside, with numerous little wooden crosses in various stages of decay which bear eloquent testimony to the toll which has been demanded by the storm king.

The *arrieros*, or mule drivers, that one may engage, never set foot on the ground if they can avoid it. It would, I suppose, be a loss of caste to walk, and they would rather ride their horses over a precipice than humiliate themselves by getting off and walking. The general appearance of these *arrieros* is decidedly picturesque, is certainly distinctive and gives them a rather striking appearance. They ride an old-fashioned Mexican saddle with a number of sheepskins strapped over the top of it. They generally have their feet encased in soft slippers made of a square piece of rawhide strapped on the foot by leather thongs, which would certainly make walking over stones decidedly uncomfortable. They are fond of silver trappings and gaudy accoutrements, and the more jingling these accessories make the better pleased is the rider, for he declares that this noise encourages the animals.

Aconcagua is distant a dozen miles from the Cumbre. The ascent of this peak has been made up a valley which runs over toward it. Vegetation gradually disappears on the upward journey, and the most of the streams contain water unfit to drink. Soon the giant cliffs and crags of Aconcagua tower over the traveller, a great mass of rock rising like the battlements of some stupendous castle. Its vast proportions are bewildering to the pygmy onlooker. Amidst this amphitheatre of peaks and valleys it would seem was the arena of one of the early-world dramas ages and ages ago. The cold becomes greater and more acute as more lofty heights are reached, especially so just before daybreak. The wind is biting. The loose round stones make a footing difficult. What looks like a mere step from one part of the mountain to another often means hours of toil to the venturesome climber.

One writer says: "The sight that met my gaze was an astounding one. An immense glacier separated us from the glacier below—the difference between twenty-three thousand feet and thirteen thousand feet. It was a precipice of gigantic size. As I looked down its dizzy sides, I saw spurs of the mountain flanking the glaciers beneath to the left and right, giving the appearance of some huge amphitheatre. The sun was low in the heavens, and did not penetrate into the vast pit, and the great masses of vapour slowly moving about in it far below, gave it the aspect of a giant cauldron, into whose depths the eye failed to penetrate, two miles vertically below. The arete, about five feet wide at this point, ran east to the summit and west to the snow-clad western peak of the mountain, growing ever narrower in that direction, until, where it sloped up to the highest point, its edge became knife-like."

In "The Highest Andes," by E. A. Fitzgerald, the following description is given of the summit of Aconcagua. "Over Argentinian territory range beyond range stretched away; coloured slopes of red, brown and yellow, peaks and crags capped with fresh-fallen snow. I had hoped to look down upon the pampas of Argentina. In this I was disappointed for, though I gazed down over the range, a sea of mountains some sixty miles in width, and averaging a height of quite thirteen thousand feet, made such a view impossible. Away over the surging mass of white cloud that lay on the glacier at my feet rose the southern frontier chain. Torlosa and the Twins, on either side of the Cumbre Pass, stood like colossal sentinels guarding the great highway between the two republics; then there were the lofty glaciers lying between the rugged crags of Juncal, the ice peaks of Navarro and Pollera, the Leones and the Cerro del Plomo, that overhangs the city of

Santiago, Chile, and some sixty miles farther on the magnificent white summit of Tupungato.

"No lens or pen can depict the view from the Chilean side. I looked down the great waste, past the western peak of the mountain to right and left, over ranges that dwindled in height as they neared the coast to where, a hundred miles away, the blue expanse of the Pacific glittered in the evening sun. The sun lay low on the horizon, and the whole surface of the ocean within the points of vision was diffused with a blood-red glow. The shimmering of the light on the water could be distinctly seen. So near did it seem that I could not realize the immense distance that separated one from it.

"All the forces of nature had been brought to bear upon this mountain giant. Visible signs lay around one of the power of the weather and rapid changes of temperature to destroy. Aconcagua, with all its cherished secrets and its mystery, lay here before one, confessing itself as nothing more than a colossal ruin, for not a single vestige of the ancient crater of this extinct volcano remains. Foot by foot the relentless forces of nature have reduced the mountain to its present proportions. The innumerable traces of ruin and decay around one, the crumbling rocks and the disappearance of the crater told of an Aconcagua of the past, whose gigantic base filled the glacier-beds around, whose sides rose towering to the heavens several thousand feet higher than the Aconcagua of to-day; of an Aconcagua of ages yet unborn, split, broken and powdered by frost and heat, pouring itself over valleys and plains in sediment and shingle, a mere shapeless mass whose height will no longer distress the mountaineer.

"I looked at the time. It was twenty minutes past six. The sun, a great ball of blood-red fire in a cloudless sky, was dipping into the waters of the Pacific. Rapidly it sank and disappeared from view, yet, as if struggling for supremacy with the fast-approaching night, an afterglow of surpassing beauty spread over land and sea in a series of magnificent changes of colour. The mighty expanse of water from north to south, together with the sky above it, was diffused with a fiery, red glow. While the red in the sky remained, the waters, through a variety of intermediate shades of colouring, turned slowly to purple and then to blue. And yet we were not in darkness, for with the sun's departure the risen moon declared itself with wondrous brightness, penetrating the thin atmosphere and flooding everything with its colder light."

CHAPTER IX
THE PEOPLE AND THEIR CHARACTERISTICS

Argentina is made up of a complex population. An Argentinian is a person born in the country, just as we class our own population. Perhaps nearly one-half of the inhabitants are foreign born, and most of them from the Latin countries. A large proportion of the remainder do not have to go back more than one or two generations until a European ancestor is discovered. The Latin races soon become mixed and cannot very easily be traced after a generation or two. The English and German settlers continue distinct and apart. They always remain foreign. The English traits in those who have lived there a generation or two are almost as marked as in those who have recently come over from the tight little island. The later Spanish and Italian immigrants are the workers and do most of the common labour. Wherever newer methods have been introduced the influences are distinctly English. The railways are all owned and operated by the English, and these have given the British touch to all the later developments.

There is an aristocracy in Argentina as in all countries. The real aristocrat here, as in other Spanish countries, is the pure-blooded Castilian, who follows unfalteringly the traditions of his native land, and who prides himself more upon the accomplishments of the past than upon anything his family or race have done in modern times. The greater aristocracy, however, is not an aristocracy of the old Spanish régime, such as one will find in Chile or Peru, but a more recent upper ten based upon wealth. The more picturesque attributes of a Spanish civilization have almost disappeared beneath the spirit of modernism in Buenos Aires. The development of social grades all over the republic has been rapid and has kept pace with the opening up of new lands. It is possible even now to watch this development, which is still in process of evolution in the newer communities. A material prosperity has sometimes overwhelmed the other virtues and inherited characteristics. Any way to make money is the aim of the Argentinian, and an aristocracy of money has grown up.

The Argentine magnate is not a man who has attained his prominence after a bitter and strenuous commercial struggle, which has developed a hard-headed, practical side, but his wealth has come through the automatic growth in the value of his expansive leagues of rich *campo*. His income has waxed greater each year through no effort of his own. So one will find the rich *estanciero*, intoxicated with his own wealth, disporting himself in the national capital on as lavish a scale as one will see in New York or London. These wealthy land aristocrats not only spend their money, but they are eternally bent on devising new ways for divesting themselves of the surplus pesos. It is spent lavishly and not always well, for the development of the finer tastes has not kept pace with the increase of material wealth.

Some of these moneyed *estancieros* are descended from honest farmers, whose fathers had no intimation of the wealth that would fall to their descendants. They lived the simplest of existences, and looked upon their broad acres only as a source of food and shelter. Then the land began to rise with almost incredible rapidity. A league that would have been wagered on a Camp race soon represented a small fortune. The approach of the railroad to his *estancia* showed the son that fortune was in his hands and he longed for excitement. A palace in Buenos Aires was added to his possessions, he joined the famous Jockey Club and became a devotee of sport—following the odds on horses even more closely than he did the price of wheat or cattle. He now visits Europe frequently and has added a sort of cosmopolitan veneer to himself, and may possibly have learned to speak two or three languages. Thus it is that this hidalgo has added up-to-date and European customs and habits to his inherited traits, of which perhaps the vices have been imbibed fully as generously as the virtues and graces. So also it is that his life passes along in smooth and easy channels, with little to worry him except the problem of amusement and sufficient excitement.

A GROUP OF PEONS

There is no doubt that the Argentinian is ambitious. We may laugh at some of his impractical ideas, or the seeming stupidity of some of the more ignorant ones, but the fact remains that each one is endeavouring to get ahead. The Porteño is aiming to make Buenos Aires the finest city in the world, the state governments vie with each other in prodigality, and the ranchman is trying to develop the very best breeds of stock on his *estancia*. They want the best modern appliances and luxuries, and even the ladies must have the very latest Parisian designed hats and gowns. The workmen join labour organizations and they are as free to strike as in any other country in the world; in every way they are breaking away from the old traditions and trying to enter into the spirit of the modern, be it for good or ill. The same trend is observable whether the person is the descendant of one of the old families, or is one of the recent importations from Spain or Italy. This modernizing spirit seems to be in the air and is as contagious as the most virulent form of fever or plague. All differences of social station fade away before this one vital force which pervades both Camp and city. It is almost as marked as in any part of the United States and cannot be overlooked by the most unobservant traveller.

A general wastefulness characterizes all classes, both urban and rural. In many cases this is probably due to ignorance. The very bountifulness of nature has no doubt accentuated a natural disinclination to attend to detail and small economies. If conservation would be studied much more profit could be realized by all. On the *estancias* this wastefulness is noted in the methods of taking care of the crops and vast herds of stock. In the city one will see it in the administration of municipal governments in the various departments. In private life one will discern it everywhere, and even the common labourer shows the same traits of improvidence and lack of thriftiness so characteristic of the German or French peasant, for example.

The railroads are wasteful oftentimes and are unprepared to handle the immense crops produced by a bountiful nature, so that thousands of tons of grain have been lost through sheer inability to get them to market, and the *estanciero* was unable to take care of his grain because he had no elevators or granaries to hold his crop. Thousands of cattle have been lost in a dry season because the owner trusted wholly to nature and had no food to keep them from starvation when the pasture failed. But then Argentina is not alone in these traits, and it is perhaps easier to find fault or give advice than to do the things ourselves if we were placed in the same position.

Like all Latin people, the Argentinian loves politics. The opera bouffe style of government, which can still be found in Central America, has disappeared, so that the melodramatic element no longer exists. With each year the people grow less inclined to indulge in revolution simply as a pastime. The risks of the revolutionists too are greater in a nation of nearly seven million people than formerly, when there were not one-fourth that number, and a country in which prosperity and education have made great strides. Furthermore, there is the feeling on the part of the Argentinians that their country is on its way to take its place as one of the great nations of the earth, and this idea has undoubtedly sobered them somewhat. There are, no doubt, many, even to-day, who enter politics with no other purpose than to enrich themselves. Their methods, however, are far more subtle than the revolutionists of old, and they hedge themselves about with an air of apparent honesty and patriotism that is difficult to penetrate. They have had good examples of genuine patriots in the not distant past, which has no doubt aided in clarifying the political atmosphere. It is in the question of government contracts where the test of honour comes. If the tales that are told are to be believed, then rich pickings often fall to officials. In some cases this has been done openly and yet caused little comment, because such a result seemed to be but natural and expected as a matter of course.

Argentina is a country that is purely pastoral and agricultural, for the proportion of those engaged in manufacturing is numerically very small. And yet one city contains nearly one-fifth of the total population. When you include the other cities, such as Rosario, Tucuman, Mendoza, etc., the proportion of city dwellers is still greater. The cities of Argentina have outgrown the rest of the country. With people of an excitable nature, such as the Latins are, it may bode serious trouble in the future. Strikes have become very common, and lawlessness in connection with them is very easy to stir up. Just before my visit the chief of police was killed in one of those disturbances. The method of the government in dealing with these exigencies is sensible but drastic. A state of siege and martial law is declared, and every suspicious character is deported as an undesirable. Following the killing of the chief of police, several hundred Italians and Spaniards were deported. It was only after several weeks of martial law that the ban was lifted and life moved along as before. Many of the Italians are, no doubt, anarchistic in their tendencies, and sometimes it might be wondered that disturbances are not more frequent and more general than they actually are. The police of the city usually show themselves competent to cope with the situation.

Notwithstanding the cosmopolitan character of the population, the republic is governed solely by the real Argentinians. No foreigner is permitted to sit in Congress or take any hand in the legislation of the country. The character of elections has undoubtedly progressed, but they are still far from being perfect or free from criticism. It is very easy to tell beforehand who will be elected by observing the forces and influences behind the various candidates. How it is accomplished might be difficult to explain, but it is done, and the man with the proper support will almost invariably win out in some way. Absolute freedom of expression is allowed the individual and press; one may listen to or read political addresses full of flowery eloquence and fire, or hear the most bitter denunciation, with no police interference whatever. The government does not worry itself about such trifles, which are merely abstract questions and do no one harm. The chances are that if the opponents of the government are allowed to work off their pent-up emotions in this way, their opposition on election day will not be very active. Hence they always treat the "not-ins" with a sort of good-natured forbearance that would be irritating to a North American.

There are perhaps fifty thousand or more persons in Argentina who might be classed as British. It would be difficult to find a community where a few of these Anglo-Saxons do not dwell. Of this number a large proportion are of Hibernian extraction. As a rule they may easily be spotted. In Buenos Aires and Rosario this colony remains entirely distinct and mingles very little in social relations with the natives. They are engaged in commerce and the other business enterprises. The Britisher is self-satisfied and the Argentinian would call him boorish, although he is welcomed, as is any one who will contribute to the development and material progress of the country. In the Camp it is sometimes different. There one will find former citizens of the British Isles who have almost forgotten their native tongue. Their children will speak Spanish in preference to English, and they have imbibed many of the characteristics of the Spaniards. If this British *estanciero* speaks English his conversation will be interspersed with Spanish phrases. The Camp seems to have a fascination for him, and he will prefer the blue and white banner of his adopted land to the British Jack. The rich land of Argentina, which can produce such abundant crops, has wielded a spell over him. This process of welding and consolidation has, in numerous instances, been at work for several generations.

The Englishman is a born sportsman. He loves horseflesh and all games, and has initiated the Argentinian into the mysteries of many. Football is now played all over the republic by thousands of the darker-hued Argentinians, side by side with the fair-haired Anglo-Saxon. Football has to all intents and purposes become the national game of Argentina. It is really astonishing what a hold this game has upon the people. The love of sport in the Camp has no doubt had an influence in leading to a closer understanding and better feeling between the two races in the rural districts; it has been a good influence and the result has been for the best interest of the nation. If the two races are to live side by side it is well for a good fellowship to exist between them.

The seal of Spain is upon everything that she has touched. The Spaniard has left his religion, language, and social creed all over the New World south of the Rio Grande, and his mark can be traced upon face, laws and landscape. Wherever he appeared the Spaniard has written his racial autograph in a hand that neither time nor political change has sufficed to efface. The Anglo-Saxon has never succeeded in accomplishing the same results except by colonization. One who is proficient can detect from what part the Spanish-American woman comes, for each national face has an individuality. The Mexicana, the Chilena, the Uruguayana and the Argentina all differ—and yet there is a kinship that can easily be traced. The olive-brown tint is there, but in different shades. The perfect *morena* (Spanish-Moorish) is a rarity, but it is as near perfection as complexion can be—so fine, so soft and so richly warmed. This type can frequently be found in the Argentina.

ONE OF ARGENTINA'S DAUGHTERS

Outside of Buenos Aires the old conservatism concerning the position of women still prevails. It must be admitted that there is something attractive about their life. The big roomy windows, and the balconies which jut out over the street on each floor, and the women seem made for each other. The balconies were first designed for the wives and daughters of the Spaniards to look out upon the street, since they were not allowed to go out freely. I know of no sight prettier or more enchanting than to see these balconies filled with women and children on the occasion of a carnival or other festive occasion. Two, three or four tiers of balconies, one above another, will be crowded with women all in white, and it is a sight upon which to feast the eyes. Then a family group in one of the big windows, with the young ladies seated on the window itself, forms a picture that will linger in the memory.

The women of Argentina are the antithesis of English or American women in many ways. The masculine type is very rare, for the restrictions and customs rather accentuate the purely feminine traits. In youth they are beautiful and none can help but admire both face and figure. They can express in the flash of an eye what an English girl could not say in a quarter of an hour. In addition to the attractiveness granted her by nature the Argentina is an adept at all the arts of the toilet, and is generally familiar with rouge, the pencil and the powder puff; in these she is a connoisseur, and does not hesitate to apply her knowledge. In many the Spanish and Italian types have been moulded together and the beauty has probably been accentuated. As a rule her carriage is graceful, but her voice—that is the one disappointing quality. The voice is generally rather shrill, and, when excited, very unpleasant. Furthermore, they always speak in a monotonous, high-keyed, sing-song manner.

BLACK-HAIRED CHILDREN OF ARGENTINA

A lack of exercise and a love of big dinners and wines soon develops a stoutness that does not add to the beauty of the Argentine woman. One will seldom see a woman in any city walking if a conveyance can possibly be had, and it is certainly a good thing for the cabbie. It is at a late hour when they arise and they seldom don other than negligée before the middle of the afternoon. In later years they become very stout—one might cruelly say, fleshy. In Buenos Aires they are beginning to look upon a little more freedom as their birthright. One will see young women on the street or in the street car unaccompanied by the duenna or other companion, which would be unknown in Spain. Whereas they used to look upon English girls as fast, because of their freedom, now they are longing to adopt the same freedom of action, and it seems to be coming by degrees. The matron becomes very much domesticated and devotes herself unstintingly to her children and their welfare. In this way many of the youngsters are really spoiled. Their devotion to their children is, however, to be greatly admired, and a great affection seems to exist for the mother among all her children, both girls and boys.

"I should think that these mothers would get tired of black hair," said an American woman to me in Buenos Aires. And then it dawned upon me with full force that all of these Latin-American children have black hair. It had not seemed to me as monotonous or tiresome before, for there is an individuality about each face, just as there is about that of children the world over. It is true that the hair of these children is almost uniformly of that hue, but I am very sure that the mothers find their children no less interesting because Carmencita, Juanita, Consuela, Maria, Juan, José, Santiago, Antonio and all their little brothers and sisters have hair of the same shade. These children of Latin-America are very numerous, for families are generally larger than they are in the United States. It is nothing unusual to see the mother or both parents get on board a train followed by six or eight children, all of whom are of tender ages.

The Spaniard has the reputation of being cruel. He is so to his horse or mule, he can view the cruelties of the bull-fight with enthusiasm, but his voice softens in speaking to a child. In fact the children are often petted and humoured too much, and the affection lavished upon them becomes a passion. And yet these bewitching little people are never unmindful of the simple courtesies of life. They learn the amenities of speech almost from the cradle. Ask some little fellow in Spanish America his name, and he will probably roll out a long name, such as Jesus Antonio Martinez y Alcorta, "at the service of God and yourself." Pass some compliment on little Carmencita and see how quickly she will say, "It is a compliment you pay me," or "*mil gracias,*" a thousand thanks. Offer her some little courtesy and she accepts "*con mucho gusto,*" with much pleasure, to which you should reply "the pleasure will be mine." It is hardly safe to admire an ornament of a little mite of only eight or ten years. She will instantly remove it and offer it to you with the expression, "It is at the disposal of your worship." The proper "disposal" is to refuse the gift in nice polite terms. It is really remarkable, and oftentimes touching, to observe these little courtesies in the *niñas* and *muchachas*. It even extends to their prayers, for here is the Spanish form of bed-time prayer:—

> "Jesus, Joseph, Mary,
>   Your little servant keep,
> While, with your kind permission,
>   I lay me down to sleep."

Most of these Argentine children are rather solemn-faced in the presence of strangers. They are not quite so free to make up with some one unknown to them as the average American child, and it is often rather difficult to coax a smile. One can even casually pinch a little cheek without provoking the smile so free with American children. It is not fear, for they do not seem afraid, but there is a certain shyness which is very noticeable. They will look up at you with their big, black eyes, but the smile which should accompany it is not forthcoming. Especially is this true of little girls, who thus early in life seem to realize the narrowness of their lives.

It has always seemed to me sad to contemplate a girl's life in these Latin lands. No sooner has one crossed the Rio Grande into Mexico than the restrictions upon a woman's freedom become evident, and these same customs extend clear to the "Land of Fire," at the southernmost limits of South America. Not only are the little girls held in a species of bondage, but in later years they miss that care-free, happy period of American girls in their early "teens," when every one considers it a privilege and pleasure to contribute to their enjoyment. They are hemmed about by servants and *duennas* during these years, and they then suddenly emerge into young womanhood, almost before one realizes that they are more than little girls. One year they are *niñas* (which means little girls), and a year or two later they are *señoritas*, or young ladies. They have almost skipped that delightful age of being "just girls," which the Spaniards term *muchachas*.

If there is one feature about them that is especially beautiful it is the eyes. Large, dark and radiant orbs are almost universal, and especially is that true in childhood. They very early begin the use of powder and paste, and oftentimes of rouge and the black pencil. It is a shame, for youth does not need these artificial aids and the evil effects are seen in the complexions of those of maturer years. This beauty of youth is more evanescent than with American girls, and the girl of even twenty has oftentimes begun to fade, and at thirty she is decidedly matronly in appearance.

Love and religion are the only two things that a Spanish woman should concern herself about, according to the theory of that land, and the same sentiment permeates even the childish amusements. Love and lovers run through all the childish rhymes of the children of Spanish-America. But more frequently it is religion. To begin with, their very names all have some religious significance. Mary is a very common name, but to it is added one of the attributes of the Virgin, such as Mary of the Sorrows, Tears, Annunciation, etc. Thus smiling little Dolores (sorrows), Lagrimas (tears) and the other little Marys bear these sad names, but their smiles come just as easy as if their names signified joys. Saints are appealed to in many of their childish amusements. "Jesus" and "Mary Most Pure" are common forms of exclamation for the tiniest of tots, and their conversation is punctuated with these sacred terms in the most innocent way imaginable. They are used just as American tots would say "oh, my," or "good gracious."

CHAPTER X
THE PEOPLE AT PLAY

S-p-o-r-t is the word you will find at the head of the sporting columns of the Spanish, as well as English newspapers, in Argentina. This word has been transferred over bodily, as no term in Spanish exactly expressed the meaning of the English word sport. Baseball has not yet become popular and cricket is little understood by the Argentinians, but they are passionately fond of the turf, and horse racing is perhaps the favourite sport of all classes. It is not the excitement of the racing alone that appeals to the Argentinian, but the opportunity it gives for indulging in his love of betting. Argentina possesses some of the finest horse flesh in the world, and sales of favourites oftentimes take place at almost fabulous prices.

Sixty millions is a tidy little sum to be placed upon horses in one year. And yet that is the amount staked upon the races in the city of Buenos Aires last year, according to the municipal statistics of that city. Estimating the population at one million, two hundred thousand, this is an average of fifty Argentine dollars for each man, woman and child in that great city. Naturally the reported figures do not include all the money that is wagered on the horse racing, so that it is impossible to give the total amount of the bets, but it was undoubtedly several million dollars in addition to the above sum. Reducing the figures to American money, the wagers would represent twenty-five million, eight hundred thousand dollars in gold coin with the American eagle stamped on the back.

THE HIPPODROMO, BUENOS AIRES

The race track of Buenos Aires, called the Hippodromo, is a monopoly of the Jockey Club in that city. This club is an exception to the general run of clubs in the world, for it has more money than it knows what to do with. The troublesome surplus in the bank is the only problem that bothers the board of directors, and it is bringing gray hairs to their devoted heads. A half million dollars (an Argentine dollar is worth forty-three cents) is devoted to charity each year, but that is only a small part of its income. Ten per cent. of the total amount of stakes on the races is the property of the club. This, together with the gate receipts and membership dues, gives the Jockey Club an enormous income, running up very close to eight figures. The several hundred members each pay dues amounting to fifteen hundred dollars annually, and the initiation fee is four thousand dollars. The membership is always full, and there is a long waiting list of eligibles. About a year ago a proposition was seriously discussed by the club to purchase a dozen blocks right in the heart of the city, construct a broad and beautiful boulevard through it and make a present of the improvement to the city. The estimated cost was in the neighbourhood of fourteen million dollars. When the proposition came to a vote it was lost by only five votes.

It was defeated, too, not on account of the cost, but simply on the question of the advisability or practicability of such a scheme. The club had the money on hand, and they are now worrying themselves again as to what to do with it.

The home of the Jockey Club is a rather unpretentious-looking building on the narrow Calle Florida, in the very heart of the city. The interior, however, is magnificent. As one enters the massive doors, a marble staircase faces you, which is the boast of the members and the pride of Buenos Aires. Then there are dining-rooms, reception-rooms, parlours and all the other apartments required in such an establishment. All of these rooms are fitted and furnished regardless of cost, and with the artistic taste which is inherent with the Latin races, so that it will compare favourably with any palace in Europe. The banquet-room is fitted with a circular table, with a running fountain in the centre. This table is so made that it can be arranged to seat twenty people, or enlarged to accommodate a hundred, and still be a perfect circle. I had the pleasure of dining in the club with the American minister, and found that one will meet with representative Argentinians of all classes, for the membership is confined to them; but few foreigners, outside of the diplomats, are able to get their names on the membership books even as honorary members. A good introduction will sometimes give the visitor a chance to take his meals there and have a hand in the games, in which fortunes are oftentimes lost in a single night. The club possesses some exquisite works of art. They have followed the plan of purchasing one picture each year, but that picture must contain merit, for the price is no object. In this way they have collected some paintings and statuary that are worthy of places in any museum of art or palace in the world.

The Argentinians are natural born gamblers, and nothing suits them better than to take a chance on a lottery or on a horse race. The Hippodromo has one of the finest race courses in the world. There are three tracks, one within another. The outer one is three kilometers, or about one and three-fourths mile, in circumference. There are three grandstands, the central one being a magnificent structure, which is reserved for members of the Jockey Club and their invited guests. The gates are as fine specimens of brass gates as one can find of modern manufacture. The big races are all held on Sundays, or national holidays, from twelve o'clock to three. Then all of the society folk put on their best bib and tucker and pour out toward the Hippodromo. A perfect stream of luxurious automobiles and fine carriages with liveried drivers will carry the society out to the races. During the races these vehicles line up along the curb facing the middle of the street, for blocks, with mounted police mingling in the line at intervals.

Here is a typical flowery description by an Argentine reporter of a race at the Hippodromo: "It was a lavish spectacle of contentment, of spirits absorbed for the moment in the coming sport—regulars eager to try their palpitos, simple-minded folk who carried the 'sure-thing' safely tucked away in their pockets. Dreamers of fortune, these, lulled by the music of the trot. And out of the vague intonation of all this multitude there came, here and there, like a breath of fresh air, the glimpses fluttering, elegant, of luxurious carriages carrying radiantly dressed ladies, the luminous note of undulating ribbons and plumes standing out like a spring-like, feminine bouquet against the black mass of these absorbed in the sport."

It is a study of Argentine life. They are not as noisy as an American crowd, but the tense faces express the keenest interest, for nearly every one, old and young, man or woman, has a personal interest in the outcome. There are none so old and few so young that they will not wage a few pesos on a favourite. Between the races the crowds leave the grandstand and wander around below or visit the betting booths, which cover a half-acre of ground. One booth will accept wagers of ten dollars, another of fifty and still others of one hundred dollars. The money is then apportioned after fixed rules. Ten per cent. is first deducted for charity, another ten per cent. for the Jockey Club and the balance is divided among the bettors. When the result has been figured up, the amount to be paid on the different horses is posted up on a black-board and the winners can draw their money. This board, it is needless to say, is eagerly scanned after each race.

More than one hundred races were given by this club last year, and they were attended by nearly three-quarters of a million of people. The big races were witnessed by a concourse of people which sometimes numbered fifty thousand. The average attendance of all the races is more than six thousand. The attendance and the money wagered is increasing rapidly each year. The statistics show an increase in the past ten years of more than three hundred per cent., and the amount of money wagered has increased still more rapidly. The Argentinians are prosperous now, and they spend their money more freely than the average American.

The Tiger—that is the meaning in English of El Tigre, the Thames of Argentina. It is situated a half-hour's ride by train from the city of Buenos Aires, and is the favourite resort of all the lovers of water sports in that city. "Going to the Tigre" is the usual expression you will hear from the passenger at Retiro station on Saturday, Sunday or a holiday, and it may be said in Spanish, English, German or Italian. It is an inaccurate expression, for the name Tigre is properly applied only to one of the most insignificant branches of the network of streams which abound in that vicinity.

A SUMMER COTTAGE AT EL TIGRE

"IMPOSING CREEPER-CLAD COTTAGES ARE DOTTED ALONG THE BANK"

El Tigre is not an old resort. Thirty years ago the banks of the many little streams which wind in and out along the shore of the Rio de La Plata for several miles were almost bare of arboreal growth, just like the plains, or pampas, are for hundreds of miles. In fact it has only been within the past dozen years that Buenos Aires in all its cosmopolitan entirety "discovered" El Tigre. At the present time the banks are all fringed with a dense curtain of vegetation. The eucalyptus, poplar and willow alternate with each other, and closely-set peach and pear orchards are very numerous, for the Tigre fruits are large and delicious, and are in great demand in that republic. The transformation has been wonderful, and the average visitor would think that the growth was natural and not planted. This class of trees grows very rapidly when once planted by the hand of man, but nature herself slighted Argentina in the matter of trees.

As one sails in and out of the numerous canals new scenes of beauty continuously open up before his eyes. The broad canal from the railroad station is taken first, for this leads past the principal club houses. Imposing creeper-clad cottages are dotted along the bank on one side, and some of them are very beautiful. On the opposite side is the Tigre Hotel, with its many flowers and refreshment grounds. As the motor boat speeds along the regatta course the procession of passing craft is never-ending. There are launches, punts, skiffs and canoes filled with cosmopolitan parties of nearly all nationalities. Among these crowds the olive faces and graceful figures of the dark-eyed Argentinian *señoritas* may easily be distinguished from the blonde, ruddy-faced English girl, or the more buxom German type. The *señoritas* have learned to skull and manœuvre the rudder, as well as their fairer haired rivals for the affections of the youths who are fortunate to be the owners of some craft that will float on these seductive waters.

An excursion to the remote waters savours of the adventurous, for the uninitiated would soon lose his bearings. One will wind in and out of the maze of streams in continual wonder as to what the next bend will reveal. There are broad streets of water, lanes, narrow passages and even blind alleys. One might follow one course and emerge upon the broad La Plata, or he might wind in and out for hours, or even days, without once doubling on his track. Along these less frequented water ways the honeysuckle and swamp flowers bloom unaided, and the large crimson blossoms of the ceibo tree add a brilliant touch of colour. Native boats laden with willow or fruits will occasionally be met, for these watery lanes furnish the only outlet for the most of the islands to the railroad station. In fact it is a sort of rural Venice, in which the water furnishes the only means of communication. Occasionally a boat will disappear into a narrow opening that you have not noticed before, for it was so well shielded by the overhanging willows.

Many and beautiful boats will be seen upon the Tigre. There is the swift motor boat decked up high so that it can glide through the waters swiftly; again there is the broader build made for carrying a larger complement of passengers. Then there are yachts of all kinds as well as row-boats of every shape. The most of them are built in Europe, but an occasional one constructed in the United States may be singled out. There are a number of boat clubs. The oldest one was established by the English, but this has been absorbed by the Argentinians and a new one built by the British colony. This is said to be the largest rowing club in the world. The Germans have a club house, and even the Italians have built their own home. There are not enough Americans in that southern metropolis to own a club house, but some of that nationality belong to the English club, and own or have an interest in some of the gasoline-propelled launches.

The people love the good things of life. In the evening those who wish to dine in a becoming manner go to the Tigre Hotel. As the light begins to fade, here and there the launches dart in and out of the shadows to the landing-stage. The dining-room quickly becomes crowded with diners in outing flannels or evening dress. After a while the tables in the dining-room become filled to overflowing with a gay and happy crowd, and they spread out upon the terrace by the river side. If there is moonlight the effect is oftentimes almost fairy-like. Then the moon and the Southern Cross look down upon such a scene of beauty and vivacity as must make the Queen of the Night smile, and cause the stars to twinkle more brightly than usual. The rays of moonlight are intersected by the reflection of the lamps, while here and there a twinkling point that denotes a launch darts in and out of the shadows. Later the notes of the guitar and mandolin may be heard on the waters, as the happy crowd disperse to the cottages, and the youthful gallants remain yet a few minutes more by the home of the charmer and breathe in the fragrance of the magnolia blossoms upon the banks. At last at a later hour all becomes quiet, save for the silent splashing of the little waves upon the banks of the canals. Then the darting glow of the fireflies and the song of the mosquito is all that remains to indicate life on El Tigre.

"Come on in; the water is fine."

It did not sound that way, for the words were in Spanish. It was in January, too, and the latitude about the same as that of Washington. There is this difference, however, that Mar del Plata is south of the "line." While we are wearing heavy wraps, the people in that part of the world are enjoying warm weather. During January and February Buenos Aires is deserted by society and officials, just as are New York and Washington in July and August. Buenos Aires can only be compared to the two cities, for it is both capital and metropolis.

Argentina has but one seaside resort. This one place is the fashionable Newport, the merry-making Coney Island, and the cosmopolitan Atlantic City, all in one. It is the English Brighton and Blackpool united. The life at Mar del Plata is like none of its prototypes or its contemporaries.

Here is an enthusiastic description of Mar del Plata by a native writer: "All at Mar del Plata suggests the refinement of a bathing resort. The waves of the Atlantic beat softly upon the sandy beaches. The magnificent hotels are filled with a *monde* cultured and sociable, that fills the summer evenings with joy. The English cottages and the luxurious chateaux are dotted upon the slopes with all their graceful architecture and modern comfort. The days are balmy and the nights perfumed; the concerts, dances, strolls upon the 'Rambla,' the gracious life of the élite—all this enlivens the sport, and causes the summer months to pass by in an enchanting fashion. And, above all, the inevitable 'flirtation' is wont to insinuate itself in the midst of this delightful frame of mind, commencing with discreet love-makings in the romantic light of the moon, in improvised excursions, during which one may enjoy with a full pulse the beauty of nature, and ending in the interchange of marriage vows to the accompaniment of delicious blushes on the part of the maiden, and nervous agitation on that of the future Benedict."

MAR DEL PLATA

A few years ago a site on a beautiful little bay of the Atlantic, two hundred and fifty miles from Buenos Aires, was chosen by a few of the wealthy residents as a summer home. At that time the property could be purchased for almost a song, as there was nothing on the site except a little fishing village. These people built commodious homes, and it was not long until this small advance guard was followed by others, and the colony began to attract attention. In the last six years alone it has increased one thousand per cent., and to-day Mar del Plata is an attractive summer resort, with scores of palatial homes, several large hotels, asphalt streets and other improvements which follow population. There are a number of low hills that line the shore, which form a pretty break in the flat plains that lie all the way to Buenos Aires. The main portion of the town is built in one of the breaks in these hills, on the largest bay, and the palatial homes are on the slopes and summits facing the sea. There are some beautiful rocky formations around the bay, deep narrow cliffs through which the waters break with thunderous noise. The finest golf links in the republic are on one of the hills which overlooks the sea, and this is the favourite spot for the English visitors to this resort. There is also a beautiful drive which extends for several miles up and down the hills and near the shore along the yellow sands, past the picturesque rocks and ever looking out upon the blue waters of the ocean.

There is not the life about Mar del Plata that one finds at an American seaside resort. Spanish conservatism still prevails, although mixed bathing is permitted. This was introduced for the first time four years ago. The people have hardly accustomed themselves to the innovation yet, as one will only see the mixed groups in small family parties. As a rule the women and children go in together and the men keep by themselves. Furthermore, no one in bathing-costume will be seen strolling on the walk, or along the beach. The women come out of the bathroom with a cloak over the shoulder, and are generally joined by an attendant. He removes the cloak as soon as the water is reached, and it is hung on a line to await her return. The suits worn are generally skirtless, but with a coat reaching half way to the knees; and they never wear stockings. The attendant accompanies them out to where the surf is breaking, always keeping near the life line. There they play around for twenty or thirty minutes and then leave the water. The cloak is placed on their shoulders again, and they immediately disappear into the dressing-rooms. The authorities are very watchful of the bathers, for the undertow at times is very strong. Scattered along the beach one will at all times see men in bathing-costumes bearing coils of rope, who are ever on the alert. These *bañeros* have saved the life of many a venturesome bather.

The bathing is generally done in the morning, for at eleven o'clock the promenade begins. This takes place along the board walk, called the "Rambla," which follows the line of the shore for a distance. This walk is open to the sea and covered with a roof, but on the shore side there are little curio stores, cafés, photograph galleries and moving picture shows. Many families also have little private bath houses along this walk; but that name is really a misnomer, for they are principally used to sit in and watch the promenade, as well as to entertain friends.

The promenade in Spanish countries is a great feature of social life. Because of the restrictive social customs there is little freedom in the life of women, and they therefore welcome this diversion. It also gives the *señoritas* a chance to exhibit their charms before the admiring young men, and very often leads to ardent love affairs. Every woman and girl who is able to get around will be on that walk just as sure as the men. And then for an hour or more the crowd will walk back and forth, until you think they would all tire themselves out. By one o'clock the promenaders have disappeared, and during the afternoon the walk is almost deserted. That is the time for the *siesta*, which is followed by a drive along the sea front. At six o'clock the promenade begins again, and is kept up for about two hours more, a repetition of the one at midday. Thus it is that life goes on day after day for three months every summer at this greatest resort in South America. This parade is a study in the life of Argentine society, for the real four hundred visit Mar del Plata. It is a place for dress and no one with a slender purse can afford to visit it, or, at least, stay any length of time. The costumers' establishments of far away London and Paris, as well as Buenos Aires, have been ransacked for gowns to be worn at this resort.

ON THE BEACH, MAR DEL PLATA

With all the increase in hotel accommodation that has been provided in recent years, the hotels were full for weeks the past season, and it was almost impossible to secure accommodation unless one had friends, or arranged for it weeks ahead. The Hotel Bristol is the largest hotel in South America. There is a main building, which contains a spacious dining and ball room, and two annexes, each of which is as large as the average city block. The prices correspond with the magnificence of the furnishings. It is a night's run from Buenos Aires, and a day train is run on Saturdays and Tuesdays, which makes the trip in about seven hours. The night that I went there were five trains, each carrying fourteen sleepers, and all of them were full. The traffic had been just as great for almost a month. The country is as flat as a barn floor, with thousands of cattle and sheep dotting the Camp as far as the eye could reach. Great, long-eared rabbits are so numerous that drives are often formed by the *estancieros* to get rid of them. Arrived at Mar del Plata, there was a close line of carriages almost a mile long waiting for "fares." As soon as one carriage was filled another moved up and took its place. At these times the "cabbie" is the real monarch, for the

Argentinians are very fond of carriages and seldom walk if a carriage is to be had.

The wealthy promoters of this resort are aiming to make it a sort of Monte Carlo. A new club has just been built, which is the largest and most imposing building in Mar del Plata. In this building three roulette tables and several games of *trente et quarante* were running in full blast, one roulette table being in a special room for ladies. The building was not quite finished at that time and only the gambling rooms were in use, they being much more necessary than the rest rooms or dining department. The most prominent men in the republic are members of this club. There had been a public *casino*, but the governor of the province had closed that. He could not reach this private club, however, without the aid of another official, who favoured the gambling. They were hoping in a few months to elect another governor who would not be so strait-laced about such an important thing as gambling. Large sums are oftentimes staked on the games at Mar del Plata, for the Argentinian is reckless enough to risk his last dollar under the excitement of the game.

Mar del Plata has become quite a fishing place and many of the inhabitants are engaged in that occupation. It is very interesting to watch the fishing boats when they come in from their excursions. First one, then two or three, and perhaps a dozen of these picturesque crafts will come around the point and head for the beach. Watching a favourable swell, one after another of the fishing smacks will head for the shore with all sail set. Awaiting them will be men with teams of horses, by means of which they are pulled up high and dry upon the sand to await the coming of morning, when they will again start out in their search for the ocean's game.

CHAPTER XI
EDUCATION AND THE ARTS

"Found schools and you will do away with revolutions," was the favourite expression of President Sarmiento. It was during this administration that education received its greatest impetus. Sarmiento, who has been called the "school-teacher president," inaugurated a most liberal policy towards popular education. He was deeply interested in this problem, had made a study of the educational systems in the United States and caused the establishment of very many schools and public libraries. The provincial and municipal authorities of the republic were everywhere encouraged and urged to establish an efficient system of public instruction, and his efforts produced beneficial results. The later administrations, however, have been absorbed in other lines, and many of the progressive ideas of Sarmiento were allowed to pass into "innocuous desuetude." There have been occasional spurts of energy, but these have been far too spasmodic.

The subject of education arouses less interest than it should with the people in general. This lack of public interest is perhaps accountable in a great measure for the indifference of the provincial and national administrations. Here is a criticism of Mr. Akers, the historian, of the educational system in Argentina. "A smattering of many subjects is taught, a sound knowledge of any one is the exception. It is not that the pupils are deficient in intelligence, but rather that teachers are lacking in experience and ability. Nor can any other result be expected under existing circumstances. The payment of officials is inadequate, and frequently salaries are months in arrears, while lack of discipline in primary, secondary and higher education is conspicuous. Provisions for the orderly exercise of authority in colleges and schools are also most defective." This criticism was written in 1903, but it is applicable to-day, except that the payment of the teachers is somewhat higher and a little more regular. The teaching profession is still greatly underpaid, as the money is turned into other channels which are more purely political. It is simply another example of that utilitarian policy of looking only to the present and letting the future generations take care of themselves.

Public instruction in Argentina is divided into three classes—primary, secondary and higher education. Primary education is compulsory by law, though seldom enforced, and is given free to all children in the republic between the ages of six and fourteen. Education in the capital and territories is under the control of the Federal Government, and there are in all five thousand, two hundred and fifty public schools for primary instruction maintained by it. Each of the provinces maintains large numbers of these schools for elementary instruction also, and in addition each city contains a number of private schools to which people of means send their children rather than to the public institutions. All of the schools having the support of the Federal Government are under the supervision of the National Council of Education, which is housed in a beautiful building in the city of Buenos Aires. Secondary education is not compulsory, but it is practically free, as only a very small fee is charged for registration. There are sixteen lyceums and thirty-five normal schools which come under this class, and they are located in all the larger cities of the nation. The national universities of Buenos Aires and Cordoba are both noted institutions, and these, together with the provincial universities at La Plata, Santa Fé and Paraná, provide the higher education. In addition to this the various provincial governments send a number of students abroad each year to complete their studies at the noted universities of Europe and North America. At the present time there are about thirty of these students at the various universities and colleges of the United States, and others are pursuing their studies in England, France, Germany and Italy.

A SECONDARY SCHOOL

Many technical schools are also maintained by the national government. Among these one of the most practical is the Industrial School of the capital. This institution has elaborate workshops which are well equipped with machinery and appliances, in which the trades and crafts are taught. The National Conservatory of Music, the School for Drawing, the School of Art, and the School of Commerce, in which instruction is given accountants and translators, are situated in Buenos Aires, and there are commercial schools in Cordoba and Bahia Blanca. There is an agricultural school in Santa Catalina, province of Buenos Aires, and agricultural experiment stations have been established at Tucuman, Bella Vista, San Juan and Tenna.

Argentina is, at the present time, spending a great deal of money for education. In the city of Buenos Aires there are sixty-seven buildings devoted to educational purposes. Many of these are very attractive structures and the total cost has run up into the millions of pesos. The general plan of education is being modelled very much after that of the United States. System and practice, however, are often two different things, and so it oftentimes happens in Argentina. In actual practice there is often a misconception of what real education means. Superficiality is too often a characteristic of the education offered. There are many finely educated persons in the country, but not many of them teachers. The positions are too often the reward of politics, although there are many very efficient women who are teaching. Graduation is easy for the scholar with a pull, for the students will bring in recommendations at graduation time in order to be sure of passing, especially if they have not been very diligent. A glitter is too often allowed to take the place of real scholarliness and learning. This superficiality is too often allowed to pass muster where solidarity should be demanded.

The University of Buenos Aires is one of the great educational institutions of the New World. It is not quite so old as the one in Cordoba, which was founded in 1613, but it has a much larger attendance of students, probably because of its location in the capital. The buildings are scattered over the city in different sections, as the various departments have been added from time to time. A few of the oldest buildings are very venerable looking indeed, and are among the oldest structures in the city. It is planned to rebuild much of the University in the suburban sections in the near future, so that more space can be utilized in quadrangle and park. Almost five thousand students receive instruction in the various departments, of which the largest number, about one-half of the whole, are matriculated in the College of Medicine, which is a large and well-equipped institution. Many departments are included in the institution, however, which do not strictly come within the designation of a medical institution proper, and that accounts for the numerical enrolment. The next largest department is that known as the Faculty of Law and Social Sciences. A recent addition to this ancient university is the National Agronomic and Veterinary Institute, which is devoted to developing what are, and perhaps always will be, the greatest sources of the national wealth of Argentina. The courses of study of the University are very complete, and contain what is best in Argentine education. It is by far the best and most thorough educational institution in the republic.

It is not to be expected that one would find in Argentina a very great number of writers. The greatest incentive to a writer, as well as to a publisher, is that a book will be read by many people. In the republics of Spanish America, with education only imperfectly spread among the masses, the number of readers has been necessarily small. Another obstacle to the development of literary activity has been in the frequent wars and revolutions which have kept most of those nations in a state of political turmoil. Furthermore the comparative isolation of those republics prevented a coöperation among them even though there was a sameness of language. Therefore the editions were necessarily small, and the remuneration consequently inadequate to encourage a literary career. In the face of these disabilities it is to the credit of Spanish-American writers that their activities have been so considerable.

Politics and journalism have always been intimately connected in Argentina, for the editorial has oftentimes been of greater interest than the news columns. Many of her writers have been intimately associated with this form of activity. Avellaneda, Pellegrini, and Bartolomé Mitre, all of whom occupied the presidential chair, first made their mark in the journalistic field. The last named wrote an able work on the history of the emancipation of South America and a biography of the Argentine patriot, San Martin. Vicente Fidel Lopez, another historical writer, gave to the world a "History of the Argentine Republic," which has taken its place among standard historical works.

Poetry and the drama have always been favourite forms of writing among Spanish writers. Perhaps no language can boast of so many dramas as the Castilian. Argentina has nourished a number of these, among whom might be named Tomas Gutierrez, Rosa Guerra and Juana Manso de Noronha, the latter writing a drama called "The Revolution of May," which is very popular in that country. There are few Spanish writers who do not at some time stray into poetic writing to which that tongue is so well adapted. Although none of the poets have secured a world-wide hearing, some very sweet poems have been penned by Echeverria, Lafinur and Figueroa. In fiction translations of French writers have generally been demanded. Only one novel by an Argentine writer has received a favourable hearing in Europe, and that was "Amalia," by José Marmol. It is an historical novel treating of the dictatorship of Rosas, and has been very highly commented upon by competent critics. It probably gives the best picture of the stirring events of that interesting period in the history of Argentina. In more recent years, since the population has increased, and better political conditions prevail, and the reading public has been so greatly augmented, writers in all fields, including philosophy and political economy have become more numerous, and the next decade will probably be marked by much greater literary activity.

The press is well represented in Argentina, for there is scarcely a town of any size that does not support a newspaper. They are well patronized too, and the towns take a pride in their publications. The press of Buenos Aires is one of the most polyglot in the world. There are in that city almost five hundred different publications, of which four hundred and twelve are printed in the Spanish language, twenty-two in Italian, eight in French, eight in English, eight in German and one in Arabic. Then the Danish, Norwegian, Swedish, Roman and Dutch tongues each have at least one representative. There are sixty-six dailies, sixty-four monthlies and almost two hundred weeklies.

La Prensa, which means The Press, is a newspaper of which any country or city might be proud. Although not a government organ, for it remains independent, this newspaper undoubtedly exerts the widest influence of any newspaper in Argentina, and perhaps in South America. It is most frequently quoted by the people and its statements are taken as facts. It has a circulation of over one hundred thousand. In appearance it is a large metropolitan sheet seldom containing less than sixteen or twenty pages. Its news columns are well written and newsy, and its editorials are weighty and well-digested. *La Prensa* publishes more foreign news than any newspaper in the world. This is its claim—certainly more than any daily in the United States. There are seldom less than two pages of foreign cablegrams from all parts of the world, principally Europe, of course. The establishment of this newspaper is on the Avenida de Mayo, in an imposing building which cost three million dollars and is one of the finest newspaper homes in the world. Here will be found not only a complete and modern newspaper plant, but a number of unique features for the good of the public and the glory of the city. At its own expense a free consulting room is provided where an able physician, aided by several assistants, administer to the sick without charge; there is a law office where, during certain hours, indigent persons can secure free legal advice; a large, well-stocked library is open to all without payment; there is a large hall for public meetings and where fine musical entertainments, as well as private operas, are sometimes given for the force. Another unique feature is a suite of finely furnished apartments where distinguished foreigners are gratuitously entertained. There are private grill rooms for the reporters and other employees, and the proprietor has a fine office which he does not occupy more than once in six months. The owner of the *La Prensa* is a very wealthy man, but he takes absolutely no part in the conduct of the paper. He engages an editor-manager, and the entire management and policy of the paper is turned over to this one man. If this man makes good he retains his position; if not, he is at once supplanted. In a long period of years there have been but four editors, which speaks well for the care with which these men have been chosen. They have all been men of prominence, and their ability is shown by the high standard of the paper which has been maintained during all of these years.

After *La Prensa, La Nacion,* which was founded in 1870 by the famous Argentine statesman, Bartolomé Mitre, is second in importance, and has a large as well as distinguished clientele. It is large and metropolitan in appearance, and might be called the government organ. The principal evening paper is *El Diario. La Argentina, El Pais, La Razon, El Tiempo, El Pueblo, Tribuna,* etc., are the names of some of the other leading dailies. There are two English daily newspapers, the *Standard* and the *Buenos Aires Herald,* each of which has a good circulation. They are both typical English papers in appearance and general style, although the Herald was founded by an American. The *Review of the River Plate* and *The Times of Argentina* are weekly publications devoted to shipping and the general financial news and interests of the country. The former has a well-established reputation as a financial authority in British commercial circles. *Caras y Caretas* is a unique illustrated weekly which has a large circulation and is exceedingly popular. *La Illustracion Sud-Americana* is a handsomely illustrated monthly, one of the best published anywhere. *La Revista de Derecho, Historia y Letras* is a literary periodical of high character.

The Spanish cavaliers left Europe just prior to the Renaissance, when the dark ages were nearing their end. Europe was then striving with the life which was soon to burst forth. The wealth of knowledge and art, which had heretofore been confined within the dark and forbidding walls of monasteries and convents, was about to be given forth to the world to which it belonged. St. Peter's was then in the hands of architects full of new ideas, the great cathedral of Seville was nearing completion and work was in progress on many of the other famous cathedrals of that continent. This genius for building crossed the seas with the new colonists, and they soon turned their attention to the upbuilding of great temples dedicated to the Almighty. It was an age of wonderful activities in art and architecture, and the New World profited by it. It was not long until hammer, chisel and trowel were busy in all the new settlements, and their accomplishments now gladden the eye of the people of this age. The oldest Spanish cathedral in the Americas is probably at Santo Domingo, as that was first settled. It was here that the body of Columbus rested for a time. Cortez marked his subjugation of Mexico by the inauguration of great public works on which the newly-enslaved inhabitants of the country were employed, as did Pizarro in Peru. The great cathedral of the City of Mexico, the most stupendous of the New World, was begun in 1573, on the site of the ancient altar of sacrifice of the Aztecs. This is said to be outranked by only three cathedrals in the world, St. Peter's, St. Paul's of London, and that of Seville. The cathedral of Lima, Peru, is the earliest and largest in South America, and was founded on the same day as the city itself, by Pizarro. The cornerstone of this magnificent structure was laid on the 16th day of January, 1535, and the bones of the founder now rest beneath its roof and are shown to the curious visitor.

THE COLUMBUS THEATRE, BUENOS AIRES

There are some old churches in Argentina which one will find in Cordoba and other old towns. The cathedral, however, is more modern, as it was not begun until comparatively recent times, although erected on the site of a chapel that was founded in 1580. Were it not for the dome surmounted by a cross its appearance would not necessarily suggest a religious edifice. The twelve massive Corinthian columns suggest the Church of the Madeleine in Paris. It shows a tendency to depart from the old models and adopt newer schemes of embellishment, just as has been the tendency in North America. Its façade, however, is imposing on the Plaza de Mayo, around which centre the commercial and political activities of this great city. It is perhaps emblematical of the new forces which are at work in Latin-America. The interior of this cathedral is commodious and will accommodate several thousand people. The Church of San Francisco is a fine example of church architecture, and has just been almost wholly remodelled. San Domingo is an historic old church, in the tower of which a number of cannon balls are imbedded, which were fired into the city by the British fleet.

The principle of subsidy to art still retains its vitality in South America. In Argentina there are several municipal theatres, or opera houses, and the finest of which is the Teatro Colon, or Columbus Theatre, of Buenos Aires. This handsome structure was erected by the municipality at a cost of two million dollars. It is three stories high. The first story represents the Ionic, the second the Corinthian and the third the Doric style of architecture. It is of recent construction and will seat nearly four thousand persons. The very best artists of the world are brought here, as the annual allotment from the municipal budget enables the management to do what the box receipts alone would not warrant, because of the long voyage necessary to bring these high-salaried artists to Buenos Aires.

CHAPTER XII
THE FORCES OF DEFENCE

No modern institution has been more talked about and written about than that of the police. The police problem is, in all cities, one to which continual thought is given by citizens as well as officials. The debt we owe to the police can more easily be understood by thinking for a moment of what city life would be without that body. In Greater New York, with a population of five millions, there are about ten thousand policemen, or one to every five hundred inhabitants. In London the proportion is one policeman for every four hundred and ninety-six dwellers in the world's metropolis. In Buenos Aires there are twice as many in proportion to the population as in New York. If these guardians of the peace were to be suddenly withdrawn, no man's property or person would be safe at any time of the day or night in these great congested centres. Men would be obliged to go armed; business places and dwellings would have to be barricaded by night; no one could leave his home with a feeling of security as to what might happen during his absence. It was so during the middle ages when the people locked and bolted their massive doors and remained at home, or went about at night in companies in order to insure safety.

In ancient times many of the duties of the modern police were performed by the soldiers. In the early days of Persia and ancient Greece guards were stationed at the gates, and at night military watchmen were placed on the walls. Rulers and persons of affluence had in addition their own personal body-guards. It was not until the days of Augustus Cæsar that the idea of a body of men trained and disciplined to maintain order for the benefit of the citizens at large was developed. The Romans were averse to the presence of soldiers within the walls, for fear that they might become a menace to public liberty. As a result of this prejudice a body of civil police grew up, a part of whose equipment were buckets of rope made waterproof with tar, for they were the firemen as well. Because of this outfit the people in derision called them "squirts," or "bucket-boys." The Anglo-Saxon system of police was not perfected until in the time of the eminent Sir Robert Peel less than a century ago. After several years of strenuous work in Parliament he succeeded in passing a law organizing the Metropolitan Police of London. Although this body of men gave security and protection to the citizens of that city it was considered an inroad upon personal liberty and the members of the force were termed in derision "bobbies" and "peelers," names which have clung to them ever since.

It has often been a query in my mind whether we fully appreciate the work of the policeman. The soldier's praise has been sung in every land and in every tongue, but the man who walks the city's streets has not succeeded in inspiring the muse to any extent. The police are a mighty army in themselves. If one could shout the one word "Police!" so that it might be heard the world over, it would call together an army of more than a million men. Among these would be the stalwart "bobbie" of London, giant Chinese policemen from Hong Kong, barefooted Zulus clothed in English helmets and suits, tens of thousands of American "cops," and last, but not least, the little brown policeman of Argentina. Buenos Aires alone could furnish five full regiments of a thousand men each.

A POLICEMAN OF ARGENTINA

These dark-skinned, undersized men are always on duty. At regular intervals a sergeant comes along and signs the officer's book, which is his record of service. The summer uniform is white, helmet and all. At night you will see one of these officers at every street intersection. As far as you can see down the narrow thoroughfares one of these white sentries may be seen on duty at every corner. Should a disturbance occur he will blow his whistle and this will be answered for many blocks. Soon policemen will be seen running from the four directions, and in a few minutes quite a force can be collected. A call to the central station would bring an additional force. In this way an incipient disturbance could soon be checked. As these men are under the pay of the national government, they form a part of the defensive forces of the country and are a really creditable body. The mounted men are well mounted and have a very smart appearance as they canter through the streets.

Since the probability of war with Chile passed away the army of Argentina has not been kept as full as prior to 1904. The proportion of soldiers to the population is perhaps less than in any other republic of South America, except Brazil. There are thirty infantry battalions, nine cavalry regiments, eight regiments of the various branches of artillery, besides the numerous special features. The cavalry in particular will compare most favourably with those of any other nation. They are recruited principally from the gauchos, the cowboys of Argentina, who are born to the saddle and sit upon the horses with a grace and naturalness that only comes with familiarity to such form of locomotion from the very cradle itself almost. The infantry are well equipped with modern arms and accoutrements, but they will not bear comparison with the troops of Uncle Sam, Germany or France. They are fighters, however, when once aroused and interested in the cause for which they are fighting. There is in addition to the permanent army a reserve army of about one hundred and fifty thousand. By the provisions of the law every Argentine citizen, from his twentieth to his forty-fifth year, a period of twenty-five years, is subject to compulsory military service. Actual service, however, except in the navy, rarely extends beyond one year. Naturalized citizens are exempt from military duty for a period of ten years after their naturalization. The fact that every one born on Argentine soil is considered an Argentine citizen has led to some unpleasant experiences among the foreign population, whose children have been born in that country. Many women have gone back to the home land so that their children would not become Argentine subjects.

General Leonard Wood, of the United States army, makes the following comment upon the Argentine army following a recent official visit to that country.

"Instruction in this army is vigorous and thorough during the entire period of service. They have a good general staff organization, and a superior school of war for training staff officers and special training of line officers, under the care of specially selected line officers. In Argentina there are excellent relations between the officers and the men. There are few court-martials and insubordination is rare. Their infantry is of a sturdy type, good marchers, well uniformed and equipped. The cavalry is well mounted and they are good horsemen. The bulk of the cavalry is armed with sabre and carbine, and there is also one regiment of lancers and one heavy regiment of cuirassiers. They are all very smartly turned out and make fine troops. Compulsory service, it has been found in Argentina, as elsewhere, is useful not only in making good soldiers, but also good citizens are so made. Men from remote districts, after a year's service with the colours, have a greater respect for the flag, for the authorities, and the national government. These men have also benefited physically and acquired habits of promptness and exactness. They return to their communities in every way improved by the service. All who enter unable to read and write are taught during their service. After the year's service with the colours men are called out at intervals, gradually decreasing in frequency, for short periods of service with the colours during manœuvres, usually about six or eight days a year. Careful track is kept of the reserves, who are almost immediately available in case their services are needed. Sufficient equipment for them is held in reserve."

In travelling over Argentina one sees very few soldiers. A man in a navy uniform will be encountered much more frequently. The standing army only numbers twenty thousand men, while the active naval force is not less than twenty-five thousand, most of whom are young men of twenty and twenty-one years of age. This force is kept recruited by conscription. All citizens are registered at birth and a number placed opposite the names on the register. Numbers are drawn each year of the young men who have reached the age of eighteen. The higher numbers pass into the navy for two years, and the lower numbers enter into the army for one year. Then after their discharge from active service these men pass into the reserves, where they are kept enrolled until they are thirty years of age. This keeps a large reserve force ready for duty in both army and navy. The Escuela Naval Militar, a naval college, is maintained where young men are trained to take positions as officers in the navy, similar to our own naval school at Annapolis. In nearly all the public schools the boys are given a military training under the direction of retired naval and military officers, and are allowed the gratuitous use of firearms and ammunition. Nearly every city and town has a shooting range where target practice is carried on under the direction of officials. The tactics are German, but the uniforms in both army and navy are of French design.

The Argentinians are very proud of their navy. There is a great jealousy between that republic and Brazil, and a consequent rivalry in building up a navy. A few years ago Brazil ordered three Dreadnaughts from English builders, the first two of which have just been received, and the other one will be delivered very soon. These boats were supposed to be the most powerful representatives of this style of war vessels ever constructed, but the Argentine naval experts believe that their new marine monsters will be still more effective. They considered the proposition for a long time, and maintained a committee in Europe for a year in order to peruse plans and keep in touch with the very latest developments in naval construction. The plans finally adopted were the result of this careful and painstaking study. The boats will be seventy feet longer than the Brazilian Dreadnaughts, twenty-five hundred tons greater displacement and will have a guaranteed speed of one additional knot.

A twenty-two million order for battleships was not a bad thing for American ship builders. And yet that was the contract given them by the Argentine Republic, after a fierce competition in which twenty-five firms from five of the leading nations of the world were engaged. The Eagle may well scream a little, for it is the first time that the United States has been considered a serious competitor in the building of battleships. The European nations used every influence, including that of their diplomatic representatives and a "knocking" of American manufacturers, to secure the order, but all to no avail. The American builders were the lowest bidders; they promised the boats in a shorter time; and the visit of the fleet a few years ago showed the Argentinos that we could build first class battleships. The writer was in Buenos Aires when the contract was let, and it awakened the people of that section of the world to the fact that the United States has become an active competitor in all lines of business.

These "Dreadnaughts," which will be known as the "Rivadavia" and "Moreno," will be 604 feet long, with a displacement of 20,500 tons, and a speed of 22½ knots will be generated by engines of 40,000 horsepower, and the normal draught will be 27 feet. The height of the turret above the water will be 26½ feet and at the poop it will be 17 feet. The armour will extend for 250 feet in the centre, 4¾ feet above and 3⅓ feet below the normal water line with a uniform thickness of one foot. The total weight of the armour will be 7,000 tons. The outward appearance of these two leviathans will be very similar to the "Arkansas" and "Wyoming," of our own navy. The armour both above and below the water line will be heavier than has heretofore been in use, while the bottom will be well protected against submarines by nickel steel. The armament will consist of twelve thirteen-inch guns in six turrets, twelve six-inch guns in the central casement and an equal number of four-inch guns well located. The coal bunkers will have a capacity of four thousand tons, besides several hundred tons of petroleum. Both of these leviathans of the deep will be delivered early in the year 1912.

THE ARMOURED CRUISER, "PUEYRREDON"

The navy of Argentina aggregates over thirty vessels, and some of them are very good boats. Among these are four armoured cruisers, all of which are 328 feet in length. Two of these, the "General San Martin" and "Pueyrredon," are twin ships of 6,773 tons displacement; the "Garibaldi" and "General Belgrano" have a displacement of 6,732 and 7,069 tons respectively. The oldest one, the "Garibaldi," was launched in 1896, and the newest one, the "Pueyrredon," in 1901, all of them being built in Italian yards. They develop 13,000 horsepower with a speed of twenty knots, and have a daily coal consumption of one thousand tons. All carry a crew of five hundred men, except the "Garibaldi," which carries only three hundred and fifty men. The cost of these vessels averaged about $3,500,000 each. The "Almirante Brown," named after the famous English-Argentine admiral, an older boat, is what is generally known as a central battery ship, and is a considerably smaller and less effective boat. There are also four cruisers. Three of these, the "Buenos Aires," "Nueve de Julio" (Ninth of July), and the "25th of May," have a speed exceeding twenty-two knots; the "Patagonia" is a smaller vessel with a speed of only thirteen knots. The coast defence vessels number two, the "Independencia" and "Libertad." The

"Espera" (hope), "Patria" (fatherland) and "Rosario" are torpedo boats with a speed of twenty knots. The "Sarmiento" is a training ship which has twice visited the United States in recent years. Fifteen new torpedo boat destroyers have also been ordered which, with the new battleships, will place the Argentine navy in a very effective condition.

The entire fleet is mobilized for four months each year. An annual review, which is held about the first of June, is made the occasion of great display. The President boards one of the vessels, which is then made the flagship, and the other vessels pass in review before it and manœuvres take place. Target practice is held and mimic engagements are "fought."

What to do with these big monsters now building is a problem which is seriously engaging the minds of the naval department. At the present time there is only one port in the republic which they can enter, and that is the Puerto Militar, at Bahia Blanca. They will not be able to reach Buenos Aires, because the waters of the La Plata are too shallow. The same is true of the other naval bases. It looks as though they will be obliged to stay near Bahia Blanca, or else anchor out on the broad Atlantic the most of the time.

In the writer's opinion Argentina has little use for a big navy. It cannot be placed on a par with European navies, and it is a big burden of expense. She has only one city on that coast, Bahia Blanca, and has not many vessels engaged in commerce, except on the La Plata and its affluents. Buenos Aires is protected from the Dreadnaughts of other nations because of its shallow harbour. One great item of cost is coal, of which great quantities are consumed, and all of which is imported either from Europe or Australia, the cost per ton being very high. The new Dreadnaughts will have a coal-consuming capacity of sixteen thousand tons per day. The annual expense at the present time of the navy is $7,500,000, and the new ships will increase this by at least $4,000,000. This will make a per capita cost of nearly two dollars for each man, woman and child in the republic. It simply resolves itself into a jealousy of and rivalry with Brazil. If the United States builders will construct Dreadnaughts that will have better armour, greater speed, and more powerful guns than the new Brazilian boats, then American manufacturers can get anything they want in Argentina.

CHAPTER XIII
RAILROADS AND THEIR DEVELOPMENT

In the Argentine railway world Buenos Aires occupies the position of ancient Rome, for all roads lead to it. A glance at the map is sufficient evidence of that fact. It has become the centre of the greatest network of railroads in South America. Like the colossal web of a spider it sends out its strands of steel north to the border of Paraguay and Bolivia, east to the trackless Atlantic, south into Patagonia and west across the Andes with a terminus at Valparaiso. There are at present about sixteen thousand miles of main track in operation in that republic. This is nearly as much as all the rest of the continent combined and shows the progressiveness of the country. All of the railroads, with the exception of the national lines and the Provincia de Santa Fé, which is a French line, were built by British capital and are under British management. Nearly all of the materials and equipment have been brought from that country, and everything has a distinctly John Bull stamp. Only one exception has been made, and that is that the compartments have been abolished in the day coaches. The sleepers, called *dormitorios*, are made into compartments and are called "Pullmans," but they lack the luxurious qualities of the cars after which they were named. The stations are generally very creditable and show a spirit of enterprise. Two-thirds of the mileage is of the broad gauge, nine and one-half inches broader than our own, which makes the seats and aisles extremely comfortable. The same English regard for safety is evident and every safeguard is applied toward that end. In fact they are English railroads transplanted to the pampas, with just a few concessions demanded by the nature of the country served.

The government of Argentina has been extremely liberal in its railroad policy. It has recognized the fact that there is no better way to develop its resources than by spreading the parallel bands of steel all over the republic. Perhaps nowhere in the world were there fewer difficulties or fewer perplexing engineering problems than here, for there was no grading and it was only necessary to take off the surface soil and dig ditches to carry off the water. A number of the concessions originally contained a government guarantee of six or seven per cent. on the investment, but most of these have since been altered as the receipts generally paid ample returns, and in consideration of release from the contractual obligation the government granted some other privileges. Many of the charters also granted an exclusive territory of about twenty miles on each side of the right of way.

The principle of consolidation has been going on in Argentina the same as in the United States. The large lines have been taking up the smaller ones until now three companies own one-half of the total mileage, and these three companies are very evenly matched. The original charters of the many lines differed greatly in their terms. They are now all being rapidly brought under a law passed in 1907, which is exceedingly liberal. Under this law the companies pay no import duties on construction materials and articles used in operating the lines, and are exempt from all taxes until 1947. During that period, however, they contribute three per cent. of their net receipts towards the construction and maintenance of the bridges and roads of the departments traversed by their tracks, particularly those roads leading to the stations. Furthermore they must convey free of charge the mails and men in charge of them. Government materials and articles for the construction of public works, war materials and stores, troops, government employees on public service, immigrants sent up country by the central immigration office, and employees of the provincial police shall be conveyed at one-half of the regular rates.

There is one American whose name stands high on the roll of honour in the development of South America, and in particular of Chile and Argentina. His name is William Wheelwright. This captain of industry was born in Newburyport, Massachusetts, March 16th, 1798. He came from that sturdy Puritan stock which has contributed so largely toward making the United States one of the most enlightened nations in the world. Not a few of his ancestors rendered conspicuous service in the French and Indian wars, and one of them served under Washington in the war of the revolution. He began life as a sailing master in charge of a vessel trading with South America. Being stranded in the La Plata he finally concluded that his destiny lay in that part of the world. One enthusiastic Argentinian biographer calls him "a new Hernando Cortez, who remained in the land of his shipwreck to conquer its soil, not by arms, but by steam; not for Spain, but for civilization." He first began his work at Valparaiso, Chile, where he transformed that city by constructing docks and sanitation. He was constantly engaged in voyages of exploration for the purpose of discovering natural resources and means for their development. The lack of transportation greatly impressed him, and through his efforts the Pacific Steam Navigation Company was organized, and he secured concessions for that company from a number of republics. United States capitalists turning down this proposition it was finally financed in England. The two vessels first placed on this route opened a new era on the west coast of South America, for they were the first transatlantic steamers to establish regular communication on that coast. At last he turned his attention to the wild and sparsely populated pampas of Argentina, at that time an undeveloped but fertile wilderness. Although his greater project for a transcontinental line failed, he succeeded in building the first important line in Argentina from Rosario to Cordoba, a distance of two hundred and forty-six miles. This was done after seventeen years of reverses due to civil strife and the Paraguayan war. The road was finally inaugurated on the 16th of May, 1870; and was opened with imposing military, religious and civil ceremonies. His last public work was the construction of a railway from Buenos Aires to Enseñada, the port for La Plata, which was opened just a half-century from the time of his own shipwreck in that same bay. He had further plans in mind but his health failed, and he sailed for London to secure medical attention. His great age was against his recovery and he died in that city on the 28th of September, 1873, and his remains were taken back to his old home in New England. A monument to his memory has been erected in Buenos Aires, and several streets have been named after him in Argentina, one in Rosario.

Just a half century after Wheelwright suggested to English capitalists the feasibility of a railroad across the Andes to connect the Atlantic with the Pacific, the road was opened to traffic, although not by the route contemplated by him. On the 27th of November, 1909, the last thin line of rock, which remained to complete the tunnel between Chile and Argentina, was demolished by the explosion of a dynamite charge. Through the opening thus made the workmen who had been employed on the two ends mingled, and a line of communication which has been the dream of two generations, was completed, that may change the political relations of South America, and which will have a marked effect on commercial relations throughout the world. On the 25th of May, of last year, this route was formally inaugurated, and an all-rail route was thus opened up between Buenos Aires, Argentina, and Valparaiso, Chile, thus establishing the first transcontinental railroad on the continent of South America. That date is a hallowed one in both republics, for it is the first centenary of the revolution which gave independence to both nations; and it is fitting that so auspicious an event should celebrate that occasion. To the South Americans it is as great an accomplishment as was the opening up of the first through line across the United States. At the present time the trip is made from one terminus to the other, a distance of eight hundred and eighty-eight miles, in thirty-eight hours, and the officials hope to reduce the running time to twenty-nine hours.

BRIDGE OF THE INCAS

This through line is made up of three different systems, and there are as many different gauges of track. The longest section is that through Argentina, which is seven hundred and seventy-eight miles in length, or seven-eighths of the entire distance. All of this is now owned and operated by the Buenos Aires and Pacific Railway, although it was built in several different sections and by different companies.

From Buenos Aires to Mendoza, a distance of six hundred and fifty-five miles, this road is built on the broad gauge plan. At Mendoza a change is made to the narrow gauge railway, known as the Trasandino Argentino, with tracks of one meter (3.28 feet) width. The scenery on this line is very beautiful as it winds around bends, passes through tunnels and continues to climb up the passes of the Andes. In several sections on this side, as well as on the Chilean side, where the grade is over 2½ per cent., the Abt system of cogs and racks is used to assist the engine on the steep climbs. On the way the famous natural bridge, known as the Bridge of the Incas, is passed, and a hotel has now been built there by the railroad company. The Trasandino Argentino ends at Las Cuevas, which is the beginning of the tunnel on that side of the "cumbre." Las Cuevas is 10,468 feet above sea level. The tunnel, which passes almost directly underneath the "Christ of the Andes," is 10,385 feet in length, of which a little more than half is on the Argentina side, which is just a few feet less than the altitude above the sea.

The Chilean terminus of the tunnel is at Caracoles, which is nothing more than a camp for labourers, and is a few hundred feet higher than Las Cuevas. From here another railroad of meter gauge, called the Trasandino Chileno, carries the traveller to the station of Los Andes, a distance of forty-five miles. It has been found necessary to construct snow sheds in many places in order to protect the track from snow slides, which are likely to occur in August and September. From Los Andes to Valparaiso the route is over the state railroad of Chile, which is of standard gauge (4 feet 8½ inches), and passes through some rich and fertile valleys on its way towards the Pacific.

This project, which has now reached completion, has had many vicissitudes. Its real history may be said to date from 1873, when the first practical step was taken by two brothers named Clark. It was while engaged in connecting Chile and Argentina by telegraph in 1869 that these brothers conceived the idea that this route was the most feasible for a transandine railway. The Clarks obtained a concession for a railroad between Buenos Aires and the Chilean boundary from the Argentine government, and were soon afterwards climbing over rock and ridge in the work of surveying these desolate mountains. Several routes were considered, but the most practical one seemed to be the old Inca trail across the Andes, and this was the shortest as well. Along this trail innumerable hordes of the primitive races have passed for unknown centuries. The Spaniard named it Camino de los Andes, the Andean Trail. For almost four centuries since the white men found this route, they have followed it on foot or on mule between the two countries. The first section was built from Mendoza to Villa Mercedes, a distance of two hundred and twenty-two miles, and completed in 1880. Three years later this line was continued to Buenos Aires. In 1887 work was begun from Mendoza toward the Chilean frontier and new sections were opened up every few years, but progress was very slow.

On the Chilean side the work progressed even more slowly because of financial difficulties. Several times construction was begun, and then stopped because money was not forthcoming from the government, as it was too costly an undertaking for private capital. In 1901, however, the financial arrangements were completed through the American firm of W. R. Grace & Co., and the final work was undertaken in an energetic manner. Argentina also took up her part again as soon as ultimate success was assured, and from that time until now the progress has been steady, but the difficult character of the work necessarily made it slow. Work on the tunnel was prosecuted from both ends, and it was a difficult undertaking because of the high altitude. Several lives were lost during its construction. It was found necessary to line the entire tunnel with a two-foot facing of cement because of the crumbling nature of the rock when exposed to the air. It is eighteen feet high and wide enough for a double track of the broadest gauge. The Chilean government guaranteed five per cent. on the capital invested in the Trasandino Chileno, almost seven million dollars, and the Argentine government practically constructed the Trasandino Argentino Railway. Thus, after thirty-seven years of work and planning, vicissitudes and discouragements, this railroad, which promises so much not only for the two governments but also for the whole of South America, has become an accomplished fact.

Heretofore it has been necessary to go around through the Straits of Magellan, a voyage of ten days, in order to reach the west coast of Chile from Buenos Aires, the metropolis of the southern hemisphere. This has been reduced to a little over a day. It brings Chile nearer to London by nine days. It is almost in the same latitude as Cape Town and Melbourne, and may eventually provide a shorter route to Australia from England, if steamers on one coast should run in conjunction with those on the other.

With the present steamship connection, via the west coast and Panama, it will be possible to go from New York to Buenos Aires, or *vice versa*, in twenty days, and this will probably be reduced to at least eighteen days before a great while. At present the best time made is twenty-four days by the east coast route, and it generally requires more, as the boats stop for two or three days oftentimes at Rio de Janeiro and Santos on their way down and back. When the Panama Canal is completed, there will no doubt be a direct line of good steamers that will run from New York direct to Valparaiso. This route will be then still more desirable and the trip will be made to Valparaiso in not more than two weeks.

North of Mendoza the Buenos Aires and Pacific Railway has pushed a line to San Juan, capital of the province of the same name. This region is rather sparsely settled, but it has a good irrigation system and will no doubt attract settlers because of the profits in fruit culture. South of Mendoza a branch has been built to San Rafael and another is being constructed to San Carlos. Although most of the country traversed by these branches presents the appearance of a hopeless, flat and unproductive desert, it possesses some of the finest soil in the republic when once irrigation is introduced. Two and even three crops of cereals can be produced, so it is said, and it is especially well adapted for grapes and alfalfa. With these and many other branches, and the extension of its lines to Bahia Blanca, the Pacific road now has the greatest mileage of any of the Argentine railroads.

The Buenos Aires and Pacific Railway may be said to bisect the country into two parts. North of this line by far the most important railroad is the Central Argentine. This company controls two thousand five hundred and thirty miles of track, and is the third system in number of miles in the republic. By the absorption of a number of smaller lines it now has a network of main lines and branches which serve that section of Argentina. The last absorption was of the Buenos Aires and Rosario Railway, which added more than a thousand miles to its lines and gave it a monopoly of railway service from the metropolis to the northwestern provinces. It now operates two main lines between Buenos Aires and Rosario. It also has under construction extensions and branches which will add nearly six hundred miles of track to its mileage.

The original section of the Central Argentine Railway was from Rosario to Cordoba, a distance of two hundred and forty-six miles, for which a concession was granted to Wheelwright and his associates. From Rosario it began to construct extensions northwards, southwards and westwards. It purchased the tracks of the Western, old Northern and lastly the Buenos Aires and Rosario Railway, until it reached its present commanding place on the railway map of Argentina. Its southern branches touch the Buenos Aires and Pacific in several places, and its western feeders reach out through the provinces of Cordoba and Santa Fé in a number of places. Northward it reaches the city of Santa Fé.

This railroad is now building a magnificent new station in Buenos Aires which will cost several millions of dollars, and which will be jointly used by it and the Pacific line. It is also making great improvements in its suburban service and dock frontage by filling in the shallow muddy shore of the river. Furthermore, it has made application to the National Congress for a franchise, or concession, to construct an underground electric railway to connect its station with those of the Southern Railway at Casa Amarillo and Plaza Constitucion. It is also elevating its tracks in Rosario so as to avoid all level crossings, and is building a large new station at Cordoba.

RAILWAY STATION, SANTA FÉ

The purchase of the Buenos Aires and Rosario line gave the Central Argentine an entrance into the rich province of Tucuman over a track of the same gauge as its own. After leaving Rosario this line passes through a rich agricultural section as far as Rafaela, and is intersected by several branch lines of the Santa Fé system. Shortly after leaving that place, which itself is only three hundred and fifteen feet above sea level, the country gradually becomes lower and swampy, being about at its lowest on the frontier between the provinces of Santa Fé and Santiago del Estero. After a considerable distance of this low, swampy land the level rises until it is over six hundred feet in elevation, where a branch four miles in length connects the main line with the city of Santiago del Estero, capital of the province of the same name. This city of fifteen thousand has nothing to distinguish it beyond the fact that it is the capital of a province. The line continues to reach higher elevation by easy grades. After crossing the frontier of the province of Tucuman it reaches a most fertile section and at last enters the pretty little city of the same name about which the Argentinian writers grow eloquent.

At Tucuman connection is made with the Central Northern Railway, a national railway of more than twelve hundred miles in length. It starts at Santa Fé and almost parallels the Central Argentine to Tucuman, at no point being distant more than fifty miles. It is a narrow gauge track. Leaving Tucuman it runs in a general northerly direction, but with many twists and turns in order to avoid the more mountainous sections of the districts through which it passes. At Tala the frontier of Salta is crossed at an elevation of two thousand six hundred and seventy feet, and a short distance further the elevation has increased to over three thousand feet. It then descends to the little town of Rosario de la Frontera noted for its thermal springs. At Guenas, one hundred and eighty miles from Tucuman, a branch runs to Salta, the capital of the province. This is a neat, well-paved city of about thirty thousand people with the usual public buildings and churches of a provincial capital. San Francisco church has a tower over two hundred feet in height which is pointed to with pride by the inhabitants. This city is very old, having been founded as early as 1582 under the name of New Seville. Pampa Blanca (the white pampa), is the first station in the province of Jujuy. Near here another branch is headed for the rather important town of Oran, but the main line soon reaches the capital. Jujuy for a long time was the northerly terminus of the Argentine railway system. This is the highest town in the republic, and, although near the tropics, the altitude gives this little city a fine and healthful climate. It has a population of ten thousand and is distant from Buenos Aires one thousand miles. The town has nothing to distinguish it, but the surrounding scenery is very beautiful. Hill and valley, wood and plain all contribute to make up a most enchanting landscape. The Rio Grande River runs through the town. It is the general bathing place as well as furnishing the power for the electric light and some mills located there. There are many thermal springs in the vicinity which are said to have splendid medicinal properties. The most noted are those of Los Reyes, the kings. There are four springs, one above another, the water being at a temperature of one hundred and twenty-five degrees Fahrenheit.

The Central Northern has recently been extended to La Quiaca, on the Bolivian frontier, where it will meet the railways of that republic when they are extended. At present the Bolivian lines reach Tupiza, and it is about a three days' journey by coach or mule between the two points. The distance still to be covered is not very great and completion is promised in about one year from this writing. There will then be a continuous railway connection between La Paz, the capital of Bolivia, and Buenos Aires. Peru is promising a road from Cuzco to Lima, and there will then be continuous connection with the Peruvian capital, except on Lake Titicaca over which there is regular steamship service.

The national government also owns a line of railway running from Cordoba northwest through the mountainous provinces of Rioja and Catamarca, more than five hundred miles in length. These lines are known as the Argentino del Norte (Northern), and there is another which is being pushed up into the Gran Chaco. The government has pursued the beneficent policy of running its lines through the districts where private enterprise was afraid to venture because of the uncertainty of the investment. They are contributing greatly to the development of those regions.

The Central Cordoba Railway is quite an important system. One line runs to San Francisco, where it connects with the Cordoba and Rosario Railway which runs to Rosario. Its principal track, however, is a narrow gauge line which runs from Cordoba in a northerly direction to Tucuman, and, with its several branches, serves an extensive territory. A goodly part of the territory traversed is forest land, but a part of it is a salty waste. An independent entrance to Buenos Aires is now being constructed. The lines known as the Provincia de Santa Fé start at Rosario and run north, following the basin of the Paraná River as far as Resistencia, a town opposite to Corrientes, touching at Santa Fé and nearly all the important places in that district. They were built by French capital and now have more than a thousand miles of track. The company is gradually extending its railhead up into the Gran Chaco, and will probably eventually reach Asuncion. They are now only a neck behind the lines on the opposite side of the river and are far ahead from a financial point of view. They have always paid handsome dividends from the quebracho wood, which they bring down from the Chaco. It would not be surprising if this line would eventually be pushed clear up into the state of Matto-Grosso, Brazil, for development is looking up that way.

The district between the Paraná and Uruguay Rivers is served by two railway systems, the Entre Rios and Northeastern systems. These two systems were formerly isolated and had a stormy career for many years. At the present time they work under a traffic exchange agreement and their financial standing is now good. These are the only railroads in the republic, with one exception, of standard gauge, 4 feet 8½ inches width between the rails. The first mentioned road serves the province of the same name. It was originally a line that ran from nowhere to nowhere. The road was built through loans contributed by the government of the province of Entre Rios in 1885, and was completed three years later. The money was squandered so recklessly that it cost twice as much as was necessary, and was built of such poor material that it had to be rebuilt within a few years. The government soon found itself unable to meet its obligations and the road was turned over to the bondholders. It was not placed on a profitable basis until the branches were completed which connected it with important points in the two provinces through which it now runs. The main line of the Entre Rios Railway cuts across this province from Paraná to Uruguay. One branch runs down to a point near Buenos Aires, and freight cars are now ferried across to that city. This is the only car ferry in operation in South America, and it is quite a novelty in that part of the world. Another branch runs to Concordia where connection is made with the Northeastern system. This road has one fork which leads up to and another which follows the Uruguay River. It was built there to carry the traffic around the rapids of that river where navigation was impossible. It will, however, soon be a much more important line, for it is gradually approaching Posadas, the commercial capital of the upper Paraná, and the most important town on the river north of Rosario. The Paraguay Central is also approaching Villa Encarnacion, on the opposite side of the Paraná, and within a short time there will be continuous communication by rail between Asuncion and Buenos Aires, with the exception of ferrying across two rivers.

South of the transcontinental line there are only two railway companies now operating. The Western Railway, or, as it is officially called, the Ferro Carril de Oeste, serves the southwestern part of the province of Buenos Aires and La Pampa. It reaches one of the richest agricultural districts of the republic and a section that is rapidly developing. The various extensions are being pushed out a few miles each year, and this company now owns fourteen hundred miles of track. The Western Railway has had a checkered career. In point of age it is the oldest line in the country, as about fifteen miles of track were built a half century ago. When this little railroad was inaugurated a great celebration was held, and the President delivered an address full of optimism and prophetic of future development. Fortune, however, refused to smile on the project, and money was scarce, so that the national government was obliged to take over the road. It was not a success until an English company took it over in 1890, and began pushing out the extensions over the pampas that are now bringing in the revenue-producing freight, which has placed the Western Railway on the road to prosperity.

The Ferro Carril del Sud, or Great Southern Railway, is the second largest railroad system in Argentina,[1] and one of the best freight producers. It has a monopoly of the greater part of the rich province of Buenos Aires, and its main station at Plaza Constitucion in the city of Buenos Aires is a busy place, with trains continually running in and out loaded with passengers for the suburbs or more distant points. It was due to the enterprise of this company that the busy port of Bahia Blanca was opened, and the seaside resort of Mar del Plata made popular. The section traversed by the Great Southern is threaded here and there by the many branches and feeders of this system, and more are being built each year. Passenger and freight traffic have increased so rapidly that the earnings per mile have almost doubled in the last ten years. It has built a strategic line several hundred miles long to Neuquen, almost directly west of Bahia Blanca, which will eventually become a transcontinental line. Engineers are now at work selecting the most feasible route across the Andes to connect with the Chilean state railways. This plan has already been approved by the directors and work will no doubt be begun before long.

The Southern has in construction a line south to the port of San Antonio, to open up the rich lands on the borders of Patagonia. It will connect with a government road which is now building from San Antonio, which is a new port on the Gulf of San Matias, westward to Nahuel Huapi, and which will be about three hundred miles long. The government is to be commended for its far-sightedness in planning this enterprise. Already a large part of the road-bed is graded and track has been laid for fifty miles or more, but service has not yet been begun. Work has also been begun on a railroad from Puerto Deseado, still farther south than San Antonio, which will run inland to Nahuel Huapi and open up an extensive country. This is but the beginning of extensive railroad development in this large southern section of Argentina, and plans have already been formulated to extend other lines into the very heart of Patagonia, and over to Lake Buenos Aires. In all the government now owns and operates a little more than two thousand miles of main track, which will be increased to fully three thousand by the new extensions of the old ones now being built.

The amount of traffic carried on these railroads is enormous and reaches big figures. I have before me the report of one of the greatest systems of Argentina for the year 1910. This states that the amount of grain carried by this line for that year, in tons of two thousand two hundred and five pounds, was as follows: linseed four hundred and two thousand one hundred and ninety-three, wheat nine hundred and ninety-one thousand one hundred and eighty-eight, corn one million one hundred and forty-two thousand four hundred. Other freight carried, not including its own supplies, amounted to five million nine hundred and eighty-three thousand one hundred and forty-three tons. Three hundred and forty-one thousand five hundred and seventy-seven head of live stock were transported. The number of passengers carried numbered almost fourteen millions. The gross receipts were twenty-five million dollars. Its capital stock is one hundred and seventy-five million dollars. It has paid for many years a regular dividend of six per cent., besides devoting large sums each year to betterments and extensions. All of these roads have been conducted along conservative lines, and their stocks are nearly all quoted on the London stock exchange considerably above par.

CHAPTER XIV
RELIGIOUS FORCES

At the time of the conquest Argentina did not possess a large indigenous population. Wandering tribes dwelt in all parts of the country from Tierra del Fuego to Brazil, but the proportion of these Indians was very small when compared with the extent of territory occupied. On the slopes of the Andes were found tribes that were very closely allied with and subject to the Incas, who ruled all along the Pacific coast from Ecuador to Chile, and there was continuous intercourse between them. No ruins of temples dedicated to the sun have been found in Argentina, although some reminders of the Inca civilization have been uncovered in the northwestern part of the republic. The principal strongholds of the native tribes were in the northeastern sections of the country, on the rich plains and low hills which border on the great rivers of the country. Indians who were related to the Tupi-Guarani tribes who inhabited Brazil, had established themselves there in considerable numbers.

These Indians were not so bloodthirsty as those in the extreme south, although some of them were given to cannibalism. Their slaying of human beings, however, was for the purpose of food and not as a part of their religious worship. They were not especially hostile to the incoming Spaniards, until the members of the tribes began to be impressed into slavery, and they then resisted the advance of that race in a feeble way. Their religion was simple and consisted of a few good deities and a number of evil ones. The former they tried to honour in their simple way, but a great deal more attention was given to appeasing the latter, in order to avoid physical suffering, for which they believed these malevolent deities were responsible. Theirs was an ignorant belief and a simple faith, and they rather welcomed the teachings of the priests who first came among them. The new doctrines were accompanied by ceremonies which appealed to their childlike natures. The chanting in an unknown but sonorous tongue, the visible emblems and the incense cast a spell over these simple people, who did not attempt to grasp the abstract idea of a trinity or the sacrifice of a Saviour.

CHURCH IN CORRIENTES, BUILT IN 1588

By far the most persistent and determined attempt to convert these aborigines was made by the Jesuit priesthood. As a result of its tireless and systematic efforts this order succeeded in establishing in Paraguay, and the country adjacent to it on the east and south, about the beginning of the sixteenth century, a seat of power which lasted for two centuries, and which has been referred to elsewhere in a general way. It developed into an ecclesiastical autocracy, with the heads of the Jesuit body as the actual as well as nominal rulers. This remarkable order subdued the Indians living between the Uruguay and Paraguay rivers, and brought all of them under its domination. This was done without resort to the sword. Although these pristine people were reduced to a condition of peonage, or serfdom, they remained loyal to the Jesuits and assisted them in repelling all invaders. So secure did the clerical rulers feel in their position, that all other white persons were forbidden to settle within the territory over which they claimed jurisdiction. It was perhaps well for the natives that they did take this position, for the Spanish adventurers would have enslaved the Indians, just as did the Portuguese "Paulistas" in Brazil.

When the Jesuits were expelled from Brazil they crossed over the Paraná River into Paraguay and Northern Argentina. Then was founded Misiones, a series of missions along the eastern shores of that river. Although these religious settlements have long since crumbled into ruins, the name still clings to one of the territories of Argentina. The Jesuit effort did not extend all over Argentina, but it was felt even to the foothills of the Andes. The Jesuit emissaries encountered the Spanish advance guard who had crossed the Cordilleras from Peru and met with a repulse. The lack of gold in the section occupied by the Jesuits was also in itself a protection, because it did not excite the cupidity of the gold-seekers. These settlements were engaged solely in agricultural pursuits. Their increasing wealth and prosperity, however, did finally excite this cupidity, and the arrogance of the order aroused an intense jealousy in the rulers of the province. As a result of these two influences this order was forcibly expelled in 1768, and their property was confiscated. Some of it was bestowed on other religious orders, but the most of it was devoted to secular uses. The power and prestige of the Jesuits among the natives were not at once destroyed by the blow. For a long time their influence was paramount, because of the blind obedience of their followers who had been gathered together in little settlements and had been taught useful pursuits.

In other parts of the country the subjugation was not so peaceful. Those Spanish troops who crossed the Andes and entered Argentina from that direction pursued different tactics. Gold was sought and everything was sacrificed to that one ambition. The conquerors were determined to acquire wealth, or at least to secure a means of livelihood without the necessity of manual labour. The natives were maltreated if they resisted, and enslaved when once subdued. Where agriculture was attempted these Indians were compelled to do the work, with no compensation except the right to live. The priests were always ready to accompany the soldiers on the most arduous campaigns. Without raising a hand against indiscriminate slaughter they held up the crucifix to the survivors, and then turned about and risked their own lives to spread the Christian faith into hitherto untrodden regions. Even the desolate interior of Patagonia was not too distant or too inaccessible for these indefatigable missionaries. Sword in one hand and the cross in the other these teachers of religion spread the doctrines of their church over the whole of the La Plata basin and the rest of South America, and gave Roman Catholicism such a grasp on the continent that it will probably never be broken. The one difficult thing to understand is how the Church of Rome could countenance the harsh and bloody methods of subjugation pursued under the very eyes of its commissioned representatives, and the violation of all the ethics of humanity as well as Christianity, unless it was simply the spirit of the age with which even the heads of the Church were also imbued. The Jesuits founded schools for the natives, in their settlements, but the other orders did not do this, although they aided in inculcating orderly ways among them.

The alliance of Church and State still exists in Argentina. The second article in the constitution reads as follows: "The federal government supports the Apostolic Roman Catholic Church." This condition exists in all the republics of South America, except Brazil. The president and vice-president must be members of that church. Religious liberty prevails and absolute freedom of worship is guaranteed to all persons of whatever belief. Protestant or Jew has the same right to erect a place of worship as the Roman Catholic. The alliance of Church and State, however, tends to weaken each. It oftentimes drags down the high office of the Church to the low level of politics and tends to cheapen its influence. It sometimes ties up the government in ways that work to its detriment. It will be better for the Church as well as government when this alliance is separated. It will probably not be many years before the final break will come in Argentina, and it is to be hoped that it will come peaceably and without a rupture of peaceful conditions.

Although the Church is a nominal partner of the State it seemed to the writer that its influence was not particularly strong. The day when the

Archbishop could dictate government policies has evidently passed away. The bond between them is weak. It appears to be an age of remarkable indifference toward religion. The men openly avow their indifference and say that they "leave religion to the women." A visit to the churches is a practical demonstration of that statement so often reiterated. The great Cathedral of Buenos Aires, which seats many thousands, will oftentimes have only a mere handful of men at the regular services within its walls. Some of the moral conditions in the republic show that the cardinal teachings of the Church are not being followed, although practically all are nominal adherents. How much of this condition might be improved by a better priesthood would be difficult to estimate. Any statement made might be construed as based upon an erroneous view, or given from a prejudiced standpoint. It is a fact, however, that there is great room for a religious awakening in Argentina, as well as the rest of South America, and the Roman Catholic Church appears to be the only one able to propagate this work aggressively among the many millions of inhabitants.

Protestantism has not gained much of a foothold among the Spanish-speaking population. There are a great many adherents of Protestant denominations among the British and German population. In Buenos Aires, Rosario and Bahia Blanca the Anglican and Scotch Presbyterian churches have edifices and support ministers. They are organized solely for the people of that faith, and do not make any effort to evangelize those speaking other languages, as their services are conducted only in English. Occasional services are held in other cities where a colony of English-speaking people resides.

The only church that is aggressively pushing its work in Argentina is the Methodist Episcopal Church. This church has about thirty missionaries at work in various parts of the republic, and a number of congregations have been successfully established. Buenos Aires is naturally the centre of their efforts, and in that city they have organized a half dozen churches. Of these the principal one is on Calle Cangallo, in the heart of the city. This is generally known as the American Church, for people who are members of the various non-Catholic bodies all unite in the services here, which are conducted wholly in English. The pastor, Rev. W. P. McLaughlin, has been in charge of this work for almost two decades and is very much beloved by all. This church is entirely self-supporting and contributes considerable sums to the work in the other churches. The other churches of this denomination in Buenos Aires are intended for work among the Spanish-speaking population, with the exception of an Italian mission. Congregations have likewise been formed in Rosario, Bahia Blanca, Cordoba, Santa Fé, La Plata, Mendoza, San Juan, Chacabuco, Junin and other cities. They claim a membership exceeding five thousand and seem to be very much encouraged in their work.

Educational work has received considerable attention from this body and a number of schools are conducted by it in which well-qualified teachers from the United States conduct the classes. These schools are recognized as worthy institutions, and many families send their children to them even though they do not accept that faith. Their influence cannot be other than beneficial and uplifting, for any effort that aims to spread enlightenment and moral ethics cannot fail to be of service in the general advancement of the country. Their work will likewise stimulate similar effort by others, and thus the general cause of education and morality is greatly furthered.

The Morris system of schools was founded by an Englishman as a missionary enterprise, but the scope of the work has since been broadened, until now it has become a great educational enterprise with several thousand students under its tutelage. The schools receive government aid, and by that means those in charge have been enabled to branch out much more than was permitted by the limited means in the early years of their history.

The Young Men's Christian Association has a very flourishing society in Buenos Aires which is doing a great work. At present they are hampered by poor quarters, but a campaign had just been ended at the time of the writer's visit and two hundred thousand dollars had been secured for a new building. A site was purchased in a central location and work was to start at once on a fine new building. With these new quarters and enlarged equipment, the work of this great world-wide organization ought to be increased many fold, and there is room for all the effort it is able to put forth. The Young Men's Christian Association forms a rallying place for young men who have broken away from home ties and started life in a foreign country. The extension of the work among the Spanish-speaking people also brings about a fraternizing between the two races which is exceedingly beneficial.

CHAPTER XV
THE STRUGGLE AGAINST OPPRESSION

The reign of Ferdinand and Isabella is perhaps the most noteworthy epoch in Spanish history. It resounded with the clash of arms and with the thirst for discovery. It was also an era of intolerance. A distinctive tendency toward cruelty has ever been a prominent trait of the Spanish character. The driving out of the Moors and the elimination of the Moorish civilization, the harsh treatment of the Jews and, finally, the establishment of the Inquisition are all indicative of that tendency. These traits were carried with them into the New World in their worst forms. The Spanish expeditions to South America were marked by ferocious cruelty, unlimited bloodshed, and an unquenchable lust for treasure. A low standard of personal relations as well as a narrow conception of public morality prevailed. It was from the very worst of the population of Spain that the early colonists to Spanish South America came. Most of them were adventurers who had nothing to lose, and who were quite willing to risk their lives for the possibility of treasure. It is not unnatural that the worst characteristics of the Spanish character should early be developed, and to an abnormal degree. One quality they had to aid them—there was no lack of personal courage. Ignorant they might be, but of personal bravery there was no question, as their deeds bear witness.

In South America there were two great racial divisions, besides the tribes dwelling in Patagonia, who were quite different to either of the others. On the Pacific slope the Incas had joined together the various tribes from north of Quito to Chile into a great community over which they exercised supreme power. The people lived under established conditions; they built towns and public works and were proficient in agriculture. On the Atlantic side of the Andes, from Venezuela to the La Plata, the Indians belonged to Tupi-Guarani stock. The features and habits of some of the tribes had become slightly modified, but they show enough similarities to leave small doubt as to their common origin. These tribes were all nomadic, and existed principally on the products of the chase or wild fruits which they gathered. The Araucanian and Tehuelche Indians of Patagonia were also nomadic, but they are of a different temperament.

For three centuries after its discovery no immigration was permitted to the South American colonies except of Spaniards. These Spaniards intermarried freely with native women. From this mixture grew up the greater part of the original population of Argentina, as well as the other colonies. The gradual development of population and wealth was little understood in the mother country. Trade with foreign countries was prohibited, all mineral wealth was heavily taxed and the Crown "milked" the colonies in every way. All of the officials were native Spaniards. A feeling of animosity gradually grew up among the colonists toward the Spaniards which finally led to the outbreak of hostilities at the commencement of the nineteenth century. South Americans perhaps give too little importance to the influence of the United States in the outcome of their struggles for liberty. The idea of America for the Americans existed long before the enunciation of the Monroe Doctrine in 1823. That idea was in the minds of Washington and his co-workers. Their success also fired the patriotism of Bolivar, San Martin and other South American liberators.

The story of Argentina is but another chapter in the history of the shortsighted attitude of Spain toward her colonies in the New World. The sole purpose of the colonial policy of Spain seemed to be to protect the trading monopoly which had been farmed out to the merchants of Cadiz, and to keep a record of the production of silver and gold, in order to insure the collection of the royal one-fifth. Every Atlantic port of South America was closed to traffic except Nombre de Dios, on the coast of Panama. Everything destined for that continent had to be taken there, transported across the isthmus and reloaded to vessels on the Pacific. Goods destined for Argentina also had to follow this route. They were carried by vessels to Callao, Peru, and from there were taken overland even as far as Buenos Aires. It was for this reason that the early settlers of Argentina mostly came in from the Andes side. To further enforce this monopoly of trade the governors of Buenos Aires were instructed to forbid all importation and exportation from that port under penalty of death and forfeiture of property to those engaged in it.

It is little wonder that a system of corruption and an evasion of such iniquitous laws was developed. The several governors recommended modifications, but the Cadiz merchants were obdurate. Smuggling and surreptitious trading grew popular, and the officials soon became silent partners in the traffic. Although the laws remained upon the statute books nothing could keep the people from trafficking with their own products. Buenos Aires became a community of smugglers. English and Dutch ships landed their goods under the very noses of officials, took their pay in hides or money and then continued their way around Cape Horn to the west coast, where the same process was repeated. Mule trains carried these goods thus illegally entered across the plains to Cordoba and Tucuman; the officials along the way winking at this evasion of unpopular laws. The profits were distributed among officials and the soldiers were hired to shut their eyes. The abstract right of the government to enact such restrictive regulations was never questioned. They broke the laws without any qualms of conscience, but contesting them was not even dreamed of. The idea that the right to trade or to practise a profession existed only by sufferance of the government has not been eradicated even to this day. It is a relic of this age. It is not surprising that office holding became the popular vocation and has remained so even to the twentieth century.

For a long period the whole of South America was under the viceroyalty of Peru. Some of the larger capitals had bodies of officials known as Audiencias. The viceroyalty was divided into provinces, each of which had a governor. Each new region occupied was organized into a municipality, which was the real unit of their political structure. The governing body of this municipality was termed the Cabildo, and was composed of from six to twelve members who were appointed and held office for life. This body exercised the civil and judicial administration. Most of these men secured their appointment through actual purchase. The territorial jurisdiction of these municipalities was generally poorly defined, and it was sometimes almost coextensive with the province. Although the colonial governor was supposed to give a full account of his administration, he often failed to do so and conducted his office as a despotic and irresponsible ruler.

The governors were always Spaniards, and only one exception appears in Argentina, Hernandarios Saavedra. This man appears as one of the brightest names during the seventeenth century. For several years he acted as governor of Buenos Aires, and he did a great deal of good in securing justice to the Indians and curbing the military power. He retained the confidence of both natives and Spaniards by his reputation for giving a square deal to all sides. Under his policy the colonies prospered and the pastoral pursuits were greatly extended. The sixteenth century contained very little of interest to the general reader. The inhabited portions were extended but little, and there were one or two uprisings of Indians against the white man's rule. Only one was serious and that was of the tribes on the Andean slopes, who were stirred up by a leader who claimed to be the direct descendant of the old Inca princes. This disturbance lasted for fifty years, but it ended with the capture and execution of the leader, who was known to the Spaniards as Bohorquez.

Some struggles took place between the Portuguese settlers of Brazil and the Spaniards, who had attempted to penetrate the regions watered by the upper Paraná. The "Paulistas," inhabitants of the state of São Paulo, resisted the encroachments of the Spaniards, as they feared the Jesuit influences, which they both feared and hated. They raided the settlements of that order in Misiones and carried off several thousand of the poor natives as captives. The Iguassú River and the east bank of the Uruguay seemed to be adopted informally as the dividing line between the two races, although later differences arose over the territory now embraced in the republic of Uruguay. The Portuguese established a settlement, called Colonia, in 1680, almost opposite to Buenos Aires, which was ever a sore spot for the Spaniards and gave rise to much trouble. It became a harbouring place for smugglers and offenders against Spanish laws, but it remained under Portuguese control for a long period.

With the eighteenth century Spain adopted a little more liberal policy toward her colonies in regard to trade. The prestige which England and Holland had obtained practically forced certain concessions. Uruguay began to be settled by Spaniards. The increase in population and greater demand for wool and hides in Europe caused a remarkable advance in trade. In 1767 the Jesuits were expelled, as they had been in Brazil some time previous. This order had accumulated enormous wealth and ruled a large section of the country with an iron hand. The members of the order were forcibly driven out and their property sold at auction or divided among other orders.

In 1776, just a few days after the declaration of independence in the American colonies, Buenos Aires was established as a viceroyalty. Lake Titicaca on the north, and the Andes on the west, were established as the boundary lines. It included the territory now divided into the four republics of Uruguay, Bolivia, Argentina and Paraguay. South of the city of Buenos

Aires, however, there was practically no development. The first viceroy was named Pedro de Zeballos, who came over with a large force of soldiers and sailors in order to drive out the Portuguese. Free commerce with Spain was now permitted and commerce greatly increased. Buenos Aires became the centre of all this trade, was greatly prospered and its population rapidly increased. Wines, brandies, hides, tobacco and maté (Paraguay tea) were the principal articles exported to Europe.

The beginning of the nineteenth century saw unrest all over South America. It began in Quito, Ecuador, and spread in every direction. It did not take long to reach the loosely cohered sections of the viceroyalty of Buenos Aires, in which the different elements had not coalesced. The Spaniards generally lived in the populated centres, while the gauchos, mostly half-breeds, had their homes on the broad pampas. It was essentially democratic as compared with more aristocratic Peru and Mexico. The only common bond was religion, and that was not strong. Spain's selfish policy had destroyed her prestige, while the revolutions in France and North America had propagated the idea of democracy among the youth.

Perhaps no one incident had greater influence upon the final events than the attempt of England, encouraged by her successes in South Africa, to capture Buenos Aires. In June, 1806, a British fleet bearing on board fifteen hundred troops appeared in the La Plata. The Viceroy immediately fled, and the British flag soon floated over his late residence. For several weeks the people acquiesced in this change, but a Frenchman, named Jacques de Liniers, headed the opposition. He organized a force in Montevideo and advanced on Buenos Aires. The citizens, reanimated by his enthusiasm, flocked to his banner and, after some bloody street fighting, the English were compelled to surrender. Their flags were captured and are still exhibited as trophies of Argentine prowess in the Church of Santo Domingo in that city. The success of the Argentinos, who had accomplished this victory without help from the mother country, greatly encouraged the patriots and aroused in them a hope of separation from Spain. Reinforcements came from England, to renew the conflict. The troops marched confidently into the city. The flat roofs of the buildings and the parapet-like fronts, however, provided excellent shelter for the defenders, and the British general was finally compelled to ask for terms. He had lost a quarter of his force but was allowed to leave on honourable terms. The attempt of Napoleon to place his brother, Joseph Bonaparte, on the throne of Spain also fermented the spirit of revolution that was becoming rampant, for the people felt no loyalty or allegiance to this upstart. A new Viceroy was sent out by the mother country, but he did not remain in peace very long. In an effort to placate the Spanish-American colonies a royal decree was issued that the colonies were considered an integral part of the monarchy and should have representatives in the Cortes. "At last you are raised to the dignity of free men," came the message to the colonists. It was too late.

A group of patriots had already risen who were holding meetings to decide what could be done in this crisis. The leader in this band was Manuel Belgrano. They decided to ask the resignation of the Viceroy and waited on him with this request. He knew that his position was untenable because of the disaffection among the troops. On the 25th of May, 1810,[2] an armed assembly met on the plaza in front of the government palace under the leadership of Belgrano, Moreno, Castelli and Valcarcel. The colours of blue and white were seen everywhere, for these were the colours adopted by the revolutionists. A provisional junta was selected who assumed the executive powers of government. For several years, however, their acts all run in the name of Ferdinand VII, King of Castile and Leon. No attempt was made at this time to secure the adherence of the other provinces, but emissaries were later sent asking their coöperation. Troops were afterwards sent, and a number of encounters occurred. Both sides killed their prisoners as a general rule, and the combats were very sanguinary.

Manuel Belgrano was a native of Buenos Aires. He had been educated in Spain and had there imbibed republican ideas. His enthusiasm, his radicalism and his ability soon placed him at the head of the revolutionary forces. Though lacking in military training he proved himself an able general. He led an unsuccessful expedition into Paraguay, whither he went to induce the Paraguayans to join in the revolt. Another great defeat had been given the Argentine forces in Bolivia. Montevideo was evacuated, and the situation was becoming desperate. Belgrano was then placed in command and gathered together the scattered forces at Tucuman. The result was a decisive victory for the patriots. The gaucho cavalry followed the fleeing Spaniards clear to the boundaries of Bolivia, and inflicted great losses upon them. Belgrano foolishly followed up this real victory by another invasion of Bolivia, and met with an overwhelming defeat at Vilapugio, and again at Ayohuma. With the remnant of his army he returned to Argentine territory, and was succeeded in command by San Martin, who proved to be the real genius of the struggle for independence.

José de San Martin first saw the light on the 25th of February, 1778, in a little town on the Uruguay River, his father being an officer in the Spanish army. While still a small boy he was taken to Spain to be educated. Entering a military school, for his father had destined him for a military career, he finished that course, and at an early age enlisted in the army. He served in the many wars of that country against Napoleon, and rose to the rank of lieutenant-colonel. He also fought for a time under the great English general, Wellington, in his campaign in the Iberian peninsula. In these conflicts San Martin had imbibed liberal principles, and a hatred of all forms of oppression and injustice filled his soul. The success of the American republic inspired him as well as others, so that he joined with many in a secret society, pledged to the work of establishing a republic in Spain.

Man proposes, but God disposes. The struggle for independence in Argentina appealed to this patriot and he decided to return to his native land. He arrived at an opportune time, for the successes of the Spanish troops had plunged the patriots into despair. In March, 1812, San Martin landed in Buenos Aires. His first step was to organize and drill some effective regiments of infantry in that city, for men trained in military tactics were wanting. He selected the finest physical and moral specimens of manhood that could be found, and subjected them to a rigid discipline. The lazy and cowardly ones were weeded out, until he had only a small force, but this body was composed of real soldiers. With these men he gained some victories, but success did not seem possible to him along these lines. He therefore planned a new move with all the genius of a great commander, who cares not for temporary success but sees only ultimate victory.

To San Martin the only hopeful plan seemed to be to drive the Spaniards out of Chile, and then attack Peru, the stronghold of Spanish power in South America. He aimed not only for the independence of Argentina, but of all of that great continent; he vowed he would not be satisfied until the last Spanish soldier had left the soil of South America, and every province was free. To this end he sought the appointment as governor of Cuyo, nestling up against the Andes on the direct route to Chile, and now known as the province of Mendoza, in Argentina. The inhabitants of that section, who breathed the free air of the mountains, were notoriously anti-Spanish, brave and enduring. Chilean patriots who had been exiled were numerous here, too, and it offered good recruiting ground. He brought with him as a nucleus a part of the troops he had drilled in Buenos Aires, and the government later sent him a corps of negro slaves, who had been freed from bondage. For three years San Martin laboured steadily building up a great war machine. Though civil war waged in and around the capital he kept aloof from all these disturbances, and busied himself in recruiting, drilling and instructing officers, as well as men, raising taxes, gathering provisions, making powder, casting guns, building portable bridges and making all arrangements for transport and commissariat on his contemplated march into Chile.

Dictator succeeded dictator, military chief followed military chief in Buenos Aires. A formal act of independence from Spain had been drawn up and proclaimed on the 9th of July, 1816, in Tucuman, where Congress had convened for that purpose. Pueyrredon was selected as supreme director. He was succeeded by Rordeau, and he again was defeated by Artigas. Then came Ramirez and other military leaders who gained more or less power and authority. San Martin paid no attention to these military or governmental affairs. One idea, one definite plan absorbed all his energy and attention. This plan he confided to no one. This taciturn general, however, was preparing a thunderbolt that would clear the Argentine sky of all these clouds, except internal dissensions. When summer came in 1817, which is our winter, and all the passes were freed from snow, he felt that he was ready to advance. Among his forces were the picked youth of Buenos Aires, reckless, enthusiastic and ambitious, who were willing to follow this leader anywhere; manumitted negroes, who were scarcely inferior to their white comrades; Chilean exiles, who preferred death to submission, and looked upon this as their only hope of again seeing their homes. All of these men had been thoroughly drilled in the arts of war as practised by the armies of Europe in the Napoleonic era. No detail had been omitted. The last few months had been spent in preparing rations of dried beef and parched corn, in gathering mules for transport, and in making sledges to be used on the slopes which were too steep for cannon on wheels. Every possible route across the Andes had been examined, and the most careful calculation of distances made. Spies were placed in all the passes, and the Spaniards were kept in absolute ignorance as to which of many passes along hundreds of miles of frontier would be used for the impending attack. These men were sworn to remain "united in sentiment and courage, in order not to suffer for the future any tyrant in America; and like new Spartans never to bear the chains of slavery while the stars shone in the sky and blood ran in their veins."

The precautions of this astute leader are shown by the fact that his real intentions were not revealed until on the very eve of the advance, through fear of treachery. In the middle of January General San Martin broke camp and left Mendoza. His army was divided into two divisions. The smaller force was sent through what is known as the Uspallata pass, which was the old Inca trail, and is now followed by the railway which has just been completed across the Andes. This trail runs across the Bridge of the Incas, one of the most famous natural bridges in the world. The other followed the more difficult pass of Las Platas, farther to the north. The solitude, barrenness and utter desolation of these Andean passes can only be fully appreciated by those who have traversed them as has the writer. Majestic Aconcagua looks down upon both routes, and all around are lofty peaks which seem like giant sentinels guarding these solitudes of nature from the invasion of man. Terrific wind and snow storms are common, and the dust blows in clouds that are almost stifling at times. It was an undertaking that would have appalled an ordinary man.

SAN MARTIN AND O'HIGGINS AT LA CUMBRE, CROSSING THE ANDES INTO CHILE

Courtesy of the Bulletin of Pan-American Union

But San Martin was no ordinary man. A high and lofty purpose thrilled his soul and steeled his heart against all discouragement. An advance guard of the Spaniards in the Uspallata pass was driven out by that wing of his little army of four thousand men. Before reinforcements could come up the two divisions had successfully accomplished the crossing and were united. Disconcerted by the report that two armies had crossed the Andes and were advancing against him, the Spanish commander retreated to Santiago for reinforcements. With admirable forethought San Martin chose his positions and awaited the conflict which was inevitable. The two armies approached each other. The Spanish commander had a superior force, composed of veterans of the peninsular wars. San Martin's men were inspired by an enthusiastic commander and a love of country. The battle raged for hours until, surrounded on three sides by the enemy, their artillery gone, a third of their number dead on the field of battle, the Spanish forces broke and fled toward Santiago. Less than half their number escaped death or capture. Thus was the decisive battle of Chacabuco won by the patriots on the 12th of February, 1817, with a loss of only twelve men killed. The next day the Spanish governor of Chile was flying from the capital, and two days later the conquerors entered that city. San Martin had won his first great victory, and was everywhere hailed as a deliverer.

Steadfast in his purpose of driving the Spaniards from all of South America the victor refused to be drawn into local fights. The Argentine patriots were fighting among themselves and his friends wanted San Martin to return and aid them. This he refused to do, and his friends were embittered. Unwilling to accept the supreme authority in Chile, General O'Higgins, who had materially assisted in the victory at Chacabuco, was selected as executive. The independence of Chile was soon after proclaimed. In connection with Lord Cochrane, an English officer, San Martin began to devote all his energies to the building of a fleet, in order to drive the hated Spaniards from Peru. Three years more were spent in these preparations. At last, in 1820, a little fleet was ready, and he sailed with a small army for that stronghold of Spanish power. In four months, without a pitched battle, he sent the enemy flying from Peru. Lima yielded and that country was declared to be independent. He then assumed the rôle of protector of Peru and commander in chief of the insurgent army. San Martin desired to coöperate with Bolivar, and a personal interview was arranged between these two liberators at Guayaquil. Bolivar refused. Without a word of explanation, without a complaint, the disappointed San Martin gave up the command of the army, resigned the dictatorship of Peru to Bolivar, and left that country. There was no place for him in Argentina, except as a leader in civil war, and this he would not indulge in. For honours or position he cared not. Thus he went into voluntary exile. Rather than jeopardize the independence secured after so much hard fighting, rather than take part in the divisions of the factions fighting among themselves, he sacrificed home, friends and honours, and even submitted to cruel charges of ingratitude and cowardice. Few finer examples of unselfishness are recorded in the annals of the world's history. If not abler San Martin was at least more unselfish than Bolivar.

General San Martin, heartbroken and disappointed, went to Boulogne-sur-Mer, in France, and established his home. The remaining years of his life were passed in obscurity and poverty, with only a faithful daughter to comfort and cheer his old age. Once he started for the land of his birth, and got as far as Montevideo. There he learned that Argentina was in the throes of a revolution. Fearing that his presence might be misconstrued, the old warrior sorrowfully turned his face back toward France. The generosity of a Spaniard was all that saved this hero from absolute want during the last few years of his life, for he lived to a good old age. Reading was the only resource left to brighten his later years, but approaching blindness deprived him of even this pleasure during the last few months. On the 17th of August, 1850, General San Martin expired in the arms of his loving and faithful daughter.

It was many years before Argentina fully appreciated the services of this grand old man, and it was then too late to bring cheer to his broken heart. His sacred remains were brought back to Buenos Aires and placed in the Cathedral, where they now repose. Honours were decreed him. There are few cities in that republic that have not erected a monument to his memory. Chile and Peru have raised statues in his honour. Only a few months ago the Argentine government dedicated a fine memorial in the French city where he died. Last year, while Argentina was celebrating her first centennial, the memory of the patriot San Martin was kept green, and the youth were taught his great and unselfish love of country. It is little wonder that the Argentinians do not go into raptures over the name of Bolivar, but hold up their own San Martin as the real liberator of at least four of the republics of South America.

For a half-century following the 25th of May, 1810, the history of Argentina is a record of wars, revolutions and other disturbances. It was the unavoidable conflict between centralizationists and autonomists, between military and civil principles of government. A detailed account of all these conflicts would be confusing and wearisome, and it can best be treated in a consideration of those involved in the struggle.

An oligarchy grew up in Buenos Aires at first that sought to rule the rest of the original viceroyalty in almost as arbitrary a manner as Spain herself had done. This caused constant friction with the other cities, each of which aspired to be an independent province. Military chieftains arose here and there who defied the authority of that oligarchy. Civil war broke out in numerous places, and bloody encounters took place followed by much devastation. Within a few years nearly all the provinces were practically independent of Buenos Aires and there were a half dozen centres of authority, although that city did not yield in her pretensions. San Martin was peremptorily ordered to return, but refused. Belgrano attempted to lead his army there, but they revolted and abandoned him, joining the local forces. The outside provinces themselves split up through local differences. Cordoba lost Rioja, from the old intendencia of Salta seceded Tucuman, Santiago del Estero and Catamarca, and Cuyo split up into Mendoza, San Juan and San Luiz. Buenos Aires itself was subdivided, losing Uruguay, Corrientes, Santa Fé and Entre Rios. Thus were formed the provinces which have since become the units of the Argentine confederation. The outside provinces were willing to unite with Buenos Aires on an equal basis, but the people of that city would not consent on such terms.

For years no really constructive statesman appeared out of the confusion and selfishness of the oligarchies. At last there loomed above all the personality of Rivadavia, who undertook the reformation of the laws and their administration. He introduced numerous reforms and founded a number of charitable institutions, and infused a more modern spirit into the government. A congress met in Buenos Aires in 1825, in which all the provinces were represented by delegates. By this time the independence of the Argentine Confederation had been acknowledged by all of the leading powers except Spain. Rivadavia and his followers gained control of this assembly. In the following year he was elected president, although this selection did not mean much because of the power of the military chieftains, called caudillos. Buenos Aires was not satisfied because of his plan to place the city under the direct control of the federal government, much as Washington in the United States. At the same time war broke out with Brazil. That country attempted a blockade, but the doughty Irish sailor, William Brown, made this ineffective. He destroyed a large part of their fleet. General Alvear defeated the Brazilians at Ituzaingo, and this victory caused great rejoicing. Negotiations for peace followed soon afterwards. Rivadavia's envoy agreed to allow Uruguay to remain a part of the empire of Brazil, and this treachery aroused such a wave of indignation that he was compelled to resign. He was succeeded by Dorrego. Dorrego did not rule long in peace. The standard of revolt was raised in Buenos Aires and General Lavalle declared himself as governor. Dorrego fled to the interior, but was pursued. He was finally captured and, without even the form of a trial, was shot by the direct order of Lavalle. This precipitated a bloody civil war which soon desolated Argentina. The gauchos arose in revolt, and a series of campaigns began in different sections of the country. It is the leader of the southern gauchos who stands out as the strongest historical character of this period.

One of the most picturesque figures in Argentine history is Juan Manuel Rosas, a native of the province of Cordoba, who soon became the chief figure in Argentine affairs. This man ruled the new nation with an iron hand for almost two decades. He became an absolute tyrant and the most bitterly hated man in the country. Descendant of a wealthy family he devoted himself to pastoral pursuits from early life. By the time he was twenty-five he was the undisputed leader of the gauchos on the southern pampas, and had a full regiment of the half-breed horsemen of the plains at his back and ready to do his bidding. He had been fairly well educated and had ability, but this talent was not supported by character. He can best be compared with the notorious Santa Anna, of Mexico, in his greed for power, his cruelty and his craving for homage. Another similar type was the half-savage Carrera of Guatemala.

Rosas first appeared in public life at the head of a troop of gaucho cavalry, in a revolution that began in 1818. During the civil war he gave valuable aid to the Federalist cause. After a decisive defeat of the famous General Lavalle in 1829 he was appointed governor over the province of Buenos Aires with the rank of Captain-General, and this made him nominal head of Argentina. This event gave this monster his first taste of power and whetted his insatiable appetite for more. The remaining provinces were gradually subdued and one after another came under the authority of this dictator, although thousands of lives were lost in the conquest. As a rule no quarter was given, and the losing side generally fought it out to the last man. On one occasion five hundred prisoners were shot in cold blood at Tucuman. From the year 1832 the power of Rosas became absolute. Says Mr. Akers: "Unitarian advocates were hunted down like wild beasts. Rosas became suspicious of his own generals, and one by one they disappeared. Quiroga was assassinated at Cordoba; Lopez died suddenly in Buenos Aires; and Cullen, Reinafe and Heredia were sentenced to death. Under the tyranny of Rosas human life had small value. If any man was a danger to the dictatorial régime he was murdered by a band of assassins retained for this purpose. Expression of public opinion was rendered impossible. Men dared not think for themselves, much less put into words their abhorrence of the dictator."

The attempt of Rosas to close the Paraná to foreign commerce led to a blockade of Buenos Aires by French and English warships in 1845, so that this attempt failed. He also endeavoured to annex Uruguay, but foreign influence prevented this also. These acts made him intensely jealous of foreign governments. Nevertheless, with all foreign powers against him, and with powerful forces in his own land opposing him, he ruled Argentina with despotic tyranny for eighteen years. Rosas placed his political favourites at the head of the provincial governments, but he was not able to keep them loyal to his interests. His arbitrary acts alienated his best friends. The longer he ruled the more united became all other factions. A common hatred of the tyrant overshadowed all other differences of opinion. Foreigners were excluded from the provinces, everything imported or exported was required to be transhipped at Buenos Aires in order that duties might be collected. It was not long until the whole population was ready to support a rebellion. The provinces which had placed this tyrant in power finally overthrew him.

The chief lieutenant of Rosas for many years had been General Urquiza, whom he appointed governor of the province of Entre Rios. The administration of Urquiza was successful, and he could always be counted on to raise troops for Rosas from among the ranchmen of that province. Urquiza was a "caudillo", but had no particular thirst for power. At last, in 1846, the rupture with the tyrant came, and from that time on Urquiza led the fight against Rosas. Three times his efforts failed, but the fourth time in alliance with some Brazilian and Uruguayan troops he crossed the river with an army of twenty-four thousand, the largest army ever assembled on South American soil up to that time. Rosas awaited Urquiza at Buenos Aires and trusted all to a single battle. Of his army half deserted him and many of his officers betrayed him. The result was a disastrous defeat for the tyrant-dictator. When General Urquiza entered Buenos Aires, Rosas fled the country. Clad as an English sailor he escaped to a British man-of-war and was conveyed to England. He lived on a farm near Southampton until his death on the 14th of March, 1877, upon the proceeds of his ill-gotten wealth.

CHAPTER XVI
THE ERA OF DEVELOPMENT

The great question that was ever disturbing peace in Argentina was the fight between the Federalists, those who favoured a centralized power, and the Unitarians, who wanted the provinces to remain supreme. It was similar to the problem of states' rights as against a strong union, which was not settled in the United States until a disastrous civil war had been waged between the two factions. The question first arose under Rivadavia, who allowed it to drift along. It did drift, and became more formidable each year until it became the pivot around which all struggles centred, and was the primary cause of forty years of strife and much bloodshed. The province of Buenos Aires was always a strong adherent of the Unitarian idea, for that meant its continued supremacy by reason of its overshadowing strength. For that reason the other provinces rejected it. As the city of Buenos Aires enlarged, the question became more and more formidable. The mooted theme caused Rivadavia to resign his office; it made possible the disastrous dictatorship of Rosas; it hampered Presidents Urquiza and Mitre in the reforms attempted by them. It was not until Buenos Aires was forcibly organized into a Federal District that this cause of perpetual friction disappeared.

Argentina felt a sense of relief upon the downfall of Rosas, and once more the people breathed freely. The supreme power naturally fell into the hands of the victorious General Urquiza. The provinces had suffered most severely during the long period of civil wars. In Rioja the government had been overthrown fifteen times in seven months. Some of them were isolated, others had been badly devastated, but all of them were poor. Buenos Aires alone had increased in wealth and population. Hundreds of liberals had left the city or been exiled, but thousands had sought that city as a refuge from the disorders of the interior. Many English and Irish had settled in that province and engaged in the raising of sheep and cattle. The city alone contained one-fourth of the entire population of the confederation, and the rest of the province had increased more rapidly than any of the others. Although military rule was ended with the change in government, the real subject of dispute was far from being solved.

As soon as he was named provisional executive General Urquiza adopted measures looking to the adoption of a constitution. The governors of the various provinces met and it was agreed to call a Congress in which each province should have an equal vote. Buenos Aires alone protested, and to avoid the predominance of that province the session was called to meet in Santa Fé. The legislature of Buenos Aires refused to assent to this arrangement. The city rose in revolt and sent an army to attack Santa Fé, while the Congress was holding its sessions. By this action Buenos Aires practically declared her independence of the other provinces, but never asked recognition of foreign governments as an independent state. Although the rest of the confederation never took any steps to force a union, they knew that it would never do to permit Buenos Aires to remain independent with its control of the La Plata and its tributaries, which furnished the only natural communication with the interior. It was the pacific policy of Urquiza alone that prevented more serious trouble at this time. He refused to become another Rosas.

On the 1st of May, 1853, a constitution was adopted which was substantially copied after that of the United States, and this constitution, with few amendments, remains the fundamental law of Argentina to-day. The Paraná River was declared free to all the world, and the city of Paraná was selected as the temporary capital, with the city of Buenos Aires as permanent capital when that province should join the union. General José Justo Urquiza was elected the first constitutional president. Under his rule the provinces greatly prospered. The connection of some of the border provinces was very slight at first, but they gradually began to see the benefits of a closer union. The relations between Buenos Aires and the confederation became so strained in 1859 that the former marched an army against Urquiza. The President defeated them and, advancing upon the metropolis, compelled them to accept the constitution and join the confederation. This was about the last national service of President Urquiza, as his term expired in 1860. For many years after that he remained governor of Entre Rios, and his influence was paramount in that section between the Paraná and Uruguay Rivers. During a revolt against his authority in 1870, the aged general and ex-President was cruelly assassinated in his own house by some followers of the opposing leader.

The successor of Urquiza was Dr. Santiago Derqui. Trouble soon arose in the new government over the intervention of the federal government in the province of San Juan, because of the assassination of the governor. His successor, who had been selected by the people, was captured by the government troops and shot. Buenos Aires protested at this summary execution, and the Congress resented their protest by refusing admittance to its members. The forces of Buenos Aires under the command of General Mitre defeated the federal army in the battle of Pavon, and Derqui was thus deposed after a brief rule, being compelled to flee from the country.

General Bartolomé Mitre, one of the most illustrious men of Argentina, was born in the city of Buenos Aires, on the 26th of June, 1821. His early education was received in his home city, but later he was sent to Montevideo. It was in this city that he imbibed revolutionary doctrines, and took up arms in 1838, in one of the disturbances so numerous in that country. A few years later, when just of legal age, he joined an expedition against Rosas, the dictator. The failure of this expedition caused Mitre to return to Montevideo and turn his fight against that usurper through the columns of the newspapers, a calling which he followed during a large part of his life. At the early age of twenty-three he headed another attack against the tyrant, and was promoted to the rank of lieutenant-colonel. Disagreements with the authorities caused the young officer to leave Montevideo, and he went to the province of Corrientes, where he took part in several engagements against Rosas. The failure of this enterprise caused him to flee to Bolivia, where he spent a number of years in newspaper work and as teacher in the military college. His career also led him to Peru and Chile, in each of which countries he joined in the political struggles, always in behalf of public liberties and generally opposed to the existing governments. His conduct in those countries led him to a number of persecutions, so that he fled from one country to another, generally being received by the people as the champion of modern political ideas. He returned again to Montevideo, where he united with Urquiza, who was at that time a leader of the movement toward liberty from political dictators. He soon separated from that leader, however, becoming an active opponent of his, and to that end founded a newspaper in that city, called *Los Debates*.

In the revolution of 1852, Mitre entered the service of the National Guard, and this movement being successful he was appointed to a cabinet position, the first political office he had held in his own country. This government did not last long, and Mitre was soon found in the military service again. For a while he edited *El Nacional*, and took a part in the forming of a new constitution. For a number of years his time was alternated between military service, literary work, editorial services and political office. In 1860 he was elected governor of the province of Buenos Aires, and in 1862, by the victory of Pavon, General Mitre succeeded to the presidency of the republic. The accession of this high-minded patriot ended the period of uncertainty in Argentina. Although he reached his high position as the representative of victorious Buenos Aires, he immediately set himself to work to remodel and strengthen the federation, a task for which he had long prepared himself. Buenos Aires became the seat of government once more. The autonomy of the provinces was not interfered with, but power and population naturally gravitated toward that city. From that time the tendency has constantly been toward strengthening the bonds of cohesion. President Mitre also sought to work out a more democratic form of government, as preventative of the uprisings which were so numerous and distracting. This work, however, was seriously interrupted by the Paraguayan war, in which he acted as Commander-General of the allied forces from 1865 to 1868. The aggressive and ambitious policy of General Lopez, the dictator of that country, united Brazil, Uruguay and Argentina in an attempt to throttle his pretensions. It was only accomplished after a bloody war of several years, and the killing or disabling of almost every man in Paraguay capable of bearing arms. In 1868 President Mitre's term of office ended, and he was presented by the people with a fine home in the capital. After his retirement he served as senator for that province, in which he did good service for his country. He did effective work as editor of *La Nacion*, a journal which he owned, and through which he propounded his political ideas. At last ripe in years, full of honours and with the universal appreciation of his fellow countrymen he departed from this life in 1906.

During the term of President Mitre Argentina made great strides in material prosperity and industrial development. The Paraguayan war furnished a splendid market for the produce of the country, for the expense of the war was mostly borne by Brazil. When the election was held in that year Dr. Domingo Faustino Sarmiento, a native of the province of San Juan, was chosen. This election was held without interference from any source and the candidate himself was in Washington as his country's representative at that time. It was a wise selection, for even the jealous Porteños could find little fault with the policy and attitude of the new President. His most bitter opponents were compelled to admit that upright dealing and a desire to promote the best interests of Argentina characterized his administration. He is best remembered for the work done in behalf of education, and for that reason has been referred to as the "school-teacher President." He was a great admirer of President Lincoln and wrote a biography in Spanish of our martyred president. One of his books closes with these words: "Without instruction liberty is impossible;" and these words seem to have been the expression of his creed. Comparative peace reigned, and prosperity again made strides in spite of the weight of the heavy debt incurred by the Paraguayan war. An epidemic of yellow fever at this time is also memorable, as it is said to have caused the death of twenty-four thousand persons in Buenos Aires within six months. Notwithstanding all these hindrances to prosperity, the termination of President Sarmiento's term in 1874 found great advances made in the republic. Education had progressed, railways had been extended, and the administration of justice had been improved. Immigration on a large scale had been turned toward Argentina. Perhaps the greatest criticism that can be offered is that his administration was practically the beginning of the policy of national and commercial extravagance which finally ended in financial disaster. Sarmiento died in 1888, at the age of seventy-seven.

The question of a successor to Sarmiento again aroused the old jealousies. At that time Argentina was a loosely-joined organization of fourteen states, each enjoying sovereign rights and each jealous of the national government. Both Mitre and Sarmiento had endeavoured to unite the provinces more closely, but with little effect. The difficulty of communication was perhaps detrimental to consolidation. Sarmiento absolutely refused to be drawn into the controversy or take any part in the selection of his successor. The provincials, however, won again when Dr. Nicolás Avellaneda, a native of Tucuman, was chosen. This election almost resulted in a serious revolution. After his inauguration, and in order to intimidate the Porteños, the President made an ostentatious parade of military strength. A meeting of prominent citizens was held, and a discussion as to the best means of combating the President followed. It was decided to found the Tiro Nacional, an organization ostensibly formed for rifle shooting, but in reality a volunteer military organization. The enthusiasm of the young men for this organization was unbounded, and every Sunday thousands attended the parade grounds to receive instruction. It was not long until the Tiro Nacional aroused the suspicion of the President and his advisors. General Mitre and other officers in the army, who were active in the Tiro, were summoned and told that their further connection with that organization would subject them to the charge of treason. As an answer to this they immediately resigned their commissions. Conflicts between national troops and members of the Tiro were narrowly averted in several instances. A compromise was finally effected which temporarily averted hostilities, as public attention was again centred upon a successor.

TYPICAL WAGONS OF THE PAMPAS

General Bartolomé Mitre might have been chosen again, but he refused to become a candidate. There was no lack of willing candidates, however, but it brought to the front one of the strongest men that Argentina has yet known, General Julio Roca. General Roca, like his predecessor, was a native of Tucuman. He had distinguished himself in campaigns against turbulent Indians, and also in command of troops in several revolutionary outbreaks. He had shown great skill and tact in organization. One of his campaigns had opened up the vast region of Patagonia to civilization. As a result of his victory, this land, which had hitherto been considered as a barren waste, was added to the national domain and given territorial government in order to avoid state jealousies. This caused General Roca to be called a national benefactor by his friends. Foreseeing that a call to arms would come sooner or later General Roca applied himself to strengthening the army, while his followers fought his political battles. For the first time the nationalists openly and strenuously advocated the confiscation of the city of Buenos Aires as the federal capital. To this Roca gave his adherence, and he became the candidate of the powerful Cordoba "League," which was a political organization of unusual strength.

Each side now began to prepare for the impending conflict, although for months these strained relations continued. The Porteños were hampered by a lack of arms and ammunition. In June, 1880, an open rupture occurred in the capital between the presidential escort and a group of citizens. The incident was reported as an attempt upon the life of President Avellaneda. The President fled the city and joined the main body of federal troops a few miles out. General Roca commanded these troops, which numbered about eight thousand, and some gunboats. The city was unfortified, but the Porteños began to throw up entrenchments and had about fifteen thousand men under arms. These troops, however, lacked military training, while the government forces had seen service in several minor campaigns. Wrangling, vacillation and jealousy all weakened the power of the Porteños. Each side delayed the conflict which all felt to be inevitable. There were minor skirmishes, but it was not until July that a serious encounter took place, on the 20th of that month. Roca decided to make an attack and placed his forces accordingly. Several points of assault were arranged. The battle began very early on the morning of that date with picket skirmishing. The defence stubbornly resisted the advance and made a valorous fight. The losses on both sides were severe; especially was this true of the Porteños, who also began to be distressed because of lack of ammunition. They had no reserve stores on which to fall back. On the second day the fighting was renewed with odds in favour of the government. The national troops finally forced their way over the Barracas Bridge into the city. The total casualties had been not less than five thousand, with the greatest loss among the city's defenders. Both sides rested for a day, the 22nd. An armistice was declared and negotiations opened. The national government, knowing the lack of ammunition, imposed onerous conditions. Participators in the revolt, however, were not to be punished, but should be denied official employment. When Congress met a few months later it ratified the election of General Roca as President. The city of Buenos Aires was proclaimed a federal district and the national capital. Thus the principal cause of friction between the provinces was forcibly removed. This was practically the last step in the process of consolidation which had been going on. This great city is now one of the strongest ties binding together the different provinces, as each one has a sense of joint ownership in and pride of their beautiful capital.

Centralization received a fresh impetus with the ascendency of President Roca. The provinces, however, got more than they had bargained for. They had succeeded in humiliating the province of Buenos Aires, but a strong central government was not one of their desires. Roca, hitherto an unknown political quantity, set himself to work to bring order out of chaos, and to develop a national spirit; to teach the people of all the provinces that first of all they were Argentinians. He surprised both his opponents and supporters; the first by his fairness, and the latter by the fact that they could not dictate to him. He did not act hastily but studied the situation. He had visited nearly every section of the country and knew the immense undeveloped resources of the country. To populate these lands and bring them under contribution to civilization was his great aim. Within a year his power was absolute, but he began no repressive measures. He never allowed militarism to become obnoxious. As a result Argentina entered upon an era of development and evolution that was simply marvellous. A reckless optimism ruled the country. Railway extension on a broader scale began; immigration agencies were opened up in Europe, government lands were sold at low rates. Public works were inaugurated, on a scale hitherto unprecedented, new docks were built in Buenos Aires and adequate drainage undertaken. European money lenders offered money for any enterprise. The petty jealousies were restrained and foreign capital encouraged. With all the skill and diplomacy of a shrewd ruler a discontented element still remained, those who were "out." In Santa Fé and Entre Rios disturbances arose which were quickly quelled, and in Buenos Aires further trouble threatened. This latter was due to the national interference in elections. The vanity of the Porteños was somewhat appeased by the efforts they made to beautify La Plata, their new capital, which was intended to rival the older city in magnificence and importance.

When the question of a successor became necessary Roca declared he would maintain absolute neutrality. Such a thing was almost unheard of in South America, and the people placed little credence in it. Among the several candidates was his brother-in-law, Miguel Juarez Celman. This man stood before the country in the guise of the official candidate. If Roca did nothing to assist, he did nothing to hinder Celman's selection. When the election arrived there was practically no contest, and Celman was chosen almost unanimously. At the election in March electors equal to twice the number of representatives in Congress are elected, who meet on June 12th and choose a president and vice-president.

Celman was an unfortunate choice. As governor of Cordoba he had shown no administrative ability, nor later in Congress. There was little to recommend him and he had been chosen by the Cordoba "Clique," because of his pliancy. The almost four years of his administration are memorable for reckless private and public borrowing. Flattery and adulation turned the head of the new President. Many thought that Roca would be the power behind the throne, but events disproved that idea. With his head turned by the servility shown him, Celman soon chafed at any restraint. He broke loose from all control, and even Roca soon cooled. Political adventurers began to fill the offices and an era of carpet-bagging followed. Elections for senators and deputies were openly manipulated. Bribery and corruption were everywhere apparent. Concessions and monopolies were scattered broadcast. A healthy activity was followed by a mad rush of speculation. The provincial governments followed suit. The corruption of former days sunk into insignificance beside the orgy of this administration. Banks of issue were established throughout the republic, whose notes were guaranteed by national bonds. The paper circulation was almost quadrupled and the premium on gold rose. As the banks were obliged to purchase bonds of the government, this gave it a ready supply of money. Soon this was squandered and the national government found itself obligated for one hundred and ninety-six million dollars on these guarantees.

The conservative element looked on this extravagance with dismay, and rumblings of discontent were heard throughout the republic, although many did not seem to have any apprehensions until the final crash came. The public continued to speculate on the scrip issued. Meetings were held by these malcontents, but the discontented centres were too far apart. A central league was formed which was called the "Union Civica," in which a number of notable names were included, men who were actuated by purely patriotic motives. This was in 1887, just a year after Celman's inauguration. Meetings were held, and literature freely distributed calling upon the people to protect themselves against the dangers threatened by this administration. During the two years following its organization the Union Civica spread its propaganda extensively. The headquarters were maintained in Buenos Aires, but local clubs were formed in nearly every town and village throughout the country. Adhesion was publicly given to the tenets of the Union Civica in many provinces, for public feeling was greatly aroused.

In 1889 the beginning of the crisis came, and by the end of that year the organizers felt they could count on the moral support of the majority of the people. The government did not sleep during this time. Meetings were broken up, newspapers were censored and editors threatened. Terrorism, however, did not check the growth of the anti-administration feeling. The President's action with the Mortgage Banks, which were practically forced to loan money on worthless securities to political favourites, was the last straw. Celman, although aware of the tremendous opposition, relied upon the strength of his army. The foreign colonies protested, and their influence was strong as they owned all the public utilities. Congress passed a resolution demanding his resignation. Force did not avail with public sentiment so aroused. An uprising was finally advocated as the only recourse, although hitherto the Union had acted within its constitutional rights. The army and navy were sounded and considerable encouragement was received. The date for the revolt was finally set for the 26th of July, 1890, and the Plaza Lavalle as the place. This plaza was barricaded and a force of fifteen hundred armed men occupied it. The government troops rendezvoused on the Plaza Libertad, a few hundred yards away. Sharpshooters were placed on the housetops to pick off the insurgents, but they were unable to dislodge them. Some vessels of the fleet attempted to bombard the government buildings, but their shells fell wide of their mark. Reinforcements of the government, as well as a shortage of ammunition, prevented the success of the revolutionary forces. An armistice was arranged and negotiations opened up for a settlement. The insurgents demanded forgiveness of themselves and the resignation of the President, and this was agreed to. His resignation caused scenes of the wildest excitement, and not until then was the real magnitude of the disaffection known. Public holidays were observed for three days. In no quarter was a good word to be said for the defeated President or his administration, and he disappeared from view almost as completely as if the earth had engulfed him. In Europe the keenest pleasure was shown, as the downfall of the President was looked upon as evidence that Argentina would thereafter insist upon honesty in the conduct of its public officials.

Dr. Carlos Pellegrini, the Vice-President, succeeded to the office of chief magistrate. The new President had already acquired a somewhat varied experience in public affairs. The name signifies his Italian descent, but his mother was an Englishwoman of distinguished family, and he had thus inherited some sturdy Anglo-Saxon qualities. He had many friends, but there were skeptics also, because he had not protested against Celman's policy. No one doubted his ability. His first duty was to organize a cabinet that would conciliate the various factions, but that was no easy task. He succeeded in getting former-President Roca to accept the portfolio of Minister of the Interior, and the other appointments were then easily and successfully filled. The new cabinet was a fortunate combination of the diverse political elements. Every one seemed fairly well satisfied, except the Cordoba "Clique."

An empty treasury and a legacy of debts of the Celman administration soon made trouble for the new President and his cabinet. Concessions which contained money guarantees had been scattered broadcast, and these obligations were being pressed. The Congress still contained the corrupt members who had been elected through the official influence of Celman. Things drifted from bad to worse, and the general inflation of public and commercial enterprises brought about an economic and financial crisis. The government had no funds with which to meet even the ordinary expenses, let alone the contractual obligations, and national bankruptcy was threatened. The resources had all been mortgaged. As a makeshift the President decided to issue inconvertible notes, and an issue of sixty millions was legalized. This gave temporary relief only and paved the way for greater complications in the future, as the currency rapidly depreciated. Foreign creditors became pressing. The government finally defaulted in its obligations. The Banco Nacional failed, and the resources of all the banks were taxed to the uttermost. Pellegrini, knowing that his tenure was only temporary, became discouraged, and no permanent solution was attempted by him. No human foresight could devise measures that would immediately bring prosperity, and the people were impatient. Dr. Pellegrini was obliged to wait until later years before his work was really appreciated. He served as national senator in after years, and passed away in 1906, mourned by the nation.

A large following began to hail General Bartolomé Mitre as the only saviour, and he finally, but with reluctance, consented to be a candidate. Another element wanted Roca, but neither of these men aspired to the presidency. The two held a conference and decided that neither would be a candidate, if a non-party candidate would be selected. Dr. Luis Saenz Peña, who had been a judge of the Supreme Court for many years, was chosen as this candidate, and was elected practically without opposition, and with the active support of Pellegrini, who imprisoned some of the opposition. Saenz Peña was sixty-eight years of age, and it was thought that his high character and broad experience of men and matters would be just the thing for the country. He had no part in the means taken to exile the opposition leaders and prevent a free election. In fact it is doubtful if he had any real desire for the position.

Thus it was that on the 12th of October, 1892, Dr. Saenz Peña took the oath of office as President, and Dr. Pellegrini retired almost unnoticed. This was the first instance where a President had assumed the office of executive without a party behind him. President Peña had no political following upon whom he could depend for support. His idea was to administer public affairs for the general good, without reference to political exigencies. Unforeseen obstacles soon arose, for the Senators and Deputies were opportunists and looking for personal advantage. The first cabinet resigned after a few stormy months. His thirty years' service on the bench had unfitted him to grasp political exigencies. He refused to use his official prerogatives to influence Congress, although the latter constantly threw obstacles in his path. Disturbances in several provinces because of local conditions stirred up the feeling of revolt and a revolution was narrowly averted. The opposition endeavoured to make it a general uprising but did not succeed. Although Saenz Peña had allied himself with those opposed to

Roca, that general took the field against the revolutionists in Rosario and Santa Fé and restored order, or at least a semblance of it. The President was determined to effect economies in national expenditures, but this was opposed by Congress. The scene of contest was transferred to Congress and the press. When Congress met in June, 1894, the relations between the two departments were strained very much. The President was too conscientious in his efforts to be free to initiate reforms to use his patronage in order to influence the legislators. Congress did nothing from month to month and neglected to pass the necessary appropriation bills. Taxes had been increased to pay the obligations of the government, so that the people were rebelling and war with Chile began to seem imminent. Congress refused to grant the request of the President for money and supplies. A ministerial crisis arose, and Dr. Peña found great difficulty in the formation of a new cabinet. The friction became more and more intense, until the President presented his resignation early in 1895, and the tension was relieved. He never again appeared in public life.

Dr. José Uriburu, who succeeded to the presidency, had been in diplomatic positions for many years. He was also unacquainted with political methods, for he had spent much of his life in foreign countries. Knowing that a repetition of the Peña failure would bring disaster to the nation former-Presidents Roca and Pellegrini decided to support Uriburu with all their resources. This assured the new President a working majority in Congress. Hardly had he assumed office before complications with Chile over the boundary threatened almost immediate war. Excitement became intense, and a large credit was voted by Congress for defence. The question was finally submitted to arbitration and war averted. President Cleveland also decided a dispute with Brazil over the limitations of Misiones adverse to Argentina, but this award was quietly accepted by the government. A default in the subsidy of the railways also caused trouble. The President asked for fifty millions of dollars in bonds to compound with the companies, and this was finally authorized. The support of Roca and Pellegrini during the three years and nine months of Uriburu's term carried it safely through a trying period, and much was accomplished in restoring the finances to a better footing.

As the election of 1898 drew near public sentiment seemed to concentrate on former-President Roca as the man to steer the ship of state, and he was elected practically without opposition. His former administration had been successful; he was at the head of the only really national party in the republic; he seemed to have the qualities of a leader who could rally around him the discordant political elements into which Argentina was divided. In October, 1898, Dr. Roca assumed office again, just eighteen years after he had first been placed in control of Argentine affairs. During his second term the boundary question with Chile was settled by W. J. Buchanan, the United States minister, as arbitrator, although a rupture in the negotiations was narrowly averted on several occasions. President Roca cleverly avoided the rupture, although it was at times difficult because of the excited state of public opinion. He scathingly rebuked the administration of justice in one of his messages to Congress, and this led to reform and the dismissal of several judges. A meeting with President Errazuiz of Chile was arranged, and this took place at Punta Arenas. On the way the President visited several of the coast settlements in Patagonia. Hitherto these southern territories had been neglected, but this visit brought them prominently into notice. President Roca also visited President Campos Salles, of Brazil, and received a return visit from that official. No revolutionary disturbances arose during this second term, but several of the provinces experienced trouble, and in Buenos Aires the national government was obliged to take charge of the provincial administration because of financial irresponsibility. Many reforms in the finances of the country were accomplished. The value of the dollar rose to forty cents and the beginning of a gold reserve was made. Dr. Roca deserves great credit for the work of his administration, and he still lives to enjoy the confidence and good will of his fellow citizens.

At the meeting of the electoral college on the 12th of June, 1904, Dr. Manuel Quintana was chosen President. Several prominent men, including former-Presidents Pellegrini and Uriburu, were candidates to succeed President Roca, but a new man was selected. President Quintana came of a distinguished family, and was a native of Buenos Aires. By profession he was a lawyer, and had been the legal advisor of many corporations, including several of the railways, so that his election was eminently satisfactory to the foreign interests. When elected he was sixty-eight years of age and had been active in politics for many years, but his record had been clear. The administration of President Quintana was marked by a steady advance in the financial standing of Argentina. Peace reigned, and there was only one slight revolution in February, 1905. At that time revolts broke out simultaneously at Rosario, Bahia Blanca and Mendoza among some government troops, but this disturbance was soon quelled. The greatest damage was inflicted in the last named city, where the revolutionists turned their cannon on the Governor's Palace and almost reduced it to ruins. Some encounters also took place in the streets of Buenos Aires. The revolution came to an abrupt end, however, after a few days, but not before a number had lost their lives. Several of the conspirators were sentenced to short terms in prison, while a larger number escaped across the border into Chile. This was a radical departure from the former custom of granting general amnesty to all who took part in revolutions against the government.

In 1906 President Quintana died and the office fell to Dr. José Figueroa Alcorta, who had been elected with him as Vice-President. President Figueroa was only forty-four years of age at the time of his inauguration and in the very prime of life. He was a native of Cordoba, and had been a National Senator from that state. He proved himself to be well fitted for the duties of that high office, and safely guided the destinies of the country without serious friction. He himself was a hard worker, and the executive could be found at work in his office early and late. He cared little for display or the social features of the position, and was a much more difficult man to meet than the average President of South America. This administration is too recent to generalize; but suffice it to say that both external and comparative internal peace reigned, and the development of the country and its resources steadily progressed.

In the campaign of 1910 there were two active candidates, Dr. Udaondo and Dr. Roque Saenz Peña, son of the former President of the same name. Many meetings were held by the followers of the former, the billboards were plastered with statements and appeals to the voters, but there was not at any time a question as to who had the "call." The official party was well organized and the log-rolling was quietly conducted. When the electors met the vote was almost unanimous for Dr. Saenz Peña. The newly-elected President, who assumed office on the 12th of October, entered upon a political career early in life. His first office was deputy in the state legislature of Buenos Aires. Later he became Minister of Foreign Affairs under President Celman. Following the fall of that man, and the scandals which were unearthed, he retired from public life for several years. Since that time he has served in several diplomatic positions, and was a member of the Pan-American Conference held in Washington. At the time of his election he was minister Plenipotentiary to the governments of Italy and Switzerland. President Saenz Peña assumes his office with the good will of the foreign colony, and promises to give Argentina a peaceful and progressive administration. His term of office will not expire until 1916.

CHAPTER XVII
TRADE CONDITIONS IN SOUTH AMERICA

Walking along the extensive docks at Buenos Aires, and going through the immense warehouses which extended one after another along those docks, I was impressed with the small proportion of the immense traffic coming into this port that belonged to the United States. It was an object lesson far more impressive than the perusal of statistics. Section after section would be visited without a single package bearing the name of one of our manufacturers, while great boxes and bales with "Hamburg" stamped upon them, French boxes of both wet and dry goods, labelled "fragile," and English shipments were piled clear up to the ceiling. The question "why is this condition?" arose in my mind, and set me upon inquiry. Are North American manufactures not adapted to the needs of our fellow Americans? Can it be that our goods are not fully known or appreciated beneath the Southern Cross?

It was just at this time that the naval commission of Argentina awarded the contract for the two battleships to United States builders, after a fierce competition from the ship-building firms of five nations, and one in which even the diplomatic representatives of more than one nation became involved. This act brought out a great deal of favourable comment upon the United States from the leading journals of Buenos Aires. A reporter of *La Prensa*, perhaps the most influential daily in that republic, came to interview me, and I took the occasion to say that the United States had entered upon an era of commercial conquest, and hereafter must be reckoned with. A number of Argentinians whom I met afterwards commented on the subject, and everywhere the encouraging words were heard: "We will welcome you; indeed we have wondered why it was not done long ago." This convinces me that no prejudice exists among the Latin-Americans against their fellow Americans of North America.

It may be that the manufacturers of the United States have been a little ignorant of conditions in South America. A little ignorance is excusable. As the United States has not been a colonizing nation, having undeveloped lands and resources at home for its surplus population, there has not been the intercourse between North and South America that there has been between South America and Europe. But there is one characteristic which I noticed everywhere and greatly admired, and that is that South Americans of every country are satisfied only with the "best." The "just as good" argument does not satisfy. When once convinced that the manufacturer of the United States is putting out a better article, it will be bought. The manufacturer of that country has oftentimes been at a disadvantage because the importing houses are mostly of European nationality, and for that reason prejudicially inclined towards their fellow-countrymen. North American-made goods have forged ahead simply and solely upon their own intrinsic merit.

"All of our printing machinery is of North American make, as is almost everything in the establishment, except the type," said the manager of *La Prensa*, as he courteously and with justifiable pride showed me through their fine office building with its humanitarian and sociological features. "We have found those goods to be the best. Furthermore, our presses, as you will see, are the North American make; and not from the branch factory in England." And so I found as we went through these offices, being taken from one floor to another on an American elevator, that the "copy" was being written up on typewriters, set up on linotype machines, and printed upon presses, all of United States manufacture; the checks to the reporters were signed by fountain-pens and the cash received over the counters was rung up on cash registers from the same land.

"Where do you purchase your paper?"

He answered: "We buy some of it in the United States but most of it in Germany. We prefer that made in North America, but it is so carelessly packed that we always figure on a ten per cent. loss. The German manufacturers carefully surround the rolls with boards to prevent the paper from damage, while the North American paper is simply wrapped with a little heavier paper, which tears or becomes water soaked, and damage results. A short time ago we returned nearly nine hundred bales to the manufacturers because of the damaged condition in which it was received."

ROLLS OF PAPER FROM GERMANY

"How does American machinery sell?" I asked of an importing merchant in Buenos Aires, who represented a few American manufacturers.

"Very well indeed, for the people generally like them. But there is one thing your North American manufacturers must learn, and that is to be very careful in putting every necessary part in the shipment. Several times we have received engines, or other complicated machinery, and when it was put together some part would be missing. As it was impossible to get that part in less than three or four months, the customer lost a season's business, and his friends bought English machinery because there was no danger of that same trouble."

It would be possible to relate numerous other instances of personal experiences, all of which would be of similar tenor to those herewith given. It is humiliating to an American to travel throughout the length and breadth of South America and see the trade which legitimately belongs to us slipping away to Europe, when some of our own factories in that line are idle because of lack of orders. It leads one to ask the questions: "What is the matter with the American business man? What is the matter with the American manufacturer?"

The South American field is an extensive one, and it is a discriminating one. The idea that anything is good enough for that continent has been exploded. Buenos Aires, for instance, is a live, hustling up-to-date metropolis. The people have money and they spend it freely. What they buy they want of the very best, and nothing is too good for them. It might also be added that nothing is too expensive for them, as they are used to paying high prices, and money seems to be of little moment when once the desire for the article exists. So it is not a cheap or a low-price market that awaits the American merchant.

Argentina is essentially British in her sympathies. That is but natural, for England owns her railroads, public improvements and government bonds. Almost two billion dollars of British gold is invested in that republic, and perhaps fifty thousand of her subjects dwell there. There is not a boat that sails for Buenos Aires from an English port which does not carry some young English boys to that city, who expect to enter commercial life there. It is only natural that this should create a preference for English-made goods, for the Englishman always carries his atmosphere with him as well as his ideas of taste and style. And yet German houses have aggressively entered this field in the past decade and have made terrific inroads on English trade. The Germans have studied the markets; they aim to cater to its demands; they grant the terms asked by the merchants, and do anything to secure the trade—and they generally get it.

One noticeable feature of the German commercial invasion is its imitation, and a desire to furnish "similar" articles at a cheaper price. As a prominent man told me: "Their goods are worth no more than you pay for them, and they are bound to lose out in the long run." It is this commercial rivalry that has caused the intense feeling between Germany and England, for the German manufacturer has been somewhat unscrupulous in his methods. If a manufacturer in the United States or England has succeeded in evolving some new and valuable contrivance, it will not be long until a German imitation will be on the market, and bearing an English name. It is well known that the North American manufacturers have evolved the best and practically only successful typewriters, cash registers and computing machines. Within the last year or two, however, German imitations have appeared in all markets. The machines in some instances have such a wholly misleading name as "Columbia," showing the plain intention of deception. In these lines their methods have had little effect. One can hardly go into an office anywhere in South America without seeing one or more typewriters with familiar labels, for a half dozen or more manufacturers are working in that field, and nearly every store has from one to a half dozen cash registers of one or two North American makes. "We are bringing them in by the shipload," said an agent in Buenos Aires, who handled both lines, and there was not much exaggeration in the statement.

It is in the practical and useful things that the genius of the United States has been most manifest. A great undeveloped country rich in natural resources stirred the inventive genius of the people, and the result has been a continual increase in time-saving and labour-saving appliances of all kinds. These same articles are equally adapted to conditions all over South America. In some places these articles are known and appreciated; in others they are still unknown. No manufacturers have evolved farming machinery of all kinds so well adapted to conditions in South America as those of the United States.

American manufacturers look with longing eyes towards the Orient as a promising field for expansion. It will be many years before China, for instance, will be a great importer of manufactured goods, because of the extreme poverty of the people and the consequent low purchasing power of the masses. The imports of that country, with its teeming population of four hundred millions, for the past year were about $333,000,000, an average of less than one dollar per capita. It will be many years before that percentage will greatly increase, because the rise in the standard of wages will be very slow owing to the abundance of labourers. Furthermore, as soon as trade has once been established, the low wages will induce manufacturers to establish factories on Chinese soil so that the cost of production will be decreased. Japan is, and will always be, a formidable competitor in the Orient, because of her ingenuity and similarly low wage scale.

South America, on the other hand, is not and will not be for a long time, if ever, a manufacturing country. Brazil has encouraged some lines of manufactures, because of her extensive water power, but still is and will ever remain an importing nation. Argentina, Uruguay and Paraguay have little available water power and scarcely any coal. Chile, Peru and all the other republics of South America remain importing nations. In none of these countries, except Chile, has coal been found in large quantities, and millions upon millions of tons are imported each year from Europe and Australia. The matter of fuel alone will always deter manufacturing in South America.

Let us glance for a moment at the purchasing power of these republics. Argentina, although not so populous as the immense republic of Brazil, easily stands at the head of the list. During the year 1909 the total foreign trade of the Argentine Republic was valued at $700,106,623, of which $302,756,095 was imports. This was an average of almost $108.00 for each man, woman and child in the nation, and an importation of more than $46.00 per capita. Thus this one republic, with a population of less than seven million, imports almost as much as China with more than fifty times the population. In the last decade the imports of Argentina have increased one hundred and fifty-four per cent., an increase exceeded only by Canada. She now ranks thirteenth in total imports and sixth in per capita imports. Those nations, such as England and Holland, which exceed in per capita imports, are large importers of raw materials and not manufactured goods, as is the case with Argentina. Furthermore, the population of Argentina is increasing rapidly, both by natural increase and immigration. There are no idle men in the country, as every able bodied man seems to be able to secure employment. Wages are about as high as in the United States, and the cost of living higher. The people spend their money freely, and the importing houses do an immense business which is increasing each year.

Brazil will one day be one of the great powers of the world, for she contains within her borders the greatest amount of undeveloped, fertile land in the world. The United States, exclusive of Alaska and the island possessions, could be set inside the territorial limits of Brazil, and leave a state as large as Texas on the outside. The Brazilian government estimates the population at a little more than twenty million, but it would probably be better to place the number at eighteen million. Brazil has fostered some lines of industry, especially the manufacture of cotton goods, where water power is an invaluable asset, but most of the goods are imported. The purchasing power of the people is not as great as in Argentina, because there are several millions of negroes and Indians included in the population. The total imports for the year 1909 were $179,690,125. This would be at the rate of ten dollars per capita, or ten times that of China. In other words, the imports of Brazil, with her eighteen million population, is equal to that of half the Chinese Empire. If the coffee situation improves there will be a great increase in Brazilian imports, for many improvements are withheld in the coffee regions at the present time on that account.

Chile, that long, narrow strip of land, whose two hundred and ninety-one thousand and five hundred square miles stretch over thirty-eight degrees of latitude, is well worthy of consideration. In 1909 the imports of this republic were $94,349,795. With a population of less than four million, this makes a per capita importation of twenty-five dollars. Peru, with a slightly greater population, but a larger number of Indians who are not purchasers, imported in the same year about $25,000,000. Uruguay ranks next to Argentina in imports in proportion to population. Larger than New York and West Virginia combined, this republic, whose physical characteristics and agricultural resources are very similar to its neighbour across the La Plata, has a population of one million one hundred thousand. It is a great stock country, and ninety-four per cent. of its $37,000,000 exports for last year were hides, frozen meat, jerked beef, meat-extracts and tallow. Its imports amounted to $35,000,000 in round numbers, making the comparatively small republic well worth consideration by the exporter. Venezuela imports will average $10,000,000, Bolivia $16,000,000, Ecuador $7,000,000, Columbia $12,000,000 and Paraguay about $4,000,000.

These figures are eloquent in themselves. They bespeak great possibilities of trade among our South American neighbours. Of the total imports of Argentina, during the year 1909, the United States sent $43,068,829. For the last two years the percentage has shown a gradual increase, as a few lines of American goods have been systematically pushed. In percentage of increase over the preceding year the United States is ahead of the other commercial nations. Specialties such as typewriters, photographic cameras, firearms, elevators, phonographs, toilet and medical articles, and petroleum products, have made their market, but it is the larger competitive field that needs attention. In this class are included motors of all kinds, electrical appliances, steel in every form, railway and tramway equipment, and a thousand and one things made by manufacturers of the United States, which are always equal to and oftentimes superior to anything of their kind made elsewhere.

We purchase more than twice as much from Brazil as any other nation, more than half the total, and sell that country less than half as much as Great Britain and less than Germany. We sell more to Argentina than we purchase from her, but Great Britain sells almost three times as much, and our percentage is only fourteen per cent. of the whole, with Germany still in the lead and France not far behind. We purchase nearly twice as much from Chile as Germany, and more than twice as much as Great Britain, and yet the latter country sells Chile more than twice as much as we do and Germany almost half as much again. And so the figures might be given for the other countries, which would show about the same ratios, and which make the American travelling through those countries lose some of his egotism.

Here are a few of the obstacles encountered: the leading banks are either British, German or Italian; the importing merchants are of the same nationality, and there is quicker transportation because of the numerous steamship lines running to European ports, although there are good steamers running direct from New York to the ports on the east coast. And the following are a few of the remedies suggested: an American bank would greatly facilitate business, as it would aid in exchange and the handling of credits; American manufacturers should study the markets and send salesmen who understand the languages, people and customs; great care in packing goods for South America should be exercised; fourthly, and lastly, establish independent houses with hustling Americans in charge, and not trust to foreign representatives who have a natural predilection for things made in their own land. The shipping question will solve itself, for boats will be run whenever business demands them. A little attention to these principles and suggestions will help in solving the question of American trade in South America. They are Americans, also, and pride themselves on that fact. They rather resent our assumption of the name "Americans," and insist that we should use the term "North Americans." They are the "South Americans." Then, as they say, as we are all "Americans," let the cry be "America for the Americans."

CHAPTER XVIII
A PROMISING REPUBLIC

Argentina has just celebrated the first centennial of her independence from Spanish domination. On the 25th of May, 1910, there was opened in the city of Buenos Aires an exposition that continued for six months. It was undoubtedly the greatest exposition ever held in the southern hemisphere, just as Buenos Aires is the largest city in that half of the globe. For almost a year active preparations had been going on for this celebration. The United States honoured the occasion by sending five warships for the opening, and appointing a special commission to represent the government in an official capacity.

The exposition really consisted of five separate exhibitions, which were located in different parts of the city and were practically independent of each other. These were the International Exhibition of Railways and Land Transports, the International Exhibition of Agriculture, the International Exhibition of Hygiene, and the National Exhibitions of Industry and Arts. The first mentioned was perhaps the most important, for it consisted of a display of every kind of land transportation from animal traction to steam and gasoline. There were special sections devoted to each phase of railways, from the building of stations to the equipment of the finest trains in the world, including all systems in general use; other sections were devoted to tramways operated by the various kinds of power, automobiles and all forms of motor cars, etc. Nothing was overlooked to make this transportation exhibit the most complete ever held in the world. Six sections in a choice location, composing about fifteen thousand square yards, were assigned for United States exhibitors. Great Britain, on the other hand, had asked for and was given more than three times that amount of space. This condition cannot be blamed upon the Argentine government, however, as the United States commission secured all the space that they asked for, and the commissioners found it difficult to fill their allotment.

The Exhibition of Hygiene was also important in this age when science has made so much advance in overcoming the obstacles placed in the way of health by nature. This included buildings devoted to hygienic sports, hygiene of dress, naval and military hygiene, ventilation and calefaction in general, sanitary work of cities, hospitals, surgical instruments, and other allied subjects. The agricultural exhibition was particularly devoted to live stock, and the other exhibitions are made clear by their nomenclature.

Each one of the foreign colonies entered heartily into the exposition spirit, and planned to present to the city some memorial in the way of a permanent work of art, in commemoration of this first centennial of the revolution which led to the independence of Argentina from Spanish rule or misrule, a date which is as sacred to the Argentinians as the Fourth of July with us. The British colony, which is one of the largest and wealthiest and numbers probably twenty-five thousand, presented a clock tower of artistic design. The German colony, of almost equal numbers, began the erection of a monumental fountain on a great and imposing terrace which was prepared by the city, and cost one hundred thousand dollars. The Austro-Hungarian collectivity offered a meteorological monument, similar to those found in the cities of Austria and Hungary, which will be adorned with meteorological implements and appliances. The Italians, who are the largest in number but not the wealthiest, built an artistic monument in Italian marble of that great discoverer, Christopher Columbus. Lastly, the three hundred Americans offered a statue of George Washington, to whose work and example more than anything else the liberty of all the Americas is due, and the government donated to them a beautiful location on one of the principal plazas. Thus, by this tribute, will another connecting link in the friendship between the two republics, each of which is predominant on its own continent, be added.

CONGRESS PALACE AND THE PLAZA, BUENOS AIRES

Courtesy of the Bulletin of Pan-American Union

All over the city of Buenos Aires men worked for months in the attempt to beautify the city for the centennial exposition. Plazas were rearranged, and new monuments erected in them; public buildings were redecorated and overhauled; the new Supreme Court Palace was hurried in order to have it ready for the sessions of the Pan-American Congress, which were held there contemporaneous with the exposition; six solid blocks were bought and condemned in order to give an approach to the new Congress Palace, and thousands of men were employed for months in tearing down these buildings, hauling away the débris, and preparing the ground for the beautiful little park into which the space has been created.

The great problem with Argentina is the settlement of the immense tracts of unoccupied land. These formerly belonged to the national government, but they are now generally owned by the various provinces. As in most Latin countries the government adopted the plan of subsidizing the railroads, instead of giving them lands which would have been an incentive to stimulate settlement along their tracks. The railways have only recently grasped the advantages of encouraging such migration. A large part of this land has already been secured by private owners. The country is overrun with land companies, and every newspaper is filled with advertisements of auction sales of lands and corner lots in projected colonies, or in estates which comprise thousands of acres. Nowhere will one find such elaborate advertisements of real estate as in the newspapers of Buenos Aires, where they spread over page after page of their bulky papers.

The government is making earnest effort to encourage immigration and has been more successful than any other republic in South America. The immigration department publishes prospectuses containing elaborate and detailed information concerning public lands and guides for prospective settlers. The efforts of the national government are ably seconded by the provincial administrations, and they are jointly endeavouring to attract a class that will adopt an agricultural life. Free transportation is given desirable immigrants, and in many places money is advanced to build a modest house. A number of European companies are also establishing colonies and bringing in settlers. Some landowners who find their estates too unwieldy are letting their land out to tenants on shares. The immigrant receives far different treatment there from what he does in the United States, where he is simply turned loose after the inspectors have passed him. It has been charged in some instances that the government does not always keep its promises with these incomers, but I do not believe that can be at all general, for they are too anxious to populate the country. The country has been pretty well surveyed and good titles can generally be obtained. It will require all of the power of the government to break the city habit and induce the people to establish their homes in the *campo*. The lonesomeness and monotony of the never-ending pampas, where distance seems limitless, will no doubt always be an objection to them as places of habitation.

Statistics show that, during the year 1909, two hundred and thirty-two thousand four hundred and fifty-eight immigrants entered Argentina. Nearly every steamer landing at Buenos Aires has a few hundred of these poor people down in the steerage quarters. They are just the same as one will see disembarking at Ellis Island from the Mediterranean steamers. During the past ten years the total number arriving over those departing was almost a million and a quarter. A great many come in for temporary work in the harvest fields or elsewhere, and after earning a few hundred dollars go back to their homes in sunny Italy. Of the number arriving nearly one-half are Spaniards and about one-third Italians. The proportion of Spaniards has greatly increased in the past two or three years. The other nationalities include Syrians, Russians (mostly Jews), French, Austrians, Portuguese, British, etc., in order of numbers. All the North Americans numbered less than three hundred. It will be seen that the overwhelming population come from Southern Europe. This is only natural for language, customs and religion are almost the same, and the transformation from Italian or Spanish to Argentino is easy. It is a fact, however, that this element does not furnish the sturdy agriculturalists that the country needs. This is not the fault of the government. It seems impossible to induce settlers from Northern Europe to go down there. Large as this emigration seems it does not nearly keep pace with the production of the nation, and there is always a scarcity of labour in the rural districts.

It has been heretofore, and perhaps always will be, the case that Europe will devote greater attention to the River Plate countries than North America. There are two good reasons for this: first, the temperate regions of South America provide an outlet for the surplus population of the Latin nations of Europe; and, secondly, these countries are depended upon to furnish a large part of the food supplies for the thickly populated nations of that continent. The Anglo-Saxon has a choice of the many colonies of his own land, such as Canada and Australia, and he, together with the German, finds the United States a congenial country in which to live. The Frenchman, Spaniard and Italian finds conditions in Argentina, Southern Brazil and Uruguay more in accordance with his traditional customs. For the Spaniard the language is the same, and the Italian soon masters the difference in idiom. So this nation forms and should form the natural haven for these people, when the struggle for existence drives them from the land of their birth. As the government improves it will become still more attractive for them, and it is to be hoped that the stream of Italian immigrants who now seek our shores will head for the River Plate. This will redound in every way to the interest of the whole world. If the production of cereals and meat in that quarter of the world is sufficiently augmented, it will mean a substantial reduction in the price of these essential foodstuffs—it will mean cheaper bread and a lowering of the present almost prohibitive prices of meats. Another reason is that the La

Plata ports are more accessible to Europe than the United States, while on the north and west coast of South America the conditions are reversed and the North American influence is much more pronounced.

The peaceful conquest of Argentina by Europe was but a natural outcome of conditions. That continent had long realized the advantages of those broad fertile plains situated in a temperate climate. Europe likewise was in need of a granary near her markets, and these rich leagues with easy access provided what she ardently wanted and greatly needed. Force was not necessary in this conquest, for the power of money alone won the day, especially for England. British gold built five-sixths of the railways, nearly all the great *frigorificos*, the port works, and many other enterprises. British banks handled the national loans, and in every way British money won its way and made that country paramount in influence, even though Spain and Italy had two million former subjects living on the country. The total amount of British money in Argentina exceeds $1,500,000,000. Germany and France also have large investments there, and Italy as well, but they are small when compared with the English sovereigns. The United States investments are hardly worth considering, as they are so insignificant. In the last few years our large meat packing firms have been endeavouring to get a foothold in Argentina, and two are already operating establishments of their own. The spectre of a meat trust is already beginning to haunt the Argentinians, and the government in particular. It is said that some of the old established concerns have been bought out by the American firms, and are simply operated under the old names. This it was impossible to verify, so I am unable to state it as a fact or simply rumour. The fact that these meat barons are entering that field is in itself significant, and they will no doubt make an effort to gather up the entire industry, and thus be able to govern the prices just as they do in the United States. Adverse legislation will probably head them off, however, unless the power of money should stifle the opposition.

The financial history of Argentina has been a checkered one and not without its scandals. In reality for years investors looked askance at all kinds of Argentine securities. The fact is that the national government suffered from its moral, if not actual, responsibility for the numerous loans floated by the various states. The national government in a real sense should have no more responsibility for a provincial debt than our Federal

Government assumes the obligation of a state under our form of government. Creditors naturally tried to press this responsibility whenever a province defaulted, and in many instances the government accepted the liability. Money was borrowed for all kinds of purposes, in particular by the notorious Celman administration, and the government became badly involved. The province of Buenos Aires became a notorious defaulter in its "cedulas," and its administrators have many times been characterized as "robbers" by the British security-holders. The municipalities of Cordoba and Santa Fé also have rather unenviable records. Many of these debts are being slowly adjusted, however, while the national government has no difficulty in placing new loans under the more recent administrations.

Argentina to-day possesses one of the largest banks in the world, the Banco de la Nacion. It succeeded another national bank which went up in smoke a few years ago after a notorious career. Foreign banks do a large part of the business of the country. The first bank, called the Casa de Moneda, was established by English and Argentine capital as early as 1822. One of the leading banks of the present day is the London and River Plate, which has been established for almost half a century. It has paid many dividends as high as twenty per cent., so that its stock is considerably above par. Interest used to be as high as twenty-four per cent. on loans, and exchange fluctuated greatly. To-day interest is much lower, though still high, and exchange is more steady. The London and Brazilian Bank, the British Bank of South America, the Anglo South American and the Bank of London and Mexico are other British banks. Then there are German, French, Italian and Spanish banks, which do an immense business. The Provincia de Buenos Aires is one of the largest native banks, and it has a number of branches.

The Argentine Commercial Code, as it exists to-day, is a well-selected and well-digested assortment of the best points in the commercial laws of other countries. Many eminent men have participated in the development of this code. The laws relating to trade and contracts are excellent, but the latter have sometimes been at the mercy of judges who were not over-scrupulous, although foreigners have had less trouble in that line than natives. The laws relating to the organization of incorporated companies are excellent. Under them each vote counts irrespective of holdings, a man with one share having as much influence as the man with a thousand. This prevents a one-man company, as there must be at least ten shareholders. Any concern working under a concession must have a fiscal agent, who is nominated by the government or municipality, and whose duty it is to supervise the accounts and general conduct of the concern. If this agent is an honest man, and not susceptible to bribes, he can have great influence for good; if, however, he is corrupt, the shareholders are doubly unfortunate.

The Bolsa, or stock exchange, in Buenos Aires is a great institution. Millions of dollars worth of securities and grains are sold on the floor of this building. It reminds one of our own stock exchanges, except for the very babel of voices. Although the cries of the brokers are all in Spanish, you will see excited groups around you talking in Italian, German and English. Most of the brokers are able to join any group and converse in that language. Argentine securities are sold on this exchange in parcels and they rise and fall rapidly, the margin in one day often being considerable. Prior to the great crash of 1890, a half billion dollars worth of securities in gold values were sold at this exchange. When the panic came ninety per cent. of the companies failed, and the shares were not worth a cent on the dollar. The great national bank, with a capital of $50,000,000 national money, which closed its doors, precipitated the crisis, and brought down with it the London house of Baring Bros. The depositors of this bank lost more than $70,000,000 by the unfortunate failure, which was brought about by crookedness on the part of the management, and high financing. Money came in so easily and rapidly that the directors thought there was no end to the golden stream headed their way. Immense sums were loaned to irresponsible politicians with no hope or scarcely expectation of having it returned. Large drafts would also be cashed from the same sources, and bribery was rampant. Its loans at one time were over four hundred million dollars in national money.

However old the history of Argentina, the civilization of the country is essentially new. One may find a beautiful mansion in the midst of a princely domain. Everything else, however, is crude. The workmen who are scattered over the *estancia* are ignorant and unprogressive, and if left to themselves would retrograde. Even near the cities the people live in a very primitive way. The roads across the pampas are hardly distinguishable from cattle trails, and they are certainly no better. The bones and carcasses of cattle and sheep that have died on the march are numerous, and do not beautify the highway. The railroad maps are no criterion of the actual settlement of the country. Names will be seen in abundance, but most of them are only stations for freight upon big *estancias*, with elevators, stockpens and perhaps a water-tank. Even a small town may be distant twenty or more miles from a farmer in some of the older settled provinces. Everything points to a country in its infancy. The habits of the natives and colonists are usually sluggish and seemingly unrefined in many ways, but the kindliness and hospitality of the Latin is everywhere in evidence. The village life of American states is missed, for the little railroad settlements seem composed of a shifting, wage-earning population different from our villagers, most of whom own their own modest little dwelling. Here a shack answers for a habitation.

Argentina could furnish homes for and feed a population of one hundred millions. In this settlement, however, it is doubtful if the Anglo-Saxon will have much part. It will be a harvest field for that race to reap the wealth, but a breeding-place for the Latin. The Anglo-Saxon does not find a companionship among the Italians and Spaniards. Furthermore the loneliness of the plain grows upon him. The poor man who attempts to make a home in this country, as the homesteaders have in our western states and in Canada, will not succeed. He must have money to begin with and ability to compete with the wealthy *estancieros* who would be his neighbours. There is still plenty of opportunity to acquire virgin land at a comparatively low price within five hundred or six hundred miles of the capital, and watch it grow in value. Some colonies or communities have been quite successful, if the management has been in good hands. Several European companies have tried the plan of bringing in colonists and selling them lands. They advance money for machinery and the necessities, receiving in payment a certain share of the products. The Baron Hirsh colony of Jews has been quite successful, but in this case unlimited money was back of the scheme in addition to the spirit of benevolence rather than the commercial and money-getting mania.

SHIPPING HIDES TO THE UNITED STATES

The number of acres of land under cultivation in Argentina has more than doubled in the past ten years. The acreage that was tilled for the season of 1909 was 47,000,000 acres. Of this number 15,500,000 was sown in wheat, 7,500,000 in corn and 3,600,000 in flax. The following are the figures of production of cereals as reported by the Department of Agriculture in metric tons of 2,205 pounds avoirdupois: wheat, 2,576,009, corn, 2,336,334, linseed, 918,413, oats, 435,540. Of this production seventy-five per cent. of the corn is available for export, seventy per cent. of the wheat and ninety per cent. of the linseed. Only a small portion of the wheat is ground into flour before it is exported. The cereals are sent to Great Britain, Germany and Belgium, although the United States has been buying considerable quantities of linseed. There were 2,723,000 frozen carcasses of mutton exported in 1909, going almost wholly to Great Britain, and 2,584,301 of beef. In addition to this a lot of jerked, or salted, beef is sent to nearby markets. The United States purchases the bulk of the hides, and for the year 1909 received 2,608,230, weighing 38,798 metric tons. Horse hides, of which two hundred and fifty thousand were exported, went to Germany, sheep hides to France and goatskins to Uncle Sam. Argentina exported 176,682 metric tons of wool, of which France took almost one half and the United States 18,961 tons more than Great Britain.

The present population of Argentina is only about five to the square mile. In 1869 the population was estimated at less than two million. A dozen years later it had risen to three million, and in 1895 it was still less than four million. From 1857 to 1897 the number of immigrants was estimated at a million and a half in round numbers. Of the total number of inhabitants those of other than Latin origin probably do not much exceed one hundred thousand in number—by this I mean those who do not inherit Latin blood from one parent or the other. This would not include the native races that dwell in considerable numbers in some of the territories. It means that Latin customs and traditions are likely to continue to prevail, although they will be considerably modified by the conditions and influence of a new land. The old conservatism and hindrance of tradition will, to a great extent, disappear before the new-world aggressiveness and progressiveness. Thus there will be a new type, which can already be traced, with perhaps a French stamp upon it, but it will nevertheless be distinctively Latin.

The growth of cities and towns in Argentina has been out of proportion to the increase in population. Buenos Aires, of course, receives the largest number, but the same disposition to reside in the crowded centres is apparent in Rosario, Bahia Blanca, Tucuman and the other cities. This massing together in municipalities is not the healthiest condition that could be devised. As none of these cities are manufacturing districts this concentration of population hinders economic development in a nation whose resources are in the cultivation of the soil. Every man thus withdrawn from farm work is a loss to the producing power of the country, for much land is lying idle for the simple reason that labourers are lacking. Until the bulk of the land is alienated from the present princely estates and broken up into smaller holdings it seems likely that these conditions will continue to prevail. A change may occur before long, as many of the big landowners borrow money at exorbitant rates of interest in order to live in luxury. This will possibly result in breaking up some of these holdings. If the government would enter upon a systematic campaign to encourage the homesteader and small farmer, much good of a permanent value might be accomplished, and a stable as well as intelligent population be built up. The fertile soil and kindly climate of this republic ought to easily support a population of more than five times the present number.

Politics has been one of the curses of Argentina. A certain class has had all the opportunity to get the benefits of office holding. The politicians work night and day—they are the counterparts of our own, and never sleep on the job. A little more tact and grace on the surface only covers the same motive—graft. The elections are always one-sided. Formerly they were conducted at the whim of a dictator or political autocrat; to-day the ballot box is stuffed and the election laws are ignored. The elections are never really an expression of the sentiment of the people. They are held on Sundays at the doors of the churches. Outside the church door are tables around which sit several men. The ballots are of paper and are dropped through slits in the boxes. Many hand their ballots to the receivers to be voted. Some voters openly repeat their ballots by giving different names, and the receivers pay no attention to the palpable fraud. In Rosario, for instance, out of forty thousand Argentine citizens qualified to vote at the presidential election of 1910, only ten thousand registered. Of these ten thousand only one-fourth took out their voting tickets, and of these all did not cast their ballot on election day. Thus less than twenty-five hundred actually voted at the June election in Rosario, in that large city. One party, calling themselves the Radicals, decided beforehand not to go to the polls, because certain electoral reforms demanded by them were not granted. Says the *Review of the River Plate*: "In electoral matters the country is as backward as it was one hundred years ago, and outside the federal capital there is no freedom of the polls, force always carries the day—and the elections. The official party say that they will not bring forward any candidate for deputy who does not subscribe fifty thousand dollars towards the funds of the party. This is a pretty stiff price, as the period is for six years and the emoluments of a deputy only amount to fifteen hundred dollars a month, which is the highest figure paid to any legislator in any part of the world. The voters' tickets, when issued, are often traded about and sometimes bring quite a premium about election day."

Mr. Carpenter tells a story about the mayor of a certain city. On the voting list was the name of a man who was dead, and some one protested: "Why, mayor, Munyoz is dead. Don't you remember we were together last month when the report of his death came in?" "Oh, yes, I remember," replied the mayor, "but if he is dead that is all the better; he can't now make any fuss as to how his vote shall be cast." Nothing to preserve the secrecy of the ballot has yet been adopted. This has led to much political unrest which has shown itself in various disturbances. Added to this has been the agitation of professional disturbers, who have come here from Italy and Spain and attempted to spread their propaganda of social revolution. It is a fertile soil for such doctrine, for nowhere is the discrepancy between wealth and poverty greater. In one generation hundreds have become wealthy by the growth in land values, the unearned increment, and they spend their money like water. Their arrogance inspires envy in those less fortunate. Argentina may well be glad that the age of demagoguery has not yet been reached, for it is fully as dangerous as open bribery and corruption, in my opinion. At present the country is materially prosperous and every one is able to find employment. The cost of living, however, is very high and rapidly increasing, so that differences between capital and labour seem to be on the increase. The enormous fortunes in the hands of the few, many of them ignorant and without tact, may cause trouble in the future.

It is a mistaken view to think that Argentina is governed by revolution alone. It is true that in the past quarter of a century there have been three more or less serious revolutions, as well as minor disturbances. Two Presidents, Celman and Saenz-Peña, were compelled to resign by these malcontents. As a rule little blood is shed, and it was simply their method of introducing a change. The majority of people simply looked upon them as an interruption to business and a nuisance in general. The government, however, has undergone a great change in recent years. The comic-opera traits have generally disappeared. The constitution is admirable, but its provisions are not always carried out to the letter. The laws are much better administered in the larger centres than in the remote Camp. Bribery used to be common, and was considered as a matter of course as much as stamp dues. This has generally disappeared, at least as an open custom. Many Argentinos no doubt still enter politics with the expectation of enriching themselves and hope to retire with a well filled purse.

It is not a rare thing for a President or other high official to quit public life after many years of service poorer than he went in. President Bartolomé Mitre was one of the more recent types of that kind, as he bore a reputation for financial integrity that was absolutely above reproach. The country is becoming too big for petty graft and petty revolutions. The increasing importance of the nation has rather sobered all classes by a feeling of responsibility for its reputation. The spirit that formerly showed itself in revolutions now occasionally makes itself felt in disorder during strikes. And yet I do not know that this disorder is much greater than has been experienced in our own land. In either country it is reprehensible and is a disgrace to pretended civilization. The authorities have a drastic way of dealing with disorders by declaring a state of siege or martial law. This submits the disturbance to be dealt with according to military law and often effectually stops it. The Italians are there, as here, often the greatest disturbers during the strikes. The bull-fight has been abolished, and they now have no sport that equals in brutality, or exceeds in gambling proclivities, the prize fight, the so-called "manly art."

Absolute freedom of the press prevails in Argentina, as well as liberty of speech. The papers are at times filled with caustic criticisms of the government which go unnoticed. Public orators also unburden themselves with the most bitter arraignments of officials with impunity. An instance of this nature occurred during the writer's own sojourn in Buenos Aires. A large meeting was held in the Plaza de Mayo where two socialist orators arraigned the President and his ministers as "a gang of thieves" in the most intemperate language. The Argentine constitution is so free in its wording that the people seem to believe it has no limitations at all. They appear to think that liberty is such an elastic and unfathomable principle that there is nothing beyond. This intemperance, unless checked, bodes trouble for the future. Orators and so-called advanced thinkers must remember that the status of free men is only possible while the beneficiary acknowledges his obligation to bestow the same privileges that he enjoys. If the citizen is protected by law against violence and calumny, he must not be guilty of a violation of the same legal precepts by calumniating the government and its officials. If the officials are forbidden to do acts which are *ultra vires*, then the citizen must be inhibited against an excessive zeal. An ignoring of these plain principles can lead to nothing else than anarchy and the subversion of all legitimate government.

One cannot study this promising republic without an awakening interest and a considerable degree of admiration. There are faults that one can easily find, and many criticisms that can be made. Its development, however, is recent, even if its history is as old as our own land. The future means much for Argentina, and its advancement during the next decade will be marvellous, unless all signs fail. The North Americans can have an important part in this development, if they desire and pursue the right policy. It is well to study the country and its needs, the people and their wants, and the result will be interesting as well as satisfactory.

THE END.

www.ingramcontent.com/pod-product-compliance
Lightning Source LLC
Chambersburg PA
CBHW081616100526
44590CB00021B/3458